Legal Language and Business Communication

Anurag K. Agarwal

Legal Language and Business Communication

palgrave
macmillan

Anurag K. Agarwal
Indian Institute of Management
Ahmedabad, India

ISBN 978-981-13-7533-0 ISBN 978-981-13-7534-7 (eBook)
https://doi.org/10.1007/978-981-13-7534-7

Cover design: eStudio Calamar

This Palgrave Macmillan imprint is published by the registered company Springer Nature Singapore Pte Ltd.
The registered company address is: 152 Beach Road, #21-01/04 Gateway East, Singapore 189721, Singapore

The original version of the book was revised: Preface, Dedication and About the Author section have been included. The correction to the book is available at https://doi.org/10.1007/978-981-13-7534-7_8.

Manjari, my wife

Preface

This book is the result of numerous discussions related to law and literature I had with my wife, Manjari, since our marriage about two decades ago. She, as a teacher of English literature and language, and I, as a lawyer and later as a business law teacher, found several overlapping and common topics to talk about while going through the morning newspaper. Usually we started with sharing our views on certain current issues, which very often meandered to a definite rift in the form of strong difference of opinions. Sometimes we were able to find common ground, and on several occasions we ended our debate with the mature bottom line, "we agree to disagree." Besides the rich conversation, the most important aspect in all these debates and discussions had been the court judgments—Indian, foreign, Supreme Court, lower courts, tribunals, landmark cases, stray cases and so on—I had cited to support my views, and copious references to English literature—prose, poetry, classics, contemporary, British, American, Indian and the like—made by her to vindicate her stand. Most of them got etched in my mind as most of the literary references were new to me.

Our mutual interest somehow wandered towards "business communication" due to my daily dose of business news—law and strategy—and her interest in the issues related to the language, both spoken and written. Frequently, we were expressing our opinions on the problems faced by businesses due to poor communication skills, or not paying due attention to legal issues, or both. We realised that the legal language is surely different from what is typically used for business communication, and that drove us to this work. She has been instrumental in the design of the book, preparation of the outline, chapter formation and sequencing, and most importantly providing invaluable literary inputs. The analysis of the use of language and different aspects of business communication has been dealt by her expertly. This work has benefitted immensely from her contribution. She has just been a step away from being the co-author of the book. This book is truly and rightfully dedicated to her.

This book is an amalgam of legal language and business communication. While communicating, a business leader has to take care of the legal periphery which she should never transgress. However, legal language in itself can be so complex and difficult that it is many a time unclear as to what the meaning can be ascribed to different words and phrases used. Also, it is easier to say that there is a boundary of law, but such a limit is not easily perceivable to the uninitiated. Occasionally even experts flounder. I do not claim to be an expert of both the fields—legal language and business communication—but with effective and pointed ideas from Manjari, I have tried to bring the best of both domains for the benefit of readers. It is surely going to be of interest to students of business and law, managers, lawyers, researchers, practitioners and readers in general.

The cases and related issues have been culled after rigorous research. Legal language and business communication as separate subjects have been studied for long; however, studying the interplay of the two has been, in all probability, not been done so far. I have tried my best to do deep research in the inter-related topics and devoted substantial time and effort in picking up highly relevant topical themes. It has not been an easy journey for me to research on these themes, which usually are very new and yet to be settled. Business practices are greatly being influenced by new developments in the fields of communication, making research in this domain extremely time sensitive and facing the risk of obsolescence too fast. Legal language, though well-established over centuries, is being continuously challenged by new dimensions of business communication in the last decade or so in a manner never experienced before. The very survival of the traditional model is being questioned. Research using pure legal databases has not been of much use as typical blending with business communication is usually absent. Also, researching pure business communication academic journals and other writings was not of much help as they did not characteristically deal with legal language and its implications. Hence, a mixed approach of researching—trial and error, random selection, picking up disparate pieces and so on—eventually bore fruit.

The book is not intimidating. It steers through legal jargon and legalese, and also the highly technical issues of grammar and linguistics. It has various case studies and current examples. Though dealing with legal language, it is in lucid language, devoid of heavy legal language as far as possible, and is interesting to read. Primarily, the book focuses on business and leadership cases; however, I have briefly discussed the relevant text on different topics covered in the book. It, hopefully, will connect well and touch upon—if not answer all—a lot many issues, concerns and queries, which often trouble a business leader. I envisage the book to be a useful companion to the business leaders.

The Introduction of the book is woven around a fantastic story *Namak Ka Daroga* (The Salt Inspector) written about a century ago by the master Hindi storyteller Munshi Premchand. The thought of using this as the initiating piece occurred to me while discussing another story *Panch Parmeshwar* by the same writer with students studying intricacies of business dispute resolution and arbitration. I have always been fascinated by Premchand's writings and his deep understanding of human behaviour in different situations, especially the business and commercial aspects intertwined with ordinary daily life of the most ordinary people. The simplicity with which he has been able to communicate the most difficult facets of human conduct in changed scenarios is unparalleled. Another story which comes closest to this ease of explaining the most difficult legal and business concepts can be Anton Chekhov's *The Chameleon*, written in 1884. This is precisely what the basic theme of this book is: different meanings ascribed to the same language and text depending on the context, and thus the importance of interpretation.

I would like to thank Sagarika Ghosh of Springer and Palgrave for her advice regarding the scope, content and relevance of the book for business leaders and lawyers. She also helped me with valuable information and comments on the initial outline and later during the preparation of the manuscript in tweaking it occasionally. I would also like to thank Sandeep Kaur of Springer and Palgrave in taking the idea forward and providing necessary support and guidance in the publication of this work.

I would like to thank my sons—Anant and Akshat—who have not been demanding in terms of time and attention. During family discussions, they have been helpful in providing their inputs and suggestions befitting their age and understanding. Sometimes, their queries made me rethink a few topics and also the manner of presenting them in the written form. Hopefully more such reflections with Manjari will bear fruit in the form of new and stimulating academic output.

Ahmedabad, India
October 29, 2018

Anurag K. Agarwal

Contents

About the Author

Anurag K. Agarwal A Harvard Law School graduate, he has been the first recipient of the prestigious Marti Mannariah Gurunath Outstanding Teacher Award at the Indian Institute of Management Ahmedabad (IIMA). As faculty at IIMA, his teaching, consulting and research interests include business leadership, negotiation, strategy and law, infrastructure and Public-Private Partnerships (PPPs), contracts and arbitration, banking, intellectual property, medico-legal issues in healthcare and related issues.

Graduated as mechanical engineer in 1990 from Motilal Nehru Regional Engineering College, Allahabad—now known as Motilal Nehru National Institute of Technology—he started his career with Bharat Petroleum Corporation Limited, where he worked for less than a year. Thereafter, he studied law at the Lucknow University, where he completed Bachelor (LLB)—gold medallist at the college—Master (LLM)—gold medallist at the University—and Doctor (LLD) of Laws. He went to the Harvard Law School for a second LL.M. He was a practising lawyer in Lucknow and Delhi for nine years. He switched over to full-time teaching in 2004, with a brief stint at Management Development Institute, Gurgaon, and joined IIMA in October 2004.

He conducts classes for several executive education programmes for government, public sector and private sector companies. He is a visiting faculty at many educational institutions. He is also on the board of some judicial, government and educational bodies.

He has authored four books: *Business Law for Managers: Kaleidoscopic Tales* (2018), *Business Leadership and Law* (2017), *Contracts and Arbitration for Managers* (2016) and *Business and Intellectual Property* (2010). He writes a weekly column "Lawfully Yours," for DNA Ahmedabad.

Introduction

The story of salt in Indian freedom movement has been of immense importance, and it was the Draconian British rule which legally imposed a tax on salt and made it illegal to produce salt or sell it without a licence granted by the British government in India. Salt is an essential commodity and everyone needs it, whether poor or rich. It was precisely because of this reason, the British made the availability of salt legally very difficult, though it was widely and easily available in India because of the very large coastline. It was only in 1930 when Mahatma Gandhi—later known as the "Father of the Nation"—started on a long walk, known as the Dandi March, and wilfully broke the law by picking up salt from the seashore. He and several others were arrested and that moment was one of the turning points of the Indian freedom struggle, which one can say started in 1857 and culminated in 1947.

With this background it will be easy to understand that in 1925 one of the finest Hindi writers, Munshi Premchand, wrote a story titled *Namak Ka Daroga* (The Salt Inspector), depicting the dilemma faced by a Salt Inspector and the allurements given by a very rich businessman of that time. The story is all about fictional characters and events; however, as literature is the reflection of what happens in the society, it can be a good barometer of the happenings in the society at that time, particularly the manner in which the successful business leaders used to communicate with government officials, so that their illegal activities could continue unhindered and technically speaking they remained on the right side of the law.

In brief, the story is like this.

Banshidhar was a capable and honest young man. He was appointed as the Salt Inspector. Once on duty at night, he saw several bullock carts illegally carrying salt on the instructions of Alopidin, a very rich landlord and businessman. Banshidhar did not allow the illegal movement of salt. Alopidin offered him huge sums of money in bribe, but he did not relent and got Alopidin arrested. When produced in the court, Alopidin managed the entire legal proceedings and was released honourably. But, after some time, Banshidhar was fired from his job, at the behest of Alopidin. Banshidhar was devastated and so was his father. Later, one evening Alopidin came to Banshidhar's house and made him the offer to become his manager at an extremely high salary and perquisites as he wanted a dead honest person to take care of his estate and business, and he stated that Banshidhar was the most suitable person for that position. Banshidhar accepted the offer, and the story ended on a positive note.

This was the social, business and legal environment in the 1920s in India, a time which was highly turbulent due to social inequality, drain of wealth by the British and general unrest in the country. Honest and talented persons were rare. The role of law in framing innocent people, or on the other hand letting go of the real culprits, was widely seen as the easiest method of controlling people by the British rulers. Communication, and business communication, was either in vernacular or in the English language—local traders used the vernacular, however, when talking to the British officers the English language was used, and this practice gave immense importance to individuals who knew the languages well. Besides the advantage of knowing two languages, the most important thing was to understand the mood of the officers so as to communicate with them the intricacies of business in such a manner that the work of the local traders got done, the officers felt happy that they had done something good and were holding the moral high ground, and in this entire process the middlemen got the illegal gratification from the traders. All this was the heady mix of business and law bringing to the fore the issues related to polite business communication blending it with the proper legal language. The art was not only in spoken communication, but had to be exhibited to a much higher level in writing.

Noteworthy issue regarding the first communication between Alopidin and Banshidhar is the fact that Alopidin wanted to bribe Banshidhar and the story dealt the interaction with great dexterity. At the outset Alopidin threw his weight around and tried to impress upon Banshidhar his status in business, government and social circles so as to browbeat him. But being a seasoned businessman, Alopidin did not threaten Banshidhar, neither in the first meeting nor later on in the court. He casually offered a big sum of money—increasing it incrementally in every offer which was rejected one by one by Banshidhar—to the extent he might have decided in his mind as the ultimate limit to which he could have gone. When it didn't work and Alopidin could gauge Banshidhar's next move very clearly—that arrest was imminent—he did not increase the offer further and got himself arrested. One may analyse Alopidin's conduct at that moment as that of a person who has resigned to his fate, accepted his arrest as predestined, and believes that nothing will change the future course of action; however, there was the shrewd mind of a businessperson working, doing cost-benefit analysis, and then taking the decision of going with the flow at that moment, and later on taking his revenge by getting Banshidhar fired from his job.

Alopidin, in this entire process, ostensibly remained suave and acted like a thorough gentleman. But, his inner core was full of guilt and manipulation. He had no remorse and did not appoint Banshidhar as his manager so as to correct the wrong he had done but to take advantage of the availability of a gem of a person like Banshidhar. The language he used with Banshidhar in the second meeting, when he made the offer to him, was extremely polite and made it possible for him to be using the courteous language laced with the legal jargon of making an offer under the contract law. At that time also he did not resort to any of the practices mentioned in the contract law which could have made the agreement between the two of them voidable or void. Alopidin had mastered the art and science of finely blending the legal language in his business communication and had further perfected it to match the taste of the person with whom he used to communicate.

Though it is not at all recommended to have evil designs and ill feelings in business, yet the importance of being tactful while conducting business communication, keeping in mind the legal contours within which one must perambulate, can never be over emphasised. One must surely try to conduct business by walking on the straight and narrow path; however, legal language, if used heavily, can make business communication unworkable besides being dry and boring. One need not start cracking a joke unnecessarily; still, there is merit in keeping the communication simple, effective and legal, according to the law of the land. There is the possibility of a business communication backfiring if too much of legality is mixed as there is a tendency of thinking and talking more about one's rights the moment there is a mention of the legal provisions. The other party, as a reflex action, usually becomes closed and suspicious at the sight of legalese.

As will be discussed in subsequent chapters, a business leader has to be conscious of the value of effective business communication while being on the right side of the law.

The book is divided into seven chapters, with each chapter dealing with a different facet of the relationship between legal language and business communication. Though the chapters can be read separately in any sequence, there is a loose connection between them with certain thoughts and ideas overflowing from one to another. Thus, the material is so placed with emphasis on certain court judgments that reading and understanding them is enjoyable and informative, without being too legalistic.

Chapter 1, "Loose Lips Sink Ships," talks about leadership communication and how the business leaders should be discreet, while trying to remain on the right side of the law. The focus of this chapter is on the maturity a business leader must develop and exhibit in making decisions and dealing with numerous individuals, in different capacities, while doing business. He cannot afford to be rigid in behaviour and attitude, as rigidity brings in obstinacy and the desire to put self at a higher pedestal than the business one is supposed to manage and lead. Being a business leader, in essence, means being flexible in approach and not to overstate according to the demands of a specific situation. Garrulity is often self-hurting and usually makes a person unconsciously slide into the grey area of law. A business leader should truly avoid being loquacious.

Chapter 2, "What's the Good Word?," highlights the importance of precision in communication, especially while writing. Use of proper words, punctuation marks and so on is emphasised. The legal vocabulary typically is full of words which may not be commonly used. A business leader is not expected to use them with perfection; however, he must have a basic understanding of some of the words and phrases used in business communication, particularly those which have a different connotation from the ordinary usage. The same is true about punctuation marks, which may make or mar a business deal, if the parties are determined to read something different from what is normally meant. Precise use, therefore, helps in avoiding future disputes. One can always take the help of a good lawyer, in case of a doubt. Getting important written business communication vetted by a legal expert is often desirable.

Chapter 3, "Should a Business Leader Talk Like a Lawyer or a Judge?," tries to answer the question which business leaders frequently ask when they face the challenge of converting simple business communication into a proper legal document. A business leader need not necessarily communicate like a lawyer or a judge, but should be careful to keep his communication simple. Being simple and straightforward in conveying one's thoughts about business is a great quality of a business leader; however, these thoughts have to be cloaked in suitable legal language to make them legally tenable according to the requirements of the particular legal environment.

Chapter 4, "It's All Greek to Me," discusses some important foreign language words, phrases and maxims, along with some cases. Despite the best intentions of using one's language to put the thoughts in words, there are occasions when foreign language words creep in oral and written communication. If we take the example of the English language for conveying our thoughts as business leaders, there are several words and phrases of foreign languages—such as French, Greek, Latin and Spanish—which find their way to the text on their own. With globalisation and international trade growing exponentially, big markets such as China and India also have their languages finding a noticeable acceptance. Due to immense technological and management advances, some of the commonly used Japanese words and phrases have already been accepted in business. But, the legal language still is dominated by Latin and Greek words, phrases and maxims.

Chapter 5, "Read My Lips!," goes into the important aspects of interpretation, which make all the difference in communication. At times whatever a person says may not be what he really wishes to convey and that may create problems for any person to understand the real meaning of the communication. These problems may be of varied nature, ranging from certain innocuous meanings to absolutely contrary meanings to what the real message is. There are different shades of confusion which may arise in between. It is, therefore, important for a receiver to understand the context and pay attention to what the sender wishes to communicate. A lot depends on the relative position of the two and the difference in their stature. In situations of one person commanding the other, it is of utmost importance that there is a certain expectation of the nature of communication made between each other, and that is met.

Chapter 6, "Man Is a Social Animal," discusses the emergence of social media in recent times and the importance it deserves in business communication, along with the legal implications. In the last decade or so there have been dramatic changes observed in the way social media has been emerging, thanks to the galloping development in technology and different business models which make this technology easily accessible to almost everyone, irrespective of the economic strata to which they belong. Businesses find it challenging in the changing times to keep pace with the revolutionary changes happening in the social media as businesses ought to be moving ahead with the changes and keeping themselves aligned with the extremely fast-changing norms lest they should fall back in the competition race. However, in this entire exercise they must maintain legal uprightness, both in content and language used.

Chapter 7, "Speech Is Silver, Silence Is Golden," discusses about exercising the option of not communicating, which is also quite effective for businesses. The chapter examines as to how silence fits in the scheme of things. Is silence always golden? Several occasions demand the least information to be shared by a business leader, and at times the least information may mean no information at all. Thus, a business leader has to decide when to keep mum and not necessarily disclose any information. At times there may be a legal requirement to speak up, and at certain different times a person may not be required to speak at all, depending on the context. Very often, business leaders opt the tactical move of remaining silent even when provoked to the fullest. In such a situation one important thing to be considered by such leaders is to take the statutory conditions into consideration so as not to be caught on the wrong foot legally.

The book, hopefully, will be of relevance to businesspersons who would like to use the communication skills in an effective manner and at the same time comply with the legal provisions.

CHAPTER 1

Loose Lips Sink Ships

It was during the Second World War in the United States that the phrase—"loose lips might sink ships"—gained popularity and was used as propaganda posters to warn and remind soldiers and officers that their indiscreet talk and unguarded speech could lead, not only them in trouble, but the entire country in avoidable trouble. During war, it is useful to get to know a lot of information about the enemy and boastful talking by anyone from the enemy side can be one of the best and easiest sources to know a lot about the enemy which otherwise would never have been accessible. Similar measures were taken across the Atlantic where the British equivalent was "careless talk costs lives," and the Germans used "Schäm Dich, Schwätzer!" (shame on you, blabbermouth!). Presently, the US Air Force warns with these words, "Loose Tweets, Destroy Fleets."[1]

Basically, the idea was to keep mum and not to disclose unwanted information. It was important to remain mum even when the soldiers and officers were off duty and were with family. Remaining silent and not indulging in loose talk was considered to be essential as while speaking, inadvertently, a person may blurt out some information which might be vital and can be used by the enemy. Later, the word "might" was dropped and the

[1] 'Loose tweets destroy fleets' US Air Force issues warning to keep social media settings secure in wake of hacker attacks; The Daily Mail, 24 Aug 2015; https://www.dailymail.co.uk/sciencetech/article-3209477/Loose-tweets-destroy-fleets-Air-Force-issues-warning-social-media-settings-secure-wake-hacker-attacks.html

A. K. Agarwal, *Legal Language and Business Communication*,
https://doi.org/10.1007/978-981-13-7534-7_1

American phrase was shortened to "loose lips sink ships," a slogan that is used in general for any communication and reminds everyone to be discreet and avoid carelessness.

One of the fascinating aspects of the phrase has been that while talking loosely one doesn't know as to who may be listening. In case a soldier reveals in any manner his location or the location of the ship—whether in simple and straightforward language or a coded language—there is always the possibility of the enemy intercepting the communication and trying to take full advantage of the information available. The young soldiers during the Second World War were seriously trained to understand the importance of silence not only in their speech but also in writing so that they did not write letters with potentially damaging information, often overtaken by emotion. Thus they were told, "silence means security," and remaining silent requires immense inner strength. The emotional stability of these individuals was reflected in their conversation and writings. Even at home they could not afford to lower the guard. They have to be on constant vigil and very well balanced in choosing the right words to convey their thoughts. Censorship was imposed on them, but it was not practical to review each and every piece of paper. Self-imposed censorship was the best way to manage things in a proper manner so that any relevant information was not leaked out. Emotionally hardened soldiers were trained not to disclose anything material if captured as a prisoner. They were also trained not to tell any lies to the enemy camp, if captured, as it was, and is, very difficult to put all the lies together in the right perspective and then to justify them.

Nine posters meant for this purpose were published in an article in the *Time* in 2016. The basic theme of the posters was *loose lips sink ships.* Following are the messages written on the nine posters:

1. Loose lips might sink ships
2. Quiet! Loose talk can cost lives
3. Free speech doesn't mean careless talk!
4. Keep it under your hat! Careless talk costs lives
5. Don't discuss: troop movements, ship sailings, war equipment
6. Silence means security: be careful what you say or write
7. If you tell where they are going… They may never get there: don't talk about troop movements

8. Don't discuss secrets on the telephone
9. A wise old owl sat in an oak; the more he saw the less he spoke; the less he spoke the more he heard. Soldier… Be like that old bird: silence means security.[2]

The posters were plastered all over the country so as to encourage the people in joining the armed forces and in general not indulging in loose and boisterous conversations related to war. These posters very well communicated to the masses the idea of keeping a secret really secret in a business-like manner. A few more slogans conveying the same thoughts were "defence on the sea begins on the shore" and "defence in the field begins in the factory." This applies to business as well as smart business leaders who consider their business to be nothing less than war.

The Business Perspective

For focussed business leaders, business is war, and nothing but war, which must be won at any cost. Just like war, in business neither they nor their lieutenants—directors, general managers, managers, executives and others—can afford to indulge in loose talk. Being indiscreet simply means being suicidal. Also, they cannot let their advisors—financial, legal, strategic consultants, technical experts, marketing wizards and so on—to ever try to take the risk of being rash even momentarily. The public relation officers and the communication executives have to be extremely cautious of not letting any information go out of the organisation and also to take every step to sensitise everyone in the organisation, especially the persons near the top of the hierarchy, not to provide even an iota of extra information in the public domain. This is particularly important as the people at the top of the pyramid in the organisation and near to the top are privy to confidential and sensitive information about the business concern.

Whether to be discreet or not is also a matter governed by legal provisions. Contractual clauses guide the conduct of executives in businesses. To remain on the right side of the law, it is often important for business leaders to understand that loose lips can invite trouble for them—both personally and professionally. The language used in communication also can be the differentiating factor as the language, usually, can be interpreted differently

[2] Hasic, Albinko, See the 'Loose Lips Sink Ships' Propaganda Posters of World War II, The Time, Dec 08, 2016, http://time.com/4591841/loose-lips-sink-ships-posters/

and may give rise to the possibility of being misunderstood. Hence, it is prudent to be careful in using the language—formal, official and business-like communication is least likely to be misinterpreted. But, if the same communication is laced with arrogance and haughtiness, there are very high chances that it will be misconstrued. Courtesy and politeness are less likely to be misunderstood and the benefit of the doubt always is given to the person who is maintaining plain and simple language, even if not titled towards higher forms of civility.

Business leaders don't work nine to five. Even if physically they are at the office during certain working hours, their mind is almost all the time engaged with business-related issues. It is quite obvious for them to mix up the work issues with their personal life and talk shop at home with family and friends. This spill-over of the conversation related to work, which may be simply to share the things at office, may sometimes be damaging for the business. Nodding acquaintance with some persons and the desire to share even some remotely connected work issues in a guarded language is not appropriate. It may be just because of sheer passion for work that a business leader is tempted to talk about his achievements at work or the dilemmas faced at the workplace. The audience matters and many a time it is the yearning to be approved and appreciated for the decisions made that a speaker goes on providing information and detailed information about work, even when there is no need to impress the audience and seek their approval. Self-confidence and courage of conviction that what one is doing is the right thing to do—without being unnecessarily reckless—essentially are enough to make the conversation sail through.

The senior and top management executives usually meet a lot many people in different settings and circumstances. All of them may not be known to them, but very often successful businesspersons are requested to share their experience and give some tips to young and inexperienced entrepreneurs, students and others in general. During such occasions there is a tendency to overstate a little bit, if not completely exaggerate, and to justify these statements, one has to divulge certain facts which could have been easily avoided. For media interactions, it can be surely miserable if the interviewer is pushing a bit too much and not leaving the issues at the surface level. For prior scheduled interviews, panel discussions and speeches to be made, it is always advisable to prepare well and anticipate the questions which can be asked. Making comments without proper thinking can be interpreted by the media and observers in a manner which the speaker never intended. Thus, forewarned is forearmed. Getting provoked easily is the surest way to commit mistake and speak the things which need not be divulged. For the individual, words spoken in rage may lead him to jail or serious legal proceedings of defamation can be initiated. Wrong choice of words, in a fit of anger, can be troublesome from the legal perspective as the employers do not wish to retain any executive in a senior position who is not able to keep his cool and does not have control over the language he uses. Professionally, loose lips always invite suffering.

For business leaders, there has to be coherence in what they think and do. Intention, expression and action should be aligned. Whenever there is a gap between these three, problems arise and may continue even after the initial damage is done. Satyam, an Indian company, faced the disgrace due to its CEO Ramalinga Raju's irresponsible utterances and actions, resulting in litigation for years in India and abroad.

Venture Global and Satyam's Raju Case[3]

This is one of those cases which have been the outcome of misdeeds of a business leader and the manner in which he had set his lips loose. It was because of his actions and loose talk, even when there was nothing concrete on the ground, that the ship—the company—had sunk. This is about the company Satyam and its founder Ramalinga Raju. The long ongoing fraud has been compared with Enron:

> The long-running fraud, which is being called India's Enron, also raised questions about the vigilance of regulators in India and the United States.[4]

Disclosure of fraud resulted in dozens of legal proceedings, both in India and in the United States. In the 2017 judgment by the Supreme Court of India, the two justices had different views which resulted in a deadlock. The matter will now be decided by a larger bench; however, the facts, discussion and analysis give us a fantastic exposure to what can happen to legal proceedings, and how long and at how many different forums these matters can continue, only because of loose talk and reckless comportment of the CEO of the company.

[3] Venture Global Engineering LLC v. Tech Mahindra Limited, Supreme Court of India, 1 November 2017, Civil Appeal Nos. 17753–17755 of 2017, Civil Appeal No. 17756 of 2017, SLP (C) Nos. 29747–29749/2013 and SLP (C) No. 8298/2014; Bench: J. Chelameswar, Abhay Manohar Sapre, JJ.

[4] Financial Scandal at Outsourcing Company Rattles a Developing Country, NYT, Jan 7, 2009, https://www.nytimes.com/2009/01/08/business/worldbusiness/08outsource.html

In 1999, Venture Global, an American company, headquartered in Michigan, formed a joint venture (JV) with Satyam Computer Services, an Indian company—now known as Tech Mahindra—with each holding 50% shareholding in the JV called, Satyam Venture Engineering Services (SVES) in Hyderabad. The shareholders agreement provided for options in case of certain events of default: purchase defaulter's shares or dissolution and liquidation of JV. The dispute resolution clause provided for arbitration. SVES entered into a contract for providing information technology (IT) services to TRW, a company engaged in automotive auxiliary business, in the year 2000. Disputes arose between Venture and Satyam, which were referred to arbitration. The award, dated 3 April 2006, ordered Venture to transfer its entire shareholding to Satyam, according to the shareholders agreement. Satyam filed for enforcement of the award in the Michigan court.

Venture challenged the award in the lower court in Secunderabad, the twin city of Hyderabad, and thereafter in the Andhra Pradesh High Court at Hyderabad—now known as the High Court of Judicature at Hyderabad—primarily on the ground that a foreign arbitral award cannot be challenged in an Indian court. Venture lost in both the courts and then moved the Supreme Court. Venture won in the Supreme Court, which decided that a foreign arbitral award could be challenged in an Indian court. In 2008, the Supreme Court restrained the transfer of shares and remanded the case to the trial court in Hyderabad.[5]

Then, Raju confessed.

Raju's Confession Letter[6]
January 7, 2009

To the Board of Directors, Satyam Computers Services Ltd.

From B. Ramalinga Raju, Chairman, Satyam Computer Services Ltd.

Dear Board Members,

It is with deep regret, and tremendous burden that I am carrying on my conscience, that I would like to bring the following facts to your notice:

(*continued*)

[5] Venture Global Engineering v. Satyam Computer Services Ltd. and another (2008) 4 SCC 190.

[6] Full text of Raju's resignation letter to the Board, The Times of India, January 7, 2009, https://timesofindia.indiatimes.com/business/india-business/Full-text-of-Rajus-resignation-letter-to-the-Board/articleshow/3946538.cms and at https://www.scribd.com/doc/9812606/satyam-raju-letter

(continued)

1. The balance sheet carries as of September 30, 2008
   (a) Inflated (non-existent) cash and bank balance of Rs 5040 crore (as against Rs 5361 crore reflected in the books)
   (b) An accrued interest of Rs 376 crore which is non-existent
   (c) An understated liability of Rs 1230 crore on account of funds arranged by me
   (d) An over stated debtors position of Rs 490 crore (as against Rs 2651 reflected in the books)
2. For the September quarter (Q2) we reported a revenue of Rs 2700 crore and an operating margin of Rs 649 crore (24% of revenues) as against the actual revenues of Rs 2112 crore and an actual operating margin of Rs 61 crore (3% of revenue). This has resulted in artificial cash and bank balances going up by Rs 588 crore in Q2 alone.

The gap in the Balance Sheet has arisen purely on account of inflated profits over a period of last several years (limited only to Satyam standalone, books of subsidiaries reflecting true performance). What started as a marginal gap between actual operating profit and the one reflected in the books of accounts continued to grow over the years. It has attained unmanageable proportions as the size of the company operations grew significantly (annualized revenue run rate of Rs 11,276 crore in the September quarter, 2008 and official reserves of Rs 8392 crore). The differential in the real profits and the one reflected in the books was further accentuated by the fact that the company had to carry additional resources and assets to justify higher level of operations – thereby significantly increasing the costs.

Every attempt made to eliminate the gap failed. As the promoters held a small percentage of equity, the concern was the poor performance would result in a takeover, thereby exposing the gap. It was like riding a tiger, not knowing how to get off without being eaten.

The aborted Maytas acquisition deal was the last attempt to fill the fictitious assets with real ones. Maytas' investors were convinced that this is a good divestment opportunity and a strategic fit. Once Satyam's problem was solved, it was hoped that Maytas' payments can be delayed. But that was not to be. What followed in the last several days is common knowledge.

(*continued*)

(continued)

I would like the board to know:

1. That neither myself, nor the Managing Director (including our spouses) sold any shares in the last eight years – excepting for a small proportion declared and sold for philanthropic purposes.
2. That in the last two years a net amount of Rs 1230 crore was arranged to Satyam (not reflected in the books of Satyam) to keep the operations going by resorting to pledging all the promoter shares and raising funds from known sources by giving all kinds of assurances (Statement enclosed, only to the members of the board). Significant dividend payments, acquisitions, capital expenditure to provide for growth did not help matters. Every attempt was made to keep the wheel moving and to ensure prompt payment of salaries to the associates. The last straw was the selling of most of the pledged share by the lenders on account of margin triggers.
3. That neither me, nor the Managing Director took even one rupee/dollar from the company and have not benefitted in financial terms on account of the inflated results.
4. None of the board members, past or present, had any knowledge of the situation in which the company is placed. Even business leaders and senior executives in the company, such as Ram Mynampati, Subu D, T.R. Anand, Keshab Panda, Virender Agarwal, A.S. Murthy, Hari T, SV Krishnan, Vijay Prasad, Manish Mehta, Murali V, Sriram Papani, Kiran Kavale, Joe Lagioia, Ravindra Penumetsa, Jayaraman and Prabhakar Gupta are unaware of the real situation as against the books of accounts. None of my or Managing Director's immediate or extended family members has any idea about these issues.

Having put these facts before you, I leave it to the wisdom of the board to take the matters forward. However, I am also taking the liberty to recommend the following steps:

1. A task force has been formed in the last few days to address the situation arising out of the failed Maytas acquisition attempt. This consists of some of the most accomplished leaders of Satyam: Subu D, T.R. Anand, Keshab Panda and Virender Agarwal,

(*continued*)

(continued)

representing business functions, and A.S. Murthy, Hari T and Murali V representing support functions. I suggest that Ram Mynampati be made the Chairman of this Task Force to immediately address some of the operational matters on hand. Ram can also act as an interim CEO reporting to the board.

2. Merrill Lynch can be entrusted with the task of quickly exploring some Merger opportunities.
3. You may have a 'restatement of accounts' prepared by the auditors in light of the facts that I have placed before you.

I have promoted and have been associated with Satyam for well over twenty years now. I have seen it grow from few people to 53,000 people, with 185 Fortune 500 companies as customers and operations in 66 countries. Satyam has established an excellent leadership and competency base at all levels. I sincerely apologize to all Satyamites and stakeholders, who have made Satyam a special organization, for the current situation. I am confident they will stand by the company in this hour of crisis.

In light of the above, I fervently appeal to the board to hold together to take some important steps. Mr. T.R. Prasad is well placed to mobilize support from the government at this crucial time. With the hope that members of the Task Force and the financial advisor, Merrill Lynch (now Bank of America) will stand by the company at this crucial hour, I am marking copies of this statement to them as well.

Under the circumstances, I am tendering my resignation as the chairman of Satyam and shall continue in this position only till such time the current board is expanded. My contribution is just to ensure enhancement of the board over the next several days or as early as possible.

I am now prepared to subject myself to the laws of the land and face consequences thereof.

(B. Ramalinga Raju)

Copies marked to:

1. Chairman SEBI
2. Stock Exchanges

Raju had been a persuasive communicator and could use his cool demeanour coupled with confident business conversation to clinch a deal in the toughest and the most unexpected negotiations. This was precisely how he got the first big client. It was long ago in 1991 when Raju had convinced the famous tractor company John Deere to give his programmers some work. His company, "Satyam Computer Services Ltd.," was just 3–4 years old and was extremely small to even be compared to big companies like John Deere. However, it was Raju's risk-bearing ability that he made an offer to John Deere which the tractor company couldn't refuse—simply don't pay us if you don't like our service. It was an offer on a platter and as John Deere had nothing to lose, it gave a chance to Raju and his company Satyam. Raju had a simple idea that without any physical contact with the executives of the client company, he and his programmers would try to do what the client required. So, from a small house very near to the client's headquarters, Raju and his team did the work wonderfully well to the client's satisfaction, and that was the beginning of the meteoric rise of Raju and Satyam. For nearly two decades, Raju and the company just went up and up and lapped up one-third of the Fortune 500 companies as their clients for a large amount of data-related work outsourced to India. The entire work was done from India without any physical contact with the clients in a routine and regular manner.

It was Raju's confidence, or overconfidence, which emboldened him to fudge certain numbers in the account books when things were not going the way he, and more importantly the market, wanted. Simply to show the world that the company was doing very well and was steadily growing, Raju played with the account books and artificially inflated the profits. Later on as it was proved that it was in collusion with the auditor, PricewaterhouseCoopers (PwC). After continuing to cook the account books for a fairly long period of time without being noticed by the regulators—neither in India nor in the United States—there was no scope for further manipulation, and Raju had to admit publicly.

The language of the letter is not that of a true confession with being apologetic from the bottom of the heart. It appears to be pure information minus remorse, professionally written and having taken into account the possibilities of future legal action. In all probability, it had been drafted by a shrewd lawyer for a business leader so as to communicate to the shareholders, company staff and most importantly the regulators and law enforcement bodies. Whatever has been revealed is the least Raju should have revealed to somehow have at least a fig leaf for his actions. In the letter, he keeps insisting that whatever wrong he did was simply to bridge the gap in the account books and that there never was any intention to personally take undue benefits. He has very smartly given himself a certificate that he was never greedy and all the actions he took were for the benefit of the company. Thus, very deceitfully he is conveying to the world that his conduct was well within the fiduciary duty—the duty of trust and faith—towards the company, which he did to the best of his ability, though he slipped both on the legal and ethical grounds. This is self-contradictory. Fiduciary duty, typically very high in the case of senior and top management in a company, is all based on trust, faith and confidence. It is not about numbers only; it is about relationship and the fine art—or science, whatever one may like to call it and define it—of balancing trust, self-interest, profit-making, shareholder-interest and public interest, all at the same time. It is the really difficult, and often seemingly impossible, herculean task, which tests the real business leader.

At that time, it was being analysed in the print and electronic media, and one of the interesting comments made was:

> Satyam's fall from pioneering iconoclast to the largest corporate fraud in India has been rapid, unexpected and shocking. Now, some analysts and investors are wondering whether the same coolness under pressure and willingness to take risks that attracted supporters, employees and investors to Raju may have laid the groundwork for fraud.[7]

This really speaks volumes about the confidence which is required for business communication, but how overconfidence can lead a person to being complacent and how he also starts believing himself to be infallible and someone who is beyond the long arm of the law. One can think about the feelings, apprehensions, thoughts and fears Raju must have had when for the very first time he had written a wrong number in place of the correct number. For any reasonable and prudent person, doing such a thing for the first time is a matter of great dilemma and a conscience shaking decision. This is also a very effective way of business communication, though illegal and unethical, which Raju had chosen and in a short period of time mastered. Was he not aware of the big question mark facing the legality of the exercise he was undertaking? Undoubtedly, he was fully aware of and had

[7] *The rise and fall of Satyam founder*, NYT, Jan 11, 2009, https://www.nytimes.com/2009/01/11/business/worldbusiness/11iht-demise.4.19257696.html

made the decision intentionally without any coercion or undue influence. He was not under any threat and still he did it, which clearly proves that it was not in a fit of anger or sudden provocation—as is mentioned and discussed in criminal law—but was done with a cool head. This makes this act unpardonable and highly condemnable. He was fully aware of the legal provisions related to account books and auditing and he must have, in all probability, consulted the concerned accounts persons and the auditors directly looking after those accounts. The legal language is not only the text and grammar of a particular language but also includes the various numbers reported in usually tabular form in several reports. All these reports, mandatorily, are to be submitted to different regulatory bodies and law enforcing agencies. Most of these reports are statutorily required to be filed at regular intervals duly cross-checked and approved by auditors.

In the legal journey, after Raju's confession, Venture filed a petition in the court to bring this fact on record on the ground that whatever had happened earlier, especially regarding accounts and transfer of shares, could not be taken as frozen with time—settled facts—as the auditors themselves had declared the unreliability of the financial statements of Satyam. Thus, Venture prayed in the court for changes to be made in the factual position of the case by incorporating additional facts, which would have changed the eventual decision of the court in the arbitration award challenge case. For this issue, the matter again went right up to the Supreme Court, which allowed incorporation of additional facts. Interesting ticklish issues regarding an arbitral award, in the light of the public policy of India, were tackled at different courts, and still there is disagreement among the judges in the two-judge bench.

The core issue has been that of fraud by Raju.

Fraud does not have a narrow meaning and cannot be defined with precision. It has a wide connotation in law and in general. Fraud has multiple facets and trying to put it in a narrow sense usually does not work. No more than a century ago, it has been observed in a House of Lords decision:

> But fraud is infinite in variety; sometimes it is audacious and unblushing; sometimes it pays a sort of homage to virtue, and then it is modest and retiring; it would be honesty itself if it could only afford it. But fraud is fraud all the same; and it is the fraud, not the manner of it, which calls for the interposition of the Court.[8]

[8] Frank Reddaway and Co. Ltd. v. George Banham, [1896] A.C. 199 at 221.

This pithy passage has been cited in the 2010 decision of the Supreme Court of India in Venture Global v. Satyam Computer Services case.[9] There was further discussion about fraud in that same judgment as the entire case has been based on the wrongdoings of Raju and misrepresentation made by him. The issue has been how to bring the fraudulent aspects within the purview of "public policy" under the Arbitration and Conciliation Act of 1996. There have been arguments from both sides: Venture Global arguing vehemently that because of fraud the entire arbitration proceedings and the award have no meaning at all; however, Satyam and Tech Mahindra have been taking the stand that the fraudulent activities of Raju had no direct bearing on the performance of the company, and thus there has been no causative relationship between Raju's confession and the arbitral award.

One of the judges in the 2017 Supreme Court of India case—Justice J. Chelameswar—has been in favour of the second view that the arbitral award is valid and should be enforced as Raju's fraud had no relationship with the arbitral award. However, the other judge—Justice A. M. Sapre—has been of the first view that because of Raju's confession, which goes to the root of the matter, the entire arbitration proceedings and the award have no meaning.

An important question arises: whether public policy of any country will permit fraud, misrepresentation, false communication and wilful concealment of facts? The answer to this question is very obvious: no. It is extremely difficult, almost impossible, to justify the establishment of any argument with the foundation laid with falsehood. Fraud and cheating can never be pardoned and thus, reasonably, should be directly hitting at the public policy clause in the arbitration law in India, and elsewhere also.

Interestingly, arbitration is the creation of a contract, and the contract law in India—the Contract Act, 1872—defines fraud in Section 17.

Section 17, Indian Contract Act, 1872
Section 17: "Fraud" means and includes any of the following acts committed by a party to a contract, or with his connivance, or by his agents, with intent to deceive another party thereto or his agent, or to induce him to enter into the contract:

(*continued*)

[9] Venture Global Engineering v. Satyam Computer Services, Supreme Court of India, 2010; 2010 INDLAW SC 609; Bench: P. Sathasivam, Asok Kumar Ganguly, JJ.

(continued)

1. the suggestion as a fact, of that which is not true, by one who does not believe it to be true;
2. the active concealment of a fact by one having knowledge or belief of the fact;
3. a promise made without any intention of performing it;
4. any other act fitted to deceive;
5. any such act or omission as the law specially declares to be fraudulent.

Explanation: Mere silence as to facts likely to affect the willingness of a person to enter into a contract is not fraud, unless the circumstances of the case are such that, regard being had to them, it is the duty of the person keeping silence to speak, or unless his silence is, in itself, equivalent to speech.

Usually wide interpretation of "fraud" is accepted in arbitration proceedings, and in the instant case it was the nexus between Raju and the auditors that relevant and material facts were concealed before the arbitrators, which in true sense makes the award redundant.

Raju's unreliable behaviour was towards the company, the people, regulators and other stakeholders. However, he was usually a sweet-talker and would not rub people the wrong way. His mellifluousness was not to be relied upon. On the other extreme there are persons who can be very straightforward, to the extent of being impolite, egoistic and abrasive. One may be highly qualified and immensely talented, but condescending attitude towards others, even if subordinates, coupled with loose lips can hardly be tolerated in an evolved and sophisticated work environment. Paul Romer learnt it the hard way at the World Bank.

Paul Romer's Exit from the World Bank

In January 2018, the World Bank's chief economist Paul Romer had to quit just after a little less than one and a half years at the position and much before his tenure was going to be completed in 2020.

For some time he had been facing difficult issues at the job, particularly relating to his abrasive nature of working which left many of his peers and colleagues miffed. It is not that everybody has a sweet-natured and amiable boss or colleague at the workplace to enjoy working or at least continue working, but it is typically rather rude and discourteous behaviour, often laced with condescending attitude, which many a time makes it impossible for a person to continue in the position, until and unless the person has all the power to behave in a dictatorial manner and get away with it.

Romer had been unpopular at the World Bank primarily for his outspoken nature and for often making unsubstantiated statements. The ultimate statement which might have cost him his job had been regarding fabricated data relating to the ranking of different countries on the ease of doing business index. He haughtily had stated that the World Bank economists did not care about the veracity of the numbers which were at times stated in different reports and presentations, and that there were rather no proven methods to vindicate the reliability of those numbers. He was particularly talking about the global ranking of Chile and how political leanings of his fellow economists at the World Bank had for the last several years ranked it much lower than it should have been, all by playing with numbers in an arbitrary manner. Later, he made a U-turn and disavowed his statement. But, by that time the damage had been done—both for him and for the highly regarded institution called the World Bank.

Unlike scientists, who require rigorous analysis and proving a hypothesis beyond doubt, economists are not expected to do so. This is very well established and quite acceptable in the socio-political and economic fraternity. It is not possible fundamentally to do as scientists do as there are numerous assumptions on which subjectivity is pushed towards objectivity using certain numbers. The assignment of any numerical value to a subjective criterion is itself a matter of exercise of discretion to a subjective problem, and, hence, even infinitesimally small amount of subjectivity can make all the difference in the final ranking.

Having a basic understanding of how economic institutions function and compile different data to come up with a ranking, any reasonable and prudent person would not complain on the ground that discretion has been exercised in subjective matters. However, Romer's allegation that while collecting the data, several responsible persons did not even bother to verify the numbers which could easily have been done with a little bit of effort creates confusion and erodes the confidence in the working of the institution, and even if the allegations are not proved as per the requirements of the jurisdiction's evidence law, at least seeds of doubts have been sowed. Simply by making Romer leave the World Bank, the institution will not be able to have the same level of confidence of the people and will, in all probability, need to immediately undertake an image-building exercise.

There have been questions raised by the opposition parties in India and the perpetual cynics as to how the ranking of India in the doing business index can move up so fast from 130 to 100 for the year 2018. If there is some merit in what Romer is talking about, who knows that there might have been certain political leaning towards India which pushed the country in the top-100 club in the global index. We, in India, would not like to believe that.

India, currently, is on the cusp of moving in the direction of high economic growth and becoming one of the favourite destinations to attract foreign investment. Any doubts about the numbers which led to the ranking being increased must be laid to rest. It is pertinent for the World Bank to conduct a thorough enquiry to investigate the allegations and clear the air. The reputation and credibility of the institution is at stake. The sooner this exercise is done the better it will be for the participating countries in the rankings, so as to restore the confidence, faith and trust in the annual exercise, which, if not tested vigorously, faces the threat of being called a sham and useless annual ritual.

Coming back to Romer and his allegations and his style of working, it was reported that he even cheekily corrected grammar mistakes and directed—whether it was a suggestion or a command, difficult to say—the staff to use "and" sparingly in their writings, and (thankfully, we are at liberty to use it as many times as we like in this book) insisted on brief emails and presentations by coming straight to the point without beating about the bush. Organisational restructuring by making several positions superfluous is a typical pruning exercise conducted by many bosses at regular interval all over the world. But, the manner in which Romer did it rubbed many persons the wrong way.

An email, which he had written internally to the World Bank staff, was quoted by the *Financial Times* which mentioned about fabricated data. Obviously, Romer hadn't been discreet in the internal communications he had made. The exact statement from his email was picked up and he was left with no option but to defend himself by justifying the email statement on his blog post of 25 January 2018. He wrote:

> My Email Quoted by the Financial Times
>
> The Financial Times quoted accurately the following sentence from an internal email that I wrote: "Imagine a field of science in which people publish research papers with data that are obviously fabricated. …" Some readers mistakenly assumed that this sentence was supposed to convey a hidden

> meaning. To be clear, I am not aware of a single instance in which someone at the Bank published fabricated data, most certainly not "obviously fabricated" data....
>
> I meant the sentence literally. It sets up a thought experiment. The thought experiment was designed to illustrate a general point. Science makes progress toward truth only if individual participants value, hence cultivate, a reputation for personal integrity. Communicating clearly is essential for anyone who wants to signal a commitment to personal integrity.
>
> In the spirit of continuous improvement, every organization should aspire to do better. At this point, any discussion about how the World Bank can do better should take place internally, not via the press, blogs or social media. This is the best way forward because World Bank Group does more than provide support for scientific research... What I did want to say is something many of us in the bank believe – that we could do a better job of explaining what our numbers mean...[10]

Romer had always been a big name in the academic circles—a professor at the New York University—and his joining the World Bank was considered to be a great achievement for the bank. There have never been doubts about his competence and capability. The World Bank president, Jim Yong Kim, was all praise for Romer when he had resigned. It might have been a statement made by Kim while adhering to sophisticated overt behaviour to a certain extent; however, no one has denied about Romer's standing among the peers. He was often shortlisted for the Nobel Prize in Economics. However, of late he had been excessively critical of the work of his peers and said that arguments could be summarised as, "Assume A, Assume B, ... blah blah blah ... and so we have proven that P is true."[11]

When it was a question about intellectual dishonesty, according to Romer, it is inexplicable as to why Romer was so indiscreet. He could have achieved the result he wanted—to flag the issue of lackadaisical approach of his fellow colleagues, if not outright dishonest—by being somewhat tactful, patient and prudent. He did no good to anyone by his bold outspokenness. The allegations he had made needed substantial vindication, which he could not provide. The only inference a reasonable person can draw from

[10] Paul Romer blog, January 25, 2018. https://paulromer.net/my-email-quoted-by-the-financial-times/

[11] Paul Romer Steps Down as World Bank Chief Economist After Rocky Stint, Bloomberg Businessweek, https://www.bloomberg.com/news/articles/2018-01-24/romer-steps-down-as-world-bank-chief-economist-after-rocky-stint.

his conduct is that the statements made by him were not well-thought out and he was, in all probability, not really serious about them. This unfortunate situation speaks volumes about the casualness with which Romer made the accusations. Legally speaking, the burden of proof was on him, and he undoubtedly failed in providing the proof.

He could have very easily avoided the disrepute had he been cautious while making the statement. Propriety demands that after making such a statement one should not leave any stone unturned in providing sufficient evidence, even overdoing it at such occasions is considered to be absolutely fit behaviour. But, withdrawing the statement is the last thing one would expect in this critical situation.

Fascinatingly Romer won the Nobel Prize in Economic Sciences for 2018 along with William Nordhaus. But, the manner of tackling the issue at the World Bank is a totally different issue altogether.

In Romer's case, he had to face the consequences of his utterances; however, an individual's conduct may put the entire company at risk. When individuals make decisions for and on behalf of a company, there is a great responsibility one is shouldering and in such cases, it is important to be doubly sure. Written word is usually preferred to the spoken word. Shakti Bhog, an Indian company, learnt it the hard way when it agreed to ship sorghum to Niger on the basis of an informal agreement with the government of Niger.

Shipping Sorghum Case

Sorghum is called *jowar* or *jwar* in the Hindi language. About 1100 Metric Tonne (MT) of sorghum started its journey from the fields in India to reach to the people of Niger but was destined to rot and become unworthy of consumption. Sorghum reached its conclusion pretty fast as compared to the legal battle, which continued for a long time, and all because of loose lips. The ship literally did not sink but the entire business deal went awry.

Sorghum is an important crop in India and is widely grown in Andhra Pradesh and Telangana (previously these were one province called Andhra Pradesh and were bifurcated in 2014), provinces in the south-eastern part of India. It is used as food for human beings, as feed for animals, and also in the alcohol industry. It is full of nutrients and is the staple for the poorest of the poor living in that area. It is rich in protein and starch which are more slowly digested than other cereals, which makes it useful for diabetics. Its starch is gluten-free. Despite its nutritional value, it was and is not widely consumed in India.

Shakti Bhog Foods Limited (Shakti Bhog) is a company dealing in the business of manufacturing and exporting food products and cereals/grains and more. It was established in 1970 and is a leading brand of wheat flour in northern parts of India. It caters to the Indian market and also exports wheat flour, rice, pulses, oils, pickles and so forth to the United States, Australia, countries in the Gulf and many more. When Shakti Bhog would have got a good bulk deal in the erstwhile Andhra Pradesh, it frankly did not know what to do with so much of sorghum. It might have explored the export market. Niger, a poor country, might have been attracted by the terms at which Shakti Bhog was offering the grain.

It was to export sorghum (hereinafter referred to as the "cargo") to the state of Niger. It negotiated with the head of the state of Niger through a lady Principal Officer for an export order. Niger is an arid land-locked country in the Sahara desert in Africa. It is one of the least-developed countries and has been for a long time under military rule. It is rich in minerals, but agriculture is in primitive stage. It is difficult for the country to feed its people and hence the reliance on import of food grains. Military coups are common and political instability is the norm. Hence, it is difficult to rely on the promise made by any political leader, as that particular individual may not be in the position of power in the near future, or the circumstances may compel him or her not to keep the promise. Thus, the business certainty is very low and despite such conditions, Shakti Bhog was willing to do business with the country.

For some reason, Shakti Bhog's proposal did not fructify. As both the parties—Shakti Bhog and Niger government—did not pay attention to the agreement and its details, there were loose talks by the parties to the promise, which had very little meaning in the eyes of law. As dependence on casual conversation and leakage of information in business can lead to disastrous consequences, Shakti Bhog and Niger found themselves in difficult situation. Niger did not face much problem, as it being a sovereign nation could order food grain from any other country, and had not to be troubled by its so-called agreement with Shakti Bhog. But, for Shakti Bhog, it was a big blow as there was hardly anything to rely on legally against a sovereign nation, with unstable political and legal environment.

A number of cases in different judicial forums finally reached the Supreme Court of India, which held:

> Taking all the matters into consideration and after examining all the materials on record, it is necessary to mention that all the facts regarding the existence of the Charter Party Agreement have been extensively deliberated in the courts below and the said courts have unilaterally accepted that there exists a Charter Party Agreement between the parties. No grounds have

> been raised in this appeal by the appellant satisfying us also that from the records, it could be said that there was no existence of any Charter Party Agreement between the parties. We, therefore, do not find any reason to interfere with the concurrent orders of the courts below.[12]

So, the Supreme Court held that arbitration in London would be the method to resolve the matter. It was on the basis of communication between Shakti Bhog and the other parties to the contract. The relevant portion of the agreement is reproduced:

> Clause 19- LAW AND ARBITRATION
>
> (a) This charter party shall be governed and construed in accordance with the English Law and any dispute arising out of this charter party shall be referred to arbitration in London in accordance with the Arbitration Acts 1950 and 1979 or any statutory modification or re-enactment thereof for the time being in force. Unless the parties agree upon a sole arbitrator, one arbitrator shall be appointed by each party and the arbitrators so appointed shall appoint a third arbitrator, the decision of the three-man tribunal thus constituted or any two of them, shall be final. On the receipt of one party of the nomination in writing of the other's arbitrator, that party shall appoint their arbitrator within fourteen days. Failing which the decision of the single arbitrator appointed shall be final. For disputes where the total amount claimed by either party does not exceed the amount stated in Box 25, the arbitration shall be conducted in accordance with the small claims procedure of the London Maritime Arbitrators Association.

In legal proceedings in the United States, Kola informed the US District Court, Southern District, New York,[13] on 23 February 2009 that the London Arbitration had resulted with an award in its favour in the amount of $1.6 million, plus costs and fees, and Kola should have been allowed to attach the property of four alter egos of Shakti Bhog, viz., Shakti Bhog Snacks Limited, Kumar Food Industries Limited, Crest Biotech Limited and Dash Exports Private Limited. The Court did not allow.

Loose lips had taken Shakti Bhog to several courts—Kakinada District Court, Delhi High Court, Andhra Pradesh High Court, Supreme Court

[12] Shakti Bhog Foods Limited v. Kola Shipping Limited, Supreme Court of India, 23 September, 2008, Bench: Tarun Chatterjee, Dalveer Bhandari, JJ.; (2009) 2 SCC 134.

[13] Kola Shipping Ltd. v. Shakti Bhog Foods Ltd., SDNY, No. 08 Civ. 8817 (GEL), dated Feb. 24, 2009; Citation 2009 WL 464202 (S.D.N.Y.).

of India, Arbitration in London, the US District Court of the Southern District of New York. Several years later, eventually, Shakti Bhog became bankrupt and proceedings were on for liquidation. The *Mint* reported:

> The National Company Law Tribunal (NCLT) on Thursday refused to initiate insolvency proceedings against Shakti Bhog Foods Ltd to recover over Rs 2045 crore since it's already undergoing liquidation.[14]

It is difficult to say how much contribution was of 1100 MT of Sorghum in its bankruptcy, but imprudence in expression and action in business might have been responsible for its sinking. After all, loose lips sink ships.

Communicating indiscreetly, without bothering about the repercussions, can be really troublesome. Free speech is one of the most important rights which we all humans have, but, all the jurisdictions do not protect it equally. There is different treatment given to this right on the basis of varied interpretations. Several organisations, especially private companies, do not allow exercise of this right fully. The periphery which they recognise for their employees is a much smaller subset of the larger set permitted by the country's legal framework. If an employee loosens his lips beyond the permissible limit of the organisation—which changes according to the context—he has to sink, as the business leaders managing the company cannot let the company sink because of loose lips of one or more employees. An internal memo circulated in Google in 2017 highlights it well.

Google's Anti-Diversity Note

In July 2017, James Damore, a Google employee, wrote an internal memo[15] to the employees of Google, which got leaked to the external world. The opening portion is reproduced:

> *Reply to public response and misrepresentation*
>
> I value diversity and inclusion, am not denying that sexism exists, and don't endorse using stereotypes. When addressing the gap in representation in the population, we need to look at population level differences in

[14] NCLT refuses to initiate insolvency proceedings against Shakti Bhog Foods; LiveMint; 9 Feb 2018; https://www.livemint.com/Companies/zMppLjW34IlZfrYV8rDjdK/NCLT-refuses-to-initiate-insolvency-proceedings-against-Shak.html

[15] Google's Ideological Echo Chamber: How bias clouds our thinking about diversity and inclusion; James Damore, July 2017; https://www.documentcloud.org/documents/3914586-Googles-Ideological-Echo-Chamber.html

> distributions. If we can't have an honest discussion about this, then we can never truly solve the problem. Psychological safety is built on mutual respect and acceptance, but unfortunately our culture of shaming and misrepresentation is disrespectful and unaccepting of anyone outside its echo chamber. Despite what the public response seems to have been, I've gotten many personal messages from fellow Googlers expressing their gratitude for bringing up these very important issues which they agree with but would never have the courage to say or defend because of our shaming culture and the possibility of being fired. This needs to change.[16]

The crux of the note was that the company had been discriminating against white male conservatives. Damore contended that women were under-represented in technology companies because of inherent psychological differences between men and women. At that time Google had been undergoing an investigation by the US Department of Labor for discriminating on the basis of gender—it was reported that Google used to pay men more as compared to women for the same job.

There was strong opposition by the female employees and a huge uproar in the company regarding discrimination and the basis and need for it. There were, ironically, similar sentiments prevailing among a section of the employees who clearly came out in agreement with the memorandum, some in open through social media, and some anonymously or by using a pseudo-name on the internal discussion groups or external world platforms. Also there were voices which are vehemently against the idea written in the memo and aggressively wanted action taken against the writer. The company, as far as the overall picture was concerned for the world at large, did not always have an image of being an equal opportunity employer, as inquiries on this very issue had been going on by the American investigative and regulatory bodies. The company was compelled to write a note to its employees. "After a number of female staff described their disgust at the document on social media, Google sent out a company-wide memo saying it did not represent the company's views."[17] Danielle Brown, at that time, had just been appointed as Google's new Vice President of Diversity, Integrity and Governance. Brown wrote to the employees:

[16] Exclusive: Here's The Full 10-Page Anti-Diversity Screed Circulating Internally at Google [Updated]; Gizmodo; 5 Aug 2017; https://gizmodo.com/exclusive-heres-the-full-10-page-anti-diversity-screed-1797564320

[17] Google staffer's hostility to affirmative action sparks furious backlash; The Guardian; 6 Aug 2017; https://www.theguardian.com/world/2017/aug/06/google-staffers-manifesto-against-affirmative-action-sparks-furious-backlash

Googlers,

I'm Danielle, Google's brand new VP of Diversity, Integrity & Governance. I started just a couple of weeks ago, and I had hoped to take another week or so to get the lay of the land before introducing myself to you all. But given the heated debate we've seen over the past few days, I feel compelled to say a few words.

Many of you have read an internal document shared by someone in our engineering organization, expressing views on the natural abilities and characteristics of different genders, as well as whether one can speak freely of these things at Google. And like many of you, I found that it advanced incorrect assumptions about gender. I'm not going to link to it here as it's not a viewpoint that I or this company endorses, promotes or encourages.

Diversity and inclusion are a fundamental part of our values and the culture we continue to cultivate. We are unequivocal in our belief that diversity and inclusion are critical to our success as a company, and we'll continue to stand for that and be committed to it for the long haul. As Ari Balogh said in his internal G+ post, "Building an open, inclusive environment is core to who we are, and the right thing to do. 'Nuff said.'"

Google has taken a strong stand on this issue, by releasing its demographic data and creating a company wide OKR on diversity and inclusion. Strong stands elicit strong reactions. Changing a culture is hard, and it's often uncomfortable. But I firmly believe Google is doing the right thing, and that's why I took this job.

Part of building an open, inclusive environment means fostering a culture in which those with alternative views, including different political views, feel safe sharing their opinions. But that discourse needs to work alongside the principles of equal employment found in our Code of Conduct, policies, and anti-discrimination laws.

I've been in the industry for a long time, and I can tell you that I've never worked at a company that has so many platforms for employees to express themselves—TGIF, Memegen, internal G+, thousands of discussion groups. I know this conversation doesn't end with my email today. I look forward to continuing to hear your thoughts as I settle in and meet with Googlers across the company.

Thanks,
Danielle[18]

[18] Google on Anti-Diversity Manifesto: Employees Must 'Feel Safe Sharing Their Opinions'; Motherboard; 5 Aug 2017; https://motherboard.vice.com/amp/en_us/article/vbv54d/google-on-anti-diversity-manifesto-employees-must-feel-safe-sharing-their-opinions?utm_medium=referral&utm_campaign=amp&utm_source=motherboard.vice.com-RelayMediaAMP

Immediate action was necessary to control the damage. There had been loose lips and the company had to make its best efforts so as to save the ship from sinking.

Google fired Damore.

It was reported:

> Like most of Silicon Valley's top tech companies, Google is overwhelmingly male, white and Asian. Women make up just 20% of the technical workforce, and African Americans just 1%, according to Google's most recent diversity report. Google is also engaged in a legal battle with the US Department of Labor, which is investigating the company for wage discrimination. A DOL lawyer told the Guardian in April that its analysis of wage data showed "that discrimination against women in Google is quite extreme, even in this industry". "At this point the department has received compelling evidence of very significant discrimination against women in the most common positions at Google headquarters," the attorney said. Google denies the charges.[19]

CEO Sundar Pichai wrote to all the employees:

Note to Employees from CEO Sundar Pichai[20]

Diversity and Inclusion, Aug 8, 2017

This note was sent to Google employees this evening. -Ed.

This has been a very difficult time. I wanted to provide an update on the memo that was circulated over this past week.

First, let me say that we strongly support the right of Googlers to express themselves, and much of what was in that memo is fair to debate, regardless of whether a vast majority of Googlers disagree with it. However, portions of the memo violate our Code of Conduct and cross the line by advancing harmful gender stereotypes in our

(*continued*)

[19] Google reportedly fires author of anti-diversity memo; The Guardian; 8 August 2017; https://www.theguardian.com/technology/2017/aug/08/google-fires-author-anti-diversity-memo

[20] Diversity and Inclusion, 8 Aug 2017, https://www.blog.google/outreach-initiatives/diversity/note-employees-ceo-sundar-pichai/; Gajanan, Mahita, 2017, Read Google CEO Sundar Pichai's Letter About the Controversial Anti-Diversity Memo, 8 August, http://fortune.com/2017/08/08/google-anti-diversity-memo-sundar-pichai-letter/ (last accessed on 23 Feb. 19).

(continued)
workplace. Our job is to build great products for users that make a difference in their lives. To suggest a group of our colleagues have traits that make them less biologically suited to that work is offensive and not OK. It is contrary to our basic values and our Code of Conduct, which expects "each Googler to do their utmost to create a workplace culture that is free of harassment, intimidation, bias and unlawful discrimination."

The memo has clearly impacted our co-workers, some of whom are hurting and feel judged based on their gender. Our co-workers shouldn't have to worry that each time they open their mouths to speak in a meeting, they have to prove that they are not like the memo states, being "agreeable" rather than "assertive," showing a "lower stress tolerance," or being "neurotic."

At the same time, there are co-workers who are questioning whether they can safely express their views in the workplace (especially those with a minority viewpoint). They too feel under threat, and that is also not OK. People must feel free to express dissent. So to be clear again, many points raised in the memo—such as the portions criticizing Google's trainings, questioning the role of ideology in the workplace, and debating whether programs for women and underserved groups are sufficiently open to all—are important topics. The author had a right to express their views on those topics—we encourage an environment in which people can do this and it remains our policy to not take action against anyone for prompting these discussions.

The past few days have been very difficult for many at the company, and we need to find a way to debate issues on which we might disagree—while doing so in line with our Code of Conduct. I'd encourage each of you to make an effort over the coming days to reach out to those who might have different perspectives from your own. I will be doing the same."

It was necessary for Pichai to intervene at the right time so that the things did not get out of hand for the company. The morale of all the employees was on the decline due to fuzzy internal scenario created by Damore's memo. Confusion had to be cleared and it could best have been done by the CEO by citing the company's policy and code of conduct.

He could have very well chosen not to get involved after Danielle's email to the employees, but the fact that Danielle had been appointed to the position of Vice President of Diversity, Integrity and Governance—a fancy post created probably to satisfy the external world and regulatory bodies more than for internal effectiveness—very recently, and, hence, did not have the moral authority to command the employees, made it almost mandatory for him to directly be in touch with all the employees and exert his authority. Damore's firing had to be handled deftly at the topmost level because there was a section of employees which believed in what he had written in the memo. Another important message from the top was of deterrence, that others should refrain from communicating such thoughts otherwise they could have faced the same consequences as that faced by Damore. Simply speaking, the message to the employees was to keep their mouths shut or be ready to be fired.

Conclusion

In the context of business communication, loose lips have a different connotation than armed forces. When it is a question of national security, everyone involved in the defence mechanism has to keep the lips tight so that not even a single word goes out indiscreetly; however, when it is a matter of business communication, it is not possible for business leaders not to speak at all the times. They have to surely speak and let others know about their plans and intentions, but they have to be extremely cautious not to tell more than what is required at that particular moment. How to determine as to what is necessary to be shared and where to draw the line are matters of discretion which is to be exercised by the business leader in that particular context. Therefore, there cannot be a simplified formula to be applied in each and every situation. Keeping silent at that moment is also an option and that often has also to be chosen keeping in mind the requirements of that particular situation and what may be the repercussions if silence is maintained or something necessarily has to be spoken. Besides the words spoken or written, the manner in which it is done has tremendous value. Choosing the medium—whether a hardcopy, or electronic communication, or through social media, or through a telephone call, or through a town hall meeting, or through a one-to-one meeting, or through a press release, or through any other method—is also a critical decision to be made.

Intervention of a business leader at the very right moment to control the damage, if done by anyone else in the business organisation by loosening the lips, is of immense value for business in the long run. Short-term benefits have to be sacrificed at that moment and some hard decisions have to be made if the top business leader decides in his wisdom to douse the fire using all possible means, but at the same time not overdoing it. It is also the moral responsibility of top business leaders in any business community to give ample opportunity to others to vent their pent-up feelings so that the situation doesn't become explosive. Again the issue is of how much freedom as to be given to the members of a business community so that a right balance is achieved of having adequate freedom yet subtle control from the top. Absolute freedom in such cases typically does not work. Human beings, by their very nature of being a living organism, love to interact. There are obviously some exceptions who are introverts and do not like to mingle with others. For them it is necessary that there are channels of communication easily available and they understand that their feelings and thoughts, expressed in whatever manner, are duly recognised and appreciated. It is of course not at all necessary that the company works upon each and every thought and idea simply to keep those persons satisfied, as there will not be sufficient merit in every such idea.

Discretion has to be exercised in letting people express themselves and also in controlling them if they become indiscreet so as to be on the right side of the law. All business communication must pass the test of legality.

CHAPTER 2

What's the Good Word?

In Lewis Carroll's *Through the Looking-Glass, and What Alice Found There (1872)*—which was the sequel to *Alice's Adventures in Wonderland* (1865)—the conversation between Alice and Humpty Dumpty highlights the importance of the use of words.

> "When *I* use a word," Humpty Dumpty said, in rather a scornful tone, "it means just what I choose it to mean—neither more nor less."
>
> "The question is," said Alice, "whether you *can* make words mean so many different things."
>
> "The question is," said Humpty Dumpty, "which is to be master—that's all."

This passage has often been used in court judgments to emphasise the significance of the use of proper words and the meaning they convey. Lord Atkin used it in the *Liversidge*[1] case pronounced by the House of Lords, and it has been used in two US Supreme Court cases—*TVA*[2] and *Zschernig*.[3]

[1] Liversidge v. Anderson, dissenting judgment by Lord Atkin, November 3, 1941, House of Lords, [1942] AC 206.

[2] Tennessee Valley Authority v. Hiram Hill et al., or TVA v. Hill, 437 U.S. 153 (1978).

[3] Zschernig v. Miller, 389 U.S. 429 (1968).

A. K. Agarwal, *Legal Language and Business Communication*,
https://doi.org/10.1007/978-981-13-7534-7_2

Use of precise words to convey the right meaning is the key to good communication. While writing or while speaking, at times it is confusing as to what can be the right word to be used. At that moment, a question often comes to mind of the writer or speaker, "what's the good word?" The problem is not unique to the English language. In most of the languages, even the native speakers find it difficult to choose the right word, assuming the language is quite well developed with a strong vocabulary. The more the number of words in a particular language, the more difficult it is to choose the right word to be used to convey the right meaning at that moment.

Most of the court proceedings in common law countries—including India—are conducted in the English language. The legal language used in the courts has evolved over centuries and to a common person it may appear to be quite difficult. Besides the legal language, the words used in the English language may at times appear to be so uncommon that their usage may either not convey the proper meaning to the reader or listener, primarily due to non-familiarity, or it might itself be improper. The language is evolving and growing and new words are added as expected by their usage and common understanding. Well-known dictionaries adopt so many different words with the passage of time that it is not practically possible for a common person to keep pace with the addition of new words. As the English language is used in a large number of countries there are certain local, territory-specific words which are commonly used in that particular geographical area and are duly accepted practically as part of the language, though their usage may not be generally known in other parts of the world. The choice of words also depends on the scope of vocabulary of the user and the context in which the communication has been made. Colloquially, a large number of words are used which may not be recognised in formal language and thus their usage is confined to casual conversations.

There have been efforts made by families, schools, colleges, societies, governments and others to popularise different languages in different parts of the world. To mix learning of language and different words with fun and entertainment, radio and television have undoubtedly played an important role. A number of programmes have been designed for this very purpose especially for children, teenagers and youngsters. There have also been efforts to come up with entertaining programmes related to adult education. One such television show had been the Canadian word-based game show, *What's the Good Word?* telecast in the 1970s. Similar game shows were broadcast on radio and telecast on television in several other countries. The Indian public television—Doordarshan—used to telecast a programme by the same name, *What's the Good Word?* in the 1970s and early 1980s hosted by the very well-known etiquette expert Sabira Merchant. This show was very popular among students and had a long run of 15 years on the national television in India.

In the United Kingdom, a wonderful television show titled *Mind Your Language* was telecast in the 1970s with the setting of an adult education college in London where the teacher had to teach the English language to students from different nationalities. The show was educational, entertaining and hilarious. Based on this show, an Indian television show titled *Zabaan Sambhal Ke*, the title means mind your language in Hindi, was telecast in the 1990s and funnily detected humorous situations of teaching the Hindi language to adult non-Hindi speakers. In all these television shows, the central theme was the use of correct words, grammar and punctuation, so that the right meaning was conveyed while communicating. How the right words have to be used in business communication is an art and can be mastered by practice.

Business Communication: The Legal Lens

In case of any business dispute, the matter may be referred to a judicial forum for adjudication. At that time, the disputing parties do not have to convince each other about their point of view, but it is the presiding officer in the judicial forum who has to be convinced. For this purpose, the parties and the judge should be on the same page. What the lawyer of a disputing party would try to convey to the judge is what his client would have told him. Now, the problem is that if other party to the dispute does not agree, which usually happens, to the meaning ascribed by the first party and his lawyer, there is a divergence of opinion about the meaning which could be ascribed to the written word. In case there is reliance on merely spoken words, the situation becomes still more uncertain, with both the parties not agreeing to the meaning as insisted by either of them.

The lawyer has the duty to use the right words so as to convey the desired meaning to the judge; however, a lawyer may find himself with hands tied behind his back if his client himself has not used the proper words in the communication with the other party. The practice of law depends on the use of proper words, which are the tools and weapons used in litigation. The language is of utmost importance in business communication so that it conveys the desired meaning, as well as can stand the test of time on the anvil of law. Is it necessary for a business leader to learn the legal language while doing business? The answer is yes and no, both. Yes, because every piece of communication—written and oral—can be tested legally and it helps to know clearly the legal implications of using or not using a particular word. No, because the business leader has many other things to bother about while doing business and he cannot be expected to become an expert in using the legally correct language.

What can be done? The business leaders can simply jot down his thoughts about the business and engage a lawyer to phrase it and write it in the legal format. However, the spirit of the message should not be lost in making it legally fit. It is not at all necessary for the business leader to learn the legal words, phrases and maxims. But, it is mandatory that he must know and use the words of any language—whether English or any other—in a precise manner and not loosely. One cannot simply make the excuse that the legal language is difficult and for any other language one doesn't have the competence of an expert. It is quite reasonable and understandable that the business leader may not use the language like an expert, but can always get the draft document vetted by experts, whether of language or law.

For a business leader there are a few definite methods to learn the art of using the right words, proper punctuation and writing or speaking it correct, grammatically. One obvious method is to learn the words as one comes across them. There are a number of words which any businessperson will stumble upon. He can be careful to learn their meaning and a little more by proactively finding more about them. Use of words in law may convey a different meaning as compared to normal English language. This may be true for other languages also; however, in the present text, we will confine ourselves to the English language only. For instance, consideration in law, particularly contract law, means something done or paid in return, however, in simple English it means attention or reflection.

So, it is important to understand the import of words through the lens of law if there is a different meaning from that of the ordinary language. Also, meaning of certain words may differ from the use in different places and context. For instance, person simply may mean an individual or a human being; however, its use can be for a juristic person also, which will include a company. There are words which have been used in the legal sense to mean certain major principle of law. For example, the word reasonable conveys the meaning of being just and fair also. It does not simply mean reasonable from the perspective of one party; it has the implied understanding of being reasonable in the larger context of law.

It is not only the words which have to be taken care of; the punctuation marks are of no less importance. The following case is about the missing comma, which cost the company about $5 million.

The Comma Case[4]

Can a comma create uncertainty? We understand that the use of punctuation marks in any language has its own importance, and wrong usage—using it when it is not required, or not using it when it is required, or using a different mark from the one which is suitable at that particular place—can bring out a different meaning from the text. It is usually the comma which is used for short pauses, and the full stop is used for ending a sentence. Presence or absence of a punctuation mark may result in litigation as can be expected in a highly litigious jurisdiction, and when the stakes involved are high. The matter can even be taken to the highest court in the jurisdiction; however, if the litigants act wisely and decide not to test it in the highest court—due to a great deal of uncertainty as to what the final decision may be—they may like to settle the matter if it had been highly contentious and both the sides had been adamantly sticking to their point of view. One such matter was decided by the US Court of Appeals for the First Circuit by accepting the view that absence of a comma had created a great deal of uncertainty, and it was not possible to find the real intention of the legislature. The case related to truck drivers and Oakhurst Dairy in the United States. Eventually, both parties settled the dispute after litigating for about four years, and it cost the dairy $5 million, not a small sum to be paid for the absence of a comma. The facts are straightforward and quite simple.

Oakhurst Dairy is a company headquartered in Portland, Maine, in the United States. It is, as the name suggests, in the business of milk and milk products, and has also diversified in fruit juices. The company takes pride in bringing the fresh and natural products to its consumers and its website reads as:

[4] Kevin O'Connor v. Oakhurst Dairy, U.S. Court of Appeals for the First Circuit, No. 16-1901; March 13, 2017.

Oakhurst Dairy: About Us[5]
"*The Natural Goodness of Maine*

It's about more than milk.

Life in Maine isn't always easy. The winters are long and the summers are short. But we've always made the most of all we have. And providing fresh, local food is part of our heritage.

From the original Oakhurst Dairy, founded by the Bennett family on Woodford Street in Portland in 1921, to the modern 100% farmer-owned dairy on Forest Avenue in Portland, Oakhurst has always stood for ***The Natural Goodness of Maine***. It's about more than milk. It's about standing up for what you believe, and doing what's right.

The Natural Goodness of Maine is our heartfelt pledge to not only offer you the freshest products day in and day out, but to conduct business transparently, in ways that honor our customers, the environment and our responsibility to next generation. All of our milk comes from local Maine farmers who took the first farmers pledge to keep artificial growth hormone out of our milk. That now-famous fight with Monsanto was the right thing to do then, and stands today as an example of our dedication to doing what's right—even when it's hard.

Today we extend this commitment by reducing our environmental impact, keeping our footprints as small as possible, and finding ways to support healthy active kids. It's a long journey we are all on. We thank you for supporting local food. We thank you for supporting quality. And we thank you for choosing Oakhurst. It's about more than milk."

To make it possible to reach to the consumers with fresh products as soon as possible, the company takes the services of truck drivers, and with the expansion in business with diversification, the number of truck drivers has also gone up. It is quite obvious that the truck drivers are crucial for the dairy business. The employment conditions are governed by the relevant laws of Maine. Title 26, chapter 7, of the Maine Revised Statutes deals with the wage and hour law and also takes care of the overtime law. It specifically provides:

[5] Oakhurst Dairy, About Us, https://www.oakhurstdairy.com/about-us/

> [a]n employer may not require an employee to work more than 40 hours in any one week unless 1½ times the regular hourly rate is paid for all hours actually worked in excess of 40 hours in that week.

The term "employee" has been defined in the same chapter elsewhere, and has been given a broad meaning:

> [a]ny individual employed or permitted to work by an employer.

The truck drivers are, undoubtedly, within the definition of employee and are entitled to overtime, if there were more than 40 hours in any one week.

The law, however, has certain exemption clauses which do not entitle the employees to overtime. Exemption F is one of them.

Case Hinges on Exemption F[6]

Exemption F states that the protection of the overtime law does not apply to:

The canning, processing, preserving, freezing, drying, marketing, storing, packing for shipment or distribution of:

(1) Agricultural produce;
(2) Meat and fish products; and
(3) Perishable foods.

The entire dispute is about the interpretation of the words ***"packing for shipment or distribution."***

The contention of the truck drivers was that the words used in exemption F, "packing for shipment or distribution," should be read as a whole, and as a single activity. That is, a single activity would mean packing, whether it is for shipment or for distribution, and, thus, "packing" is an integral word used in this particular activity. Until and unless the employee was involved in the activity of packing the goods, the exemption would not apply to him. Therefore, the drivers insisted that as they had no role in packing the goods—though they handled the dairy products while

[6] 26 M.R.S.A. § 664(3)(F).

transporting them—by any stretch of imagination and even with extremely wide interpretation given to the word packing. In the final analysis, the truck drivers vehemently argued that the words “packing for shipment or distribution” had to be read together as one activity and they could not be exempted from claiming overtime for the number of hours put in beyond the stipulated 40 hours every week.

Obviously, Oakhurst Dairy strongly opposed the view taken by the truck drivers and insisted that exemption F did not mean what the drivers were interpreting it to be. According to the Dairy it had very clearly mentioned that the exemption should be for the employees who were involved in either packing for shipment, or distribution, and it would have been wrong to read it in a manner that brings together the words as packing for shipment or distribution. For perishable goods like dairy products and fruit juices, it was and is quite natural that distribution of the goods has to be done in a speedy manner which is, in such industries, undertaken 24×7. There cannot be, by any stretch of imagination, a meaning which could have been ascribed to the phrase “packing for shipment or distribution” as words to be read together. According to the dairy, the drivers were outside the purview of the law for overtime protection, as they were clearly covered under exemption F.

Though it appears, on plain and simple reading, as one single activity, yet in practical sense one truly understands that “packing for shipment” and “distribution” surely are two different activities, and these typically are done by a separate set of employees in most of the business organisations, except very small enterprise which may not have sufficient number of staff to manage different activities specifically. In the instant matter, on a technical ground, it can very well be said that the drivers do have a case for getting proper interpretation of the legal provision by a court of competent jurisdiction. This is the most interesting aspect of interpretation of the provisions of law which may be read by both the parties to litigation in their own favour, and it becomes the duty of the courts to try to find out the intention of the legislature at the time of making of the law, and thereafter extrapolate it to the present conditions so as to give it a workable and sensible interpretation.

In 2014, drivers filed a case against Oakhurst Dairy in the US District Court for the District of Maine and claimed the overtime wages which had not been paid to them under the federal Fair Labor Standards Act[7] and the Maine overtime law. The District Court, on the basis of the ruling by the Magistrate Judge, decided in favour of the Oakhurst Dairy on the ground

[7] 29 U.S.C. §§ 201 et seq.

that exemption F read better in favour of the dairy and not the drivers. Thus, the District Court decided that distribution was a stand-alone activity and hence was exempted from the overtime payment category. Having lost the interpretive battle in the lower court, the drivers appealed in the Court of Appeals for the First Circuit as to what should be the proper meaning of the phrase "packing for shipment or distribution."

The detailed arguments made by both sides were based on two pillars: legislative history, and grammar and syntax. It is very interesting to note how the arguments were woven around the principles of English grammar and the lawyers for both the parties must have put in long hours in understanding the fundamental principles of the language so as to argue in favour of their clients. Some of these arguments as discussed by the court in the judgment are culled out.

Oakhurst Dairy's Arguments[8]

"…In considering it, we do not simply look at the particular word "distribution" in isolation from the exemption as a whole. We instead must take account of certain linguistic conventions – canons, as they are often called – that can help us make sense of a word in the context in which it appears. Oakhurst argues that, when we account for these canons here, it is clear that the exemption identifies "distribution" as a stand-alone, exempt activity rather than as an activity that merely modifies the stand-alone, exempt activity of "packing." Oakhurst relies for its reading in significant part on the rule against surplusage, which instructs that we must give independent meaning to each word in a statute and treat none as unnecessary.

…To make this case, Oakhurst explains that "shipment" and "distribution" are synonyms. For that reason, Oakhurst contends, "distribution" cannot describe a type of "packing," as the word "distribution" would then redundantly perform the role that "shipment" – as its synonym – already performs, which is to describe the type of "packing" that is exempt…By contrast, Oakhurst explains, under its reading, the words "shipment" and "distribution" are not redundant. The first word, "shipment," describes the exempt activity of "packing," while the second, "distribution," describes an exempt activity in its own right.

(*continued*)

[8] Kevin O'Connor v. Oakhurst Dairy, First Circuit, pp. 8–10, http://media.ca1.uscourts.gov/pdf.opinions/16-1901P-01A.pdf

(continued)

Oakhurst also relies on another established linguistic convention in pressing its case – the convention of using a conjunction to mark off the last item on a list… Oakhurst notes, rightly, that there is no conjunction before "packing," but that there is one after "shipment" and thus before "distribution." Oakhurst also observes that Maine overtime law contains two other lists in addition to the one at issue here and that each places a conjunction before the last item…

Oakhurst acknowledges that its reading would be beyond dispute if a comma preceded the word "distribution" and that no comma is there. But, Oakhurst contends, that comma is missing for good reason. Oakhurst points out that the Maine Legislative Drafting Manual expressly instructs that: "when drafting Maine law or rules, don't use a comma between the penultimate and the last item of a series."… In fact, Oakhurst notes, Maine statutes invariably omit the serial comma from lists. And this practice reflects a drafting convention that is at least as old as the Maine wage and hour law, even if the drafting manual itself is of more recent vintage."

Drivers' Arguments[9]

"The drivers contend, first, that the inclusion of both "shipment" and "distribution" to describe "packing" results in no redundancy. Those activities, the drivers argue, are each distinct. They contend that "shipment" refers to the outsourcing of the delivery of goods to a third-party carrier for transportation, while "distribution" refers to a seller's in-house transportation of products directly to recipients. And the drivers note that this distinction is, in one form or another, adhered to in dictionary definitions. See New Oxford English American Dictionary 497, 1573–74 (2001); Webster's Third New International Dictionary 666, 2096 (2002)….

The drivers' argument that the legislature did not view the words to be interchangeable draws additional support from another Maine

(continued)

[9] Kevin O'Connor v. Oakhurst Dairy, First Circuit, pp. 10–15, http://media.ca1.uscourts.gov/pdf.opinions/16-1901P-01A.pdf

(continued)

statute. That statute clearly lists both "distribution" and "shipment" as if each represents a separate activity in its own right...

Next, the drivers point to the exemption's grammar. The drivers note that each of the terms in Exemption F that indisputably names an exempt activity – "canning, processing, preserving," and so forth on through "packing" – is a gerund. By, contrast, "distribution" is not. And neither is "shipment." In fact, those are the only non-gerund nouns in the exemption, other than the ones that name various foods.

Thus, the drivers argue, in accord with what is known as the parallel usage convention, that "distribution" and "shipment" must be playing the same grammatical role – and one distinct from the role that the gerunds play.... In accord with that convention, the drivers read "shipment" and "distribution" each to be objects of the preposition "for" that describes the exempt activity of "packing." And the drivers read the gerunds each to be referring to stand-alone, exempt activities – "canning, preserving ...."

By contrast, in violation of the convention, Oakhurst's reading treats one of the two non-gerunds ("distribution") as if it is performing a distinct grammatical function from the other ("shipment"), as the latter functions as an object of a preposition while the former does not. And Oakhurst's reading also contravenes the parallel usage convention in another way: it treats a non-gerund (again, "distribution") as if it is performing a role in the list – naming an exempt activity in its own right – that gerunds otherwise exclusively perform.

Finally, the delivery drivers circle back to that missing comma. They acknowledge that the drafting manual advises drafters not to use serial commas to set off the final item in a list – despite the clarity that the inclusion of serial commas would often seem to bring. But the drivers point out that the drafting manual is not dogmatic on that point. The manual also contains a proviso – "Be careful if an item in the series is modified" – and then sets out several examples of how lists with modified or otherwise complex terms should be written to avoid the ambiguity that a missing serial comma would otherwise create..."

Regarding the legislative history, Oakhurst Dairy had pointed out that the overtime law impacted in 1965 had used the definition of employee in a law enacted four years earlier which excluded the workers handling "aquatic forms of animal and vegetable life," which later on became exemption F, the bone of contention in this case. According to the Dairy, a proper meaning would include meats, vegetables and perishable foods. The court did not agree with this argument and concluded that, according to the legislative history, there was no clarity about the purpose of the exemption and at best it could be said to be speculative. Interestingly, the court itself analysed that even if, for a moment, one believes what is speculated, it would be difficult to explain why the legislature would exempt packing but not distributing the perishable goods. It would not be proper for the court, the judge observed, to draw a firm conclusion on the basis of speculated and presumed legislative purpose. The legislative history was not of much use for making a final decision as the court did not find direct linkage between the laws enacted in the 1960s and their application in the twenty-first century so as to make a dramatic change in the meaning of the phrase in the present time.

While making the final decision based on the arguments made by the drivers and the Oakhurst Dairy, the court used the default rule of construction, especially used in the state of Maine, that for any ambiguous provision in the law related to wages and overtime and so on it should be done to enhance the purpose for which the law had been enacted. It should be liberally interpreted and that is precisely what the court did in the instant case—interpreted in favour of the drivers, as the wages and overtime law had been made to take care of the vulnerable party in case of a contract between a big entity and minions. The basic purpose of the wages and overtime law is to protect the workers from exploitation and strengthen their position vis-à-vis their employers, and, hence, the First Circuit was in favour of accepting the argument of the drivers that the phrase "packing for shipment or distribution" should be read as a whole. The court also relied on the introductory portion of the subchapter of Maine law containing the overtime statute which declared clearly the legislative purpose: "It is the declared public policy of the State of Maine that workers employed in any occupation should receive wages sufficient to provide adequate maintenance and to protect their health, and to be fairly commensurate with the value of the services rendered."

The First Circuit finally ordered reversal of the District Court's partial summary judgment—a major victory for the drivers against the Oakhurst Dairy.

Comments and Questions

The case is all about a serial comma, also known as series comma, or Oxford comma, or even a Harvard comma. However, it is most commonly known as the "Oxford comma." It is the comma which is placed in a series of three or more terms, just before the conjunction "and" connecting the last term with the second last term. For example, when mentioning friends, a person may say that his friends are Tom, Dick, and Harry. The comma just after Dick makes it very clear that the person has three friends and their names are Tom, Dick, and Harry. However, if the comma is absent after Dick, it may mean that the person has two friends, and their names are Tom, and "Dick and Harry." This may sound to be a little far-fetched; however, another example will surely highlight the importance of the Oxford comma.

After receiving a lifetime achievement award for playing wonderful tennis, the recipient issued a press note: "For this award I would like to thank my parents, Jimmy Connors and Martina Navratilova." Without Oxford comma, the sentence can be understood by a reader to convey that Jimmy Connors and Martina Navratilova were his parents. As these names are very well known and in the public domain, most of the readers would understand that the recipient wishes to thank his parents, Jimmy Connors, and Martina Navratilova. However, it requires putting a few things together and not simply picking up the meaning from plain and simple reading. The sentence would have been unambiguous and easy to understand if the Oxford comma had been used: "For this award I would like to thank my parents, Jimmy Connors, and Martina Navratilova."

There is no one single opinion about the use of Oxford comma, as it depends on the usage—which typically is the case with any language, and the English language being used in so many countries in the world, regional differences are bound to happen—and also the purpose for which the work is being written. Academy writing, usually, mandates the use of the Oxford comma, whereas journalistic writing is more liberal. It is not much used in British English, however, the Oxford style manual—and that's why the name Oxford comma—makes its usage a requirement to prevent ambiguity.

Oxford Style Guide, 2014[10]
"Use a comma between items in a list.

I ate fish, bread, ice cream and spaghetti. (correct)
I have nothing to offer but blood, toil, tears and sweat. (correct)

Note that there is no comma between the penultimate item in a list and 'and'/'or', unless required to prevent ambiguity—this is sometimes referred to as the 'Oxford comma'. However, always insert a comma in this position if it would help prevent confusion.

He took French, Spanish, and Maths A-levels. (wrong)
I ate fish and chips, bread and jam, and ice cream. (correct)
We studied George III, William and Mary, and Henry VIII. (correct)
She left her money to her parents, Mother Theresa and the pope (wrong)"

The relevant law—Exemption F—in the state of Maine has been amended in 2017 after the First Circuit decision, and now reads as follows:

> The overtime provision of this section does not apply to:
> ...
> F. The canning; processing; preserving; freezing; drying; marketing; storing; packing for shipment; or distributing of:
>
> 1. Agricultural produce;
> 2. Meat and fish products; and
> 3. Perishable foods.
>
> ...
> [2017, c. 219, §15 (AMD).][11]

[10] University of Oxford Style Guide, Michaelmas term 2014, p. 13, https://www.ox.ac.uk/sites/files/oxford/media_wysiwyg/University%20of%20Oxford%20Style%20Guide.pdf

[11] Maine Revised Statutes, Title 26: Labor and Industry, Chapter 7: Employment Practices, Subchapter 3: Minimum Wages; §664. Minimum wage; overtime rate, https://mainelegislature.org/legis/statutes/26/title26sec664.html

The previous text—prior to the 2017 amendment—is reproduced here for a quick comparison:

> The canning, processing, preserving, freezing, drying, marketing, storing, packing for shipment or distribution of:…

We can easily note that the commas after canning, processing, preserving… have been replaced with semicolons for greater clarity, and a semicolon has been placed after shipment to separate it without any doubt from distribution. Also, "distribution" has been changed to "distributing" so as to be fully consistent with the other words in the sentence like canning, processing, preserving and so on. The activity "distribution" has been written in the gerund form "distributing" to be in line with other activities mentioned.

Such is the importance of punctuation marks that businesses have to be extremely careful about their usage. However, a question arises as to how a business leader can really understand and anticipate the usage of punctuation marks by the legislature itself in the black letter law? There is no clear-cut answer to this issue as a business leader has to rely on the previous decisions made by different courts, and also the norms in the industry. Despite all the precautions taken, it can always be extremely risky to fully rely on the previous decisions as there can be a new issue arising out of something absolutely unexpected which may prove to be uncertain and costly for the company. In such a scenario, it is prudent to settle the matter rather than taking the litigation to a complete finality. Oakhurst Dairy could have appealed in the US Supreme Court against the decision of the First Circuit, but true business wisdom must have prompted the dairy to settle the matter with truck drivers rather than going into the zone of uncertainty and taking a huge business risk. No one knows how the matter would have been dealt in the appeal—it could have gone either way as the interpretation of the Oxford comma is not really scientific and objective but depends heavily on the discretion of the judges. In that sense, business communication has its own limitations of using the legal language to its advantage. Commenting on the settlement, the *New York Times* wrote:

> …But the resolution means there will be no ruling from the land's highest courts on whether the Oxford comma—the often-skipped second comma in a series like "A, B, and C"—is an unnecessary nuisance or a sacred defender of clarity, as its fans and detractors endlessly debate. (In most cases, The

> Times stylebook discourages the serial comma, often called the Oxford comma because it was traditionally used by the Oxford University Press.)...[12]

While writing a detailed article about the Oakhurst Dairy case and use of commas, the British Broadcasting Corporation (BBC) illustrated as to how commas have been used in international conventions to somehow get consensus:

> ...Early climate change conventions included this line:
>
> "The Parties have a right to, and should, promote sustainable development."
>
> The sentence ensures those signing the agreement have the ability to promote sustainable development – and should do so.
>
> But in its original draft, the second comma was placed after "promote", not before it:
>
> "The Parties have a right to, and should promote, sustainable development."
>
> Some countries weren't happy with the original wording because they didn't necessarily want to be locked into promoting sustainable development. Moving the comma kept the naysayers happy while placating those who wanted stronger action...[13]

Whether it is a matter of international conventions or business contracts, the language—including the punctuation marks—is very important, and just like computer programming, one word or mark this way or that way can make a huge difference. A typographical error, if not rectified through a corrigendum in time, can prove to be very costly. Legal documents are read with extreme care and attention whenever a dispute arises. At that time, it is the interpretation which matters for the disputants. Contracts, just like cars undergo a crash test, should be tested under most unreasonable conditions of interpretations chosen by the most unreasonable persons.

As discussed in the beginning of this chapter, proper word power develops with practice. Vocabulary can't be built in a day. Word games are a good method to improve the vocabulary. Proper use of words can help avoid legal disputes. But how to develop word power?

[12] Oxford Comma Dispute Is Settled as Maine Drivers Get $5 Million, NYT, February 9, 2018, https://www.nytimes.com/2018/02/09/us/oxford-comma-maine.html

[13] The Commas That Cost Companies Millions, Chris Stokel-Walker, BBC, 23 July 2018, http://www.bbc.com/capital/story/20180723-the-commas-that-cost-companies-millions

Word Power

Sometimes problems in life may lead to something beneficial and interesting, and then it is realised that those problems were blessings in disguise. The educated and intellectual class in Nigeria, often troubled with spending spare time in the evening without electricity, somehow channelised the children towards playing board games like Scrabble to help develop their vocabulary, rather than idling their time. This exercise resulted in rich dividends as over decades Nigerians have developed a love for board games, particularly Scrabble and have numerous clubs for this very purpose.

Nigeria is home to a good number of top 100 players in Scrabble in the world and the talent for this game is identified and polished at a young age in schools itself. Tournaments are frequently organised with a substantial sum of money as the price for winning players. The money itself is not the only motivating factor as good Scrabble players are given due respect in society and it is quite common for someone who considers himself to be a good player to challenge someone for a game of Scrabble.

These are interesting facts considering the overall lack of infrastructural development in the country and the pace at which the country has to develop to catch up with the first world. Training the children and nurturing the talent to use the right word is a big thing as the same children and youngsters could have been indulging in all sorts of mischievous activities full of vices.

Scrabble is a board game popular globally for the last almost 70 years. The intellectual property in the game is owned by Hasbro in the United States and Canada, and by Mattel in the rest of the world. Primarily, the intellectual property comprises the trade name and trademark for the game itself, and the copyright in the expression of the idea that a player gets some letters and he is supposed to make words out of those letters in a particular manner to earn maximum number of points. When launched, the idea in itself was quite unique and became popular and commercially successful principally because of its novelty. It greatly appealed to the educated people who considered the English language as the coveted medium of education, and, thus, being the passport to success in elitist circles. The game became very popular in English-speaking countries, and later on as the English language—willy-nilly—became one of the foremost, if not the only one, languages for communication in the world.

Nigeria had been a British colony for a pretty long time which easily explains the use of the English language and the game Scrabble might have been introduced to native Nigerians either by certain colonial masters, or some of the highly educated Nigerians who might have travelled abroad either to the United States or Great Britain. Nigeria also follows the common law system—the legal system followed in most of the Commonwealth countries, typically based on the development of law by judicial pronouncements and strictly following the doctrine of precedents. The lower courts are bound by the decisions made by the higher courts for similar matters. It is, in fact, the role of the lawyer to use the right words in the petitions and arguments—more importantly in the written text—and also to be assertive about a favourable interpretation of a word or phrase used either in the statute or in any other written text being considered for the matter heard by a court of law.

Similar circumstances can be experienced in most of the parts of India, as India had been under the British rule for a long period of time which resulted in perceptible shift towards the English language as the medium of education even in the latter part of the nineteenth century resulting in a class divide between the people who could easily read, write and speak English—and were considered to be superior and elite—as compared to those who did not possess these skills. India, being a part of the Commonwealth, has now been for a long time a common law country with huge emphasis laid on perfect drafting of plaints, petitions, applications, affidavits, deeds, conveyancing documents and the like.

The city of Calcutta had been the capital of British India till 1911, when the capital was shifted to New Delhi. Interestingly, two young brothers—Rajat and Jayant Agarwalla—from the same city of Calcutta, now known as Kolkata, launched in 2008 an online word game by the name "Scrabulous," which was, undoubtedly and admittedly, based on Scrabble. Most probably, the word Scrabulous was coined by bringing together Scrabble and fabulous.

The brothers launched the Scrabulous website in 2005 and posted it on Facebook in 2007 and it became very popular with a couple of million Scrabble players addicted to it. In January 2008, it was reported that Mattel and Hasbro had decided to take legal action against them as the companies claimed that the online version of the game was a breach of the copyright they had in the game.

It will be useful to know and remember that the protection of intellectual property in the United States and other parts of the developed world is several notches higher than that in most of the developing countries, including India.

Also, one can have copyright protection for the expression, not for an idea. Thus, the idea that one can use different letters to form words on a board with points associated with them is incapable of getting copyright protection per se; however, once this idea is expressed in the form of fixation to a tangible medium with details about how the game is to be played, along with different coloured tiles, squares and points, and more, then the idea as expressed is surely capable of being protected by the copyright law in the said jurisdiction. The moment it is a matter between two different jurisdictions, it has to be seen whether there is any bilateral treaty for protection of the right in the other jurisdiction or not. Here comes the importance of the bilateral and multilateral treaties for protection of intellectual property signed between different countries, and very popular since 1995 in the form of the World Trade Organisation and Trade-Related Aspects of Intellectual Property Rights (TRIPS) Agreement.

India is a signatory of the TRIPS Agreement since the beginning and hence Indian courts are duty bound by law to protect the intellectual property of foreign companies and individuals. As the brothers were living in Kolkata, the companies filed a petition in the Calcutta High Court seeking an injunction on the online version of the game. It was estimated that the brothers were making almost $25,000 a month at that time from revenue earned from advertising on Facebook.[14] The brothers took the stand that the online version was their contribution to make the game accessible and more popular online as they had been playing the game since their childhood and were almost addicted to it. Scrabble had been a cash cow for these companies, and to move with the times, just a year before the companies had sold the online rights for a Scrabble to another video game maker company, Electronic Arts. Experts had commented that though there were notable differences in Scrabble and Scrabulous, yet the look and feel of online Scrabulous were the same as that of Scrabble, and, hence, there was a clear infringement of the copyright.

The authorised online version of Scrabble for American and Canadian Facebook users was released in July 2008. Both the authorised and unauthorised versions of the game were free. Thereafter, Hasbro immediately filed a suit against the brothers in the US District Court in New York asking for unspecified damages. Facebook was not made a party to this

[14] Why brothers' Facebook homage to Scrabble spells L-A-W-S-U-I-T, The Guardian, 17 Jan 2008. https://www.theguardian.com/technology/2008/jan/17/internet.facebook.scrabulous

litigation and it clearly refused to block the game as it had taken the steadfast stand that it was simply providing a neutral platform to different parties to use it in an amicable manner. However, Facebook took the legal risk as it was exempted from several legal proceedings till the time it became aware of certain issues. Till that time it had no knowledge, it could have got away by taking shelter under the umbrella of ignorance, however, it can be no one's case that one is unaware of something, which one should in any case be aware of, or one did not make any reasonable efforts to know about certain obvious things. If one may call it "voluntary" or "negligent" ignorance cannot be a defence.

In another petition filed by Mattel, owner of rights in India, in the Delhi High Court—domestic courts of course have greater and more effective execution powers as compared to a foreign court, and the brothers have been living in India—it was able to get an order in its favour, but it was a sort of mixed decision which allowed the brothers to retain the right to post the game online but did not allow them to use the name Scrabulous, Scrabble or any other confusingly or deceptively similar name.[15] The game was removed from Facebook and later from the Scrabulous website. Just a little later, a new website named "Lexulous" was launched, which was for all practical purposes a new avatar of Scrabulous. In December 2008, Mattel and Hasbro withdrew the legal petitions against the brothers and their companies, and since then they all have been doing business in a legal manner, as interpreted by the courts of law. However, one may still be not fully convinced as to how a complete rip-off—with a few changes here and there—can be permitted legally. That is, at times, the beauty of legal language and how it is used in business and legal communication.

New words keep getting added to the world of words. Some of them are politically motivated and have a tremendous impact on businesses, directly or indirectly. Business leaders have to choose these new words and phrases very carefully while using them in written or oral communication. Two such words are alt-right and alt-left.

Alt-Right and Alt-Left

Civilised societies do care about the rights of all the people, and dissenting voices are allowed to be heard loudly and strongly. Communication in evolved societies is usually free-flowing and is protected from the whims

[15] Mattel, Inc. and Others v. Jayant Agarwalla and Others, Delhi High Court, 17 September 2008, 2008 INDLAW DEL 1238.

and fancies of the rulers of the day. This protection is guaranteed by the law of the land and is crucial for peaceful living. Businesses require peace to develop and prosper. What may happen to voices which are not considered mainstream is a good test to understand the tolerance level of the government, judiciary and the people at large in such societies.

In August 2017, the United States witnessed racial clashes in Charlottesville. It was reported that the intolerance levels were extremely high, unfortunately in the country that is supposed to be the melting pot and amalgamation of various cultures and civilisations. Business, directly or indirectly, is always affected when an area undergoes unrest and violent clashes. Political masters at that time, in general, resort to rhetorical speeches giving rise to numerous words and phrases which later on become part and parcel of the language used by the media. Some of the words and phrases which have been coined in the last several decades deserve to be discussed as these can be the subject matter of interpretation in different legal fora giving rise to the possibility of more than one meaning, making at times the work of lawyers, as well as judges, difficult. One can, therefore, understand the difficulty faced by the common people who may use these words and phrases in a manner which is not truly fit for usage, but ignorance and lack of awareness about such words and phrases may create legal issues in the absence of clarity on the subject and vagueness of usage.

During the French Revolution in the late eighteenth century, the terms "left" and "right" wing politics were used for the first time according to the seating arrangement in the French Parliament. Members seated on the right side of the chair were broadly supportive of the beliefs of hierarchy, social orders, tradition, conservatism, social differences, old order and so on—all of these were emanating from the belief of inequality among human beings, which may be due to natural law, or economics, or any other reason. Members seated on the left side of the chair were broadly supportive of the beliefs of social equality, egalitarianism, social justice, secularisation, unorthodoxy, republicanism as opposed to monarchy and the like—all of these were emanating from the belief of equality of human beings under all circumstances, and to work towards reducing and abolishing inequality.

Later, the left-wing politics came to bring most of the new ideas under its ambit, such as the civil rights movements, feminist movements and environmental movements. Depending on the period of time in which these ideas emerged, the intensity of their sharpness varied. These were relative to the right-wing thoughts prevailing at that time and, thus, have been highly contextual, thus, heavily dependent on the geographical area, the nature of the government of the day, the legal framework existing at that time and above all the aspirations of the people taking into consideration the real decision-making power the people commanded.

For instance, *Antifa* means anti-fascist. The members of this group work against the right-wing groups, who are wedded to the idea of white supremacy. The word Antifa has lately been used on several occasions in the United States particularly after the racial incidents in Charlottesville. However, the word has many a time been used loosely to convey anything against the establishment. Such interpretation has made any sort of voices raised against the government as Antifa. The liberal usage has diluted the real meaning and deviated from the original purpose for which the word was coined and used. Thus, prior to branding any group as Antifa, it is important to ascertain that the word fits well and the meaning is truly conveyed.

Similarly, a term being used to convey the meaning of Antifa is *Alt-left*, which is used to denote the extreme left views—the views on the otherwise forbidden domain not to be considered in discussions and to be just rejected at the outset. American President Donald Trump has often used this term, as he equates this term with violence, vitriolic attack and now using electronic forum to spread extremism. The notion that the people on the fringes subscribed to this idea or not at all in the mainstream and represent the worst type of leftist thoughts has prompted the political leaders to resort to coining terms to forcefully and convincingly communicate with their followers. Alt-left is supposed to be broader than Antifa and does not agree with mainstream beliefs. No doubt it follows liberal ideas, but it is moving far away from them in the direction of, one may say, liberal liberalism, just like whitish white.

Political nicknaming is also in vogue due to another reason. It is to typically label certain thoughts and believers with a new term, and thereafter define it according to one's own convenience and willingness. President Trump is confidently an expert in doing so. However, communication experts do ask the simple questions as to whether such new terms are useful in conveying the ideas in a simpler manner, and also do these terms have a reasonably long life, or are they short lived. There is hardly any unanimity among experts as it is difficult to generalise about different terms which keep on getting coined by political leaders, corporate leaders, researchers and academicians, and at times popularly by movie stars.

Along with alt-left, the term on the other extreme is *alt-right*. This term represents the extreme far end, the fringe of the right-wing political class and is short for alternative right. It was brought into the mainstream by Hillary Clinton during the presidential campaign in the United States in 2016 when she on several occasions highly criticised Trump for his megalomaniac, narcissistic and self-acclaimed and practised lifestyle. According to her, Trump and his followers were soaked deep down into hierarchy, class and beliefs which were responsible for division of the society, particularly on the basis of economic well-being. Alt-right was typically connected with conservatism and nationalism to the extent of being xenophobic. Easy and obvious antonyms are multiculturalism, tolerance and egalitarianism. Again, the question arises as to what is the extent to which this term can help people communicate better and allow them to conduct their daily business in a more orderly manner. There is hardly any evidence to support the argument that such new coinage of terms is really helpful in the society, though there has been stray research work to support either of the views.

The society with more far right and far left—alt-right and alt-left—radicals is moving away from consensus-building and is demeaning the value of compromise. This is a dangerous trend and uncontrolled, unintentional and liberal use of newly coined terms makes it even more dangerous. The use of electronic media and social media is truly giving rise to unintended consequences, with a large number of them being because of wrong or inadvertent interpretation of the terms by different sections of society. The use of these terms is growing exponentially and social media, which, largely, is neither censored nor monitored. The damage which can be caused is almost instantaneous, and even if any legal remedy is sought, it is time taking, usually circuitous and ends up in legal hair-splitting.

It is difficult, well-nigh impossible, to say that either left or right has an exclusive right over virtue or vice. Similarly, being tolerant or violent is not attributed to any of these exclusively. It all depends on the context, the exigency, the relativity of different situations, the players involved, their aspirations and their appetite for risk-taking, which determines as to whether a particular ideology and belief system can be accepted by the society or not. As the world is not flat, but round, the thought process may also be said to be coming back to the other extreme if one moves a little bit too much and tries to push the frontier on its side by transgressing into the other direction. Moving to the extreme, on either side, may possibly be equally intolerant. Civilised societies do work with the idea of compromise and following the middle path.

Those preferring to follow the middle path may be called the centrists, who, by and large, accept a balanced view of left and right—a little bit of social equality and a little bit of social hierarchy. At times they may lean in one direction leading to centre-left and centre-right politics. Some political commentators, however, call the centrists as weak-kneed and the term is supposed to be pejorative in sense. Though rationality may forcefully aver that anything is neither absolutely good nor absolutely bad, politics ultimately likes to eliminate all but two choices, typically on the two extremes of either good or bad, with nothing in between.

What are the words used by businesses—whether traditional words used for conservative meanings or words with multiple meanings typically in conjunction with other words—that can be problematic from the legal perspective while communicating the same to the consumers in the form of advertisement.

Misleading Advertisements: Words, Images and Intentions

There is a direct connect between businesses and consumers through advertisements and typically the attention span of the consumers is for a very short period of time while going through any advertisement whether in print form or electronic form. Very often advertising companies adopt the strategy of sensationalising the advertisements by using words, phrases and images in a manner which may not be truly acceptable socially and legally. Advertisements can be misleading which can be quite damaging for the reputation of an established company and may simply kill the prospects of getting a firm ground for newer businesses.

The British Advertising Standards Authority, in 2011, forced the cosmetics company L'Oréal to withdraw two advertisements which were misleading. The allegations had been that the company had used digital technology to create the misleading advertisements, which featured well-known actress Julia Roberts and supermodel Christy Turlington and were meant for a Lancôme brand foundation, named "Teint Miracle," and for a Maybelline brand foundation, named "Eraser," respectively. These advertisements had featured in women's fashion magazines *Red* and *Grazia*.

The advertisement showed parts of their faces covered by the make-up and parts of their faces not covered by the make-up. The company showed that the parts which were covered by make-up had fewer wrinkles as compared to the number of wrinkles on the part of the face which was not covered by make-up. The company admitted that it had used digital retouching to create the advertisements. Interestingly, both the women naturally had beautiful skin and it was beyond comprehension why the company wanted any retouching.

Earlier that year, beauty queen, former Miss World and well-known Indian actress Aishwarya Rai had complained that her photographs in the magazine *Elle* were airbrushed to make her skin lighter. She claimed that her photograph was digitally bleached. This was again very surprising why the companies would like to do any such thing because just like the two ladies mentioned earlier, Aishwarya Rai also had beautiful and glowing skin.

The question which arises for consideration is what do the companies want to communicate and convey to the readers and consumers through such advertisements? Is it that even if someone has beautiful skin, she should also use those products to make the skin look even better or is the idea that anyone who does not have such glowing skin needs to use those products and with the passage of time, she will see the change herself?

Whatever the purpose of these advertisements is, one thing is certain: no company can come up with any misleading advertisements as this is not permitted by law in evolved jurisdictions. Advertising itself is a big industry and it is well known that the impact of visual advertisements, as compared to anything in text, on the minds of the consumers is immense. Photographs, video clippings and the message along with these make a consumer not to think the reality for a moment and make her live in the world of fantasy, at least for some time.

These advertisements try to make some people believe that even the impossible is possible. For certain advertisements, it is very clear that they are not meant to be believed. These are clear-cut examples of hyperbole: for instance, after eating two biscuits of a particular brand, a kid is able to lift a very heavy table like a small flower. But some of the advertisements which are not so obvious may convey the message that whatever has been exhibited or expressed in words is "possible," and the advertisements mentioned above fall in that category. This is a very dangerous situation which may prompt a good number of consumers to buy those products, based on the misleading advertisements, and hence making the company liable for cheating consumers, although in an indirect manner.

It is remarkable to note as to how the government and its agencies respond to advertisements. At one point of time when Sushma Swaraj was the Information and Broadcasting Minister in India between 2000 and

2003, all the advertisements for fairness creams, such as Fair and Lovely, were banned on television for the simple reason that these were considered to be against the very notion of "Indian womanhood." The minister had said that there was no need for the women to be obsessed with fairness and all women—irrespective of their complexion—were beautiful. As soon as she relinquished this position, advertisements for fairness creams were back on the idiot box with a vengeance. Not only the advertisements were and are being telecast for fairness creams for women, but there are now creams for men also. Shahrukh Khan is featuring in one of them and proudly tells his fellow countrymen to use Fair and Handsome. Most probably, the days of "tall, ***dark*** and handsome" are over.

There has been another repulsive advertisement. It was by Sony in Holland. In 2006, Sony started an advertising campaign for the new white version of its PlayStation Portable (PSP) video game player which portrayed a white woman aggressively grabbing the face of a black woman, and it read:

PlayStation Portable White is Coming.[16]

This advertisement had hurt the feelings of a number of people and an association for coloured people protested. Sony defended itself and said that the two women were shown to depict the colour contrast between the existing black PSP and the new ceramic white PSP. Sony later apologised and withdrew the advertising campaign.

A couple of questions arise: did Sony not know that such advertisements would obviously be racial in nature and may create trouble? If Sony did not know this, then it is surely a failure on the part of its management. In case they were able to anticipate, the question is why did Sony's management allow the advertising campaign? Was Sony desperate like a new entrant in the market? Was Sony trying to create a controversy to get cheap publicity? Now, if this is true, then it does not speak very highly about Sony's management.

Sony could have surely used some other words to convey the same message to the consumers.

As a big multinational company, Sony, L'Oréal, or any other well-established companies need not indulge in cheap gimmicks. This may be fine to a certain extent only in certain cases of clash of the Titans. For

[16] Sony ad provokes race accusations, The Guardian, 5 July 2006, https://www.theguardian.com/technology/gamesblog/2006/jul/05/sonyadcasues

instance, Coke and Pepsi have a series of advertisements disparaging each other's product. The same is true, to a lesser extent, about Hindustan Unilever Limited (HUL) and Procter & Gamble Company (P&G) in India. For example, the rivalry between Rin and Tide—it forced one company to seek legal action. It is also true about the toothpastes (Colgate, Close-Up, Pepsodent), soaps (Dove and Olay), health drinks (Horlicks, Complan, Bournvita) and so on. The list is fairly long and Indian courts, as well as courts in other countries, have also witnessed legal battles between warring companies regarding advertisements.

It depends on the legal business and environment in the country as to what can be accepted as a reasonable advertisement. Undoubtedly, whatever is said must be true and nothing should be concealed. The companies—whether in India or abroad—need to figure out where to draw the line. Choice of words, phrases and images can really make the difference between legally permissible and impermissible.

One of the words used and misused is "privacy" and has often been interpreted by journalists and individuals in a very different manner, giving rise to practical meaning which can be poles apart. What would the phrase "reasonable expectation of privacy" mean, particularly in cases where celebrities are involved? These issues have been dealt with in a case related to the BBC and the singer Sir Cliff Richard.

BBC and Cliff Richard: Meaning of Privacy

In July 2018, Cliff Richard, the famous British singer—who had sung the very popular number "Congratulations and celebrations, when I tell everyone that you're in love with me..." recorded 50 years ago in 1968—won a lawsuit and damages of £210,000 against the BBC for infringing his privacy. This is a real test of the tussle between an individual's privacy and the right of the society to be informed. The matter pertained to the United Kingdom; however, it might set an example, if not a precedent, for the press to follow, in liberal democratic countries.

There has been, of late, considerable concern regarding the privacy aspects of individuals which are being threatened increasingly due to invasive technologies and extremely aggressive media coverage. Often, somewhat routine matters are converted into sensational news, which does not serve the purpose of informing the public but only helps in creating sensationalism. Freedom of press is necessary and fundamental in an evolved society, especially in a democratic setup as effective debate, dialogue, discussion and deliberation can only take place when the people are well informed. Transparency, rather than opacity, is the rule. But, there is a thin dividing line between what is acceptable and what is not acceptable.

The facts of this case are intriguing as there is a celebrity involved and it is well known that the celebrities find it next to impossible to maintain their privacy. The media persons are infamous for following the celebrities almost everywhere, usually stepping into the forbidden private domain. There are, on the other hand, young and promising performers who are always on the lookout for an opportunity to be in the news somehow, and if they don't get one, they would rather create one on their own by doing something absolutely stupid so as to draw the attention of the media. Even for such persons who have on their own tried to grab the headlines, there is undoubtedly an impermissible sphere where no one is allowed to enter without the individual's consent. Thus, for all solicited and unsolicited, formal and informal, official and unofficial, professional and personal, and other different categories, there is a periphery, which at times may be very clear and at times it may be blurred. At that moment it depends on the individual's judgment to understand the limit to which one can go.

In 2014, the police had raided Richard's apartment relating to certain allegations for alleged offences in the 1980s. He was neither arrested nor charged. However, the BBC had covered the police investigation intensively and even used a helicopter hovering over Richard's apartment to get better coverage. From a media person's point of view, there was nothing wrong and the BBC was just doing its job in the best possible manner to report to the world about the details of the police investigation and what was being talked about the suspect. It is interesting to note that the police have already agreed to pay Richard £400,000 after settling with him without contesting the case in a court of law. It appears to be a matter of excessive enthusiasm shown by the BBC in covering the matter as a celebrity was involved. The question to be asked is, had it been a common man would the BBC be equally interested in reporting the matter and also use a helicopter to get to know the finer details? In all probability, the answer would be no.

The judge in this case, in the judgment, has written that every suspect in police investigation "has a reasonable expectation of privacy" which was obviously denied to Richard, and whatever had been investigated by the police might have been of interest to gossipmongers, but it would be difficult to say that it was a case of real public interest.

This is a little difficult to accept. Imagine superstars—Bollywood actors, political leaders and cricketers, for example—in India. People surely are more interested to know about them and in case there is police investigation into any of their activities, it is quite natural for the people to be curious to know more and more about them. They are like demi-gods. It is not easy for their fans and followers to accept any allegation against them, and if something wrong is proved against them, they are devastated, shattered and wrecked. There are a number of instances when some of them have self-immolated themselves. Hence, it is not correct to say that there is no real public interest, but using a helicopter was a bit too much and the BBC later decided not to appeal as interpretation of the word "privacy" may go against the BBC's aggressive reporting tactic. The Director General of BBC, Lord Tony Hall, stated that the BBC would not appeal. The *Guardian* reported:

> Hall said his own view of the BBC coverage, which used a helicopter to fly over the Richard's Berkshire home to film a police raid on the property in 2014, was that "we overdid it".[17]

Sir Richard and his fans must have been merrily singing "Congratulations and celebrations…" for giving due recognition to his *privacy*.

Conclusion

Enhancing one's vocabulary for general usage can be done by following any of the time-tested methods, which include learning a few new words every day and by trying to master their usage properly. Fine differences between close words, conveying almost the same meaning, have to be understood and practised to attain familiarity. Continued usage and interaction with experts lead to building good vocabulary. Reading better quality literature, which includes works of writers known for using uncommon words, surely helps in expanding one's vocabulary.

However, for a good knowledge of legal terms—words, phrases, maxims and so on—one can read legal literature, and the most obvious material is the judgments pronounced by different courts. Presently, almost all such judgments are easily available on the internet. There is no copyright on the judgments and all of them in almost all the jurisdictions are in public domain. Most of the important judgments are commented upon and

[17] BBC coverage of Cliff Richard raid was over the top, says Tony Hall; The Guardian; 11 Sep. 2018, https://www.theguardian.com/media/2018/sep/11/bbc-to-cut-back-online-services-to-fight-netflix-say-reports

analysed by the press and commentators. Reputed journalists and columnists typically pick up the latest court judgments and discuss them in detail in their writings and deliberations. Going through these works is one of the best methods to learn new legal terms and their updated interpretation.

Words such as consignor and consignee; mortgagor and mortgagee; offeror and offeree; bailor and bailee; lessor and lessee and so on are very common and with repeated usage the meaning becomes quite clear. But, the difficult problem is when newer meaning is assigned to a particular word—either by expansion or by contraction of the scope—by interpretation by courts. Such updated knowledge is possible by keeping track of at least the landmark judgments reported in the press. For business leaders, it is highly rewarding in the long run to know about the proper usage of words and phrases relevant to their business as interpreted by the courts. Linguistic understanding and precision result in better drafting and near-perfect business communication. A business leader need not be a linguistic professional to start his business activities—however, he must not neglect and belittle proper usage of legal terms. He ought to aspire to develop the ability of getting the right word, phrase and punctuation mark while communicating.

CHAPTER 3

Should a Business Leader Talk Like a Lawyer or a Judge?

Business leaders work with the primary goal of making profit. Most of them work with a great deal of passion and fire in the belly. They do not, usually, work in a mechanical manner. While working with high levels of enthusiasm and energy to take the business forward, it is a little bit too much to expect the business leader to think like a lawyer—always to choose the language, words, grammar and syntax properly. It is, therefore, for a business leader to make the right decision as far as business issues are concerned and not get unnecessarily bogged down with legalese and legal jargon. However, it helps to blend the business leader's thinking with the basic aspects of a lawyer's thinking process. So, while a business leader's thinking process is guided by profit, a lawyer's thinking process is guided by the idea of how to remain on the right side of the law. Also, a lawyer's mind is constantly looking for the lurking dangers and threats, and, hence, what needs to be avoided is necessarily on his agenda. A lawyer's mind is tuned to the wishes, needs, demands and aspirations of his client. He steps into the shoes of the client. Some lawyers in a lighter vein comment that along with the fees a lawyer takes all the headache of his client. There is some merit in this statement. A judge's mind works in altogether a different manner. His mind is relentlessly in a quest for justice. He uses various legal tools to reach the goal of justice, fairness, equity and reason.

While communicating their thoughts, business leaders must have the capability of articulating themselves to the audience. They need to have clarity of thought so that their ideas are unambiguously communicated to

A. K. Agarwal, *Legal Language and Business Communication*,
https://doi.org/10.1007/978-981-13-7534-7_3

the target audience. This has to be done through either speaking or writing, or both. Very often, global business leaders have to communicate with audiences of different cultures and it is important to keep in mind the aspects of culture so as not to offend anyone. Business leaders, at different times, have to interact with diverse audiences who may be the individuals at the lowest level of the organisation, or at the highest levels of the organisation. Communicating with people in regulatory bodies and government is totally different from communicating with people in your own organisation, or for that matter the different company also. A business leader has to be truly professional, business-like, and choosing words carefully so that communication is formal and can be successfully passed through the test of official and legal language. A business leader also has to take care of relations with competitors, suppliers, vendors, contractors, media, consumers and so on. The tone and tenor of communication with different audiences cannot remain the same; it has to change according to the context. Every time it is not desirable to apply the filter of legal language while communicating as a business leader. For instance, while replying to a consumer complaint in the first instance, a business leader has to be firm, but polite and courteous without bringing in the issues of legal rights and duties. The purpose is to resolve the matter then and there itself and not give any chance to the aggrieved consumer to escalate it.

However, when the same business leader has to communicate with the government, or regulatory authority, or submit a response in a tribunal, the language used has to be formal, featuring proper use of legal words and phrases to convey the right meaning, and it has to be to the point. Legal rights and duties according to the different provisions of applicable laws have to be clearly cited so as to strengthen one's case in a judicial forum. It is also necessary that whatever communication is made is not only approved by someone using the legal lens, but it must also be exuding ethical values, that is, must be prima facie honest and truthful. A business leader needs to keep positivity as an integral part of his communication, whether informal or formal. At times the circumstances may be excruciating, however, the formal and official language can of course be nicely blended with positivism. Using proper legal language does not in any way means that the communication should look doomed and dark. There must be a desire to achieve positive results by the communication made. It is not at all necessary for the business leader to think either like a lawyer or like a judge to move towards bright, colourful and cheerful picture painted for the stakeholders. The converse is also not true—that if a business leader thinks like a lawyer or a judge, the business leader can never paint a positive picture. Thus, the possibility lies somewhere in between, and which is quite practical, that it helps a business leader to think a little bit like a lawyer and a judge.

The Language of the Law and Business

Is it necessary that the ordinary language used in speaking and writing be different from the language of the law? Not always. There may be a marked difference in the language used in literary writings and the language used in the judgments, pleadings and arguments. However, the difference may not be as obvious as will be evident from the following passage:

M. C. Mehta v. Union of India[1]

"Taj Mahal – The Taj – is the "King Emperor" amongst the World – Wonders. The Taj is the final achievement and acme of the Moghul Art. It represents the most refined aesthetic values. It is a fantasy like grandeur. It is the perfect culmination and artistic interplay of the architects' skill and the jewellers inspiration. The marble-in-lay walls of the Taj are amongst the most outstanding examples of decorative workmanship. The elegant symmetry of its exterior and the aerial grace of its domes and minarets impress the beholder in a manner never to be forgotten. It stands out as one of the most priceless national monument, of surpassing beauty and worth, a glorious tribute to man's achievement in Architecture and Engineering.

Lord Roberts in his work "Forty one years in India" describes The Taj as under:

> Neither words nor pencil could give to the most imaginative reader the slightest idea of all the satisfying beauty and purity of this glorious conception. To those who have not seen it, I would say, – Go to India; the Taj alone is well worth the journey.

A poet describes The Taj as under:

> It is too pure, too holy to be the work of human hands. Angels must have brought it from heaven and a glass case should be thrown over it to preserve it from each breath of air.

(*continued*)

[1] M. C. Mehta v. Union of India, Supreme Court of India, AIR 1997 SC 734.

(continued)

Sammuel Smith in his Book about The Taj explains the impact as under:

> We stood spell-bound for a few minutes at this lovely apparition; it hardly seems of the earth. It is more like a dream of Celestial beauty, no words can describe it. We felt that all previous sights were damned in comparison. No such effect is produced by the first view of St. Peter's or Milan or Cologne Cathedrals. They are all majestic, but this is enchantment itself. So perfect is its form that all other structures seem clumsy.

The Taj is threatened with deterioration and damaged not only by the traditional causes of decay, but also by changing social and economic conditions which aggravate the situation with even more formidable phenomena of damage or destruction. A private sector preservation organisation called "World Monuments Fund" (American Express Company) has published a list of 100 most endangered sites (1996) in the World. The Taj has been included in the list by stating as under:

The Taj Mahal – Agra – India

The Taj Mahal, Marble Tomb for Mumtaz Mahal, wife of Emperor Shah Jahan, is considered the epitome of Mughal monumental domed tombs set in a garden. The environment of Agra is today beset with problems relating to the inadequacy of its urban infrastructure for transportation, water and electricity. The densest pollution near the Taj Mahal is caused by residential fuel combustion, diesel trains and buses, and back-up generators.

Construction of the proposed Agra Ring Road and Bypass that would divert the estimated daily 6,50,000 tons of trans-India truck traffic awaits financing. Strict controls on industrial pollution established in 1982 are being intensively enforced following a 1993 Supreme Court Order. The Asian Development Bank's proposed $300 million loan to the Indian Government to finance infrastructure improvements would provide the opportunity to solve the chronic problems. Agra contains three World Heritage Sites, including the Taj Mahal."

The afore-cited passage is from the landmark judgment pronounced by the Supreme Court of India in the *Taj Mahal case* and it blurs the legal language and literary language. At times to forcefully and very convincingly put across the point, judgments cite from literature and pieces of writing. Sometimes the language of the judgments is not typically dry but lucid, easy to read and simple to understand. Surprisingly, these judgments are a pleasure to read as they are blended with philosophy of life beautifully.

Here is an example:

Raj Kapoor v. State[2]

I am not persuaded that once a certificate under the Cinematograph Act is issued the Penal Code, pro tanto, will hang limp. The Court will examine the film and judge whether its public display, in the given time and clime, so breaches public morals or depraves basic decency as to offend the penal provisions. Statutory expressions are not petrified by time but must be up-dated by changing ethos even as popular ethics are not absolutes but abide and evolve as community consciousness enlivens and escalates. Surely, the satwa of society must rise progressively if mankind is to move towards its timeless destiny and this can be guaranteed only if the ultimate value-vision is rooted in the unchanging basics, Truth-Goodness-Beauty, Satyam, Shivam, Sundaram.

The relation between Reality and Relativity must haunt the court's evaluation of obscenity, expressed in society's pervasive humanity, not law's penal prescriptions. Social scientists and spiritual scientists will broadly agree that man lives not alone by mystic, squints, ascetic chants and austere abnegation but by luscious love of Beauty, sensuous joy of companionship and moderate non-denial of normal demands of the flesh. Extremes and excesses boomerang although some crazy artists and film directors do practise Oscar Wilde's observation: "Moderation is a fatal thing. Nothing succeeds like excess".

All these add up to one conclusion that finality and infallibility are beyond courts which must interpret and administer the law with pragmatic realism, rather than romantic idealism or recluse extremism.

[2] Raj Kapoor v. State, Supreme Court of India, 1980 AIR 258, 1980 SCR (1)1081, V. Krishna Iyer and R. S. Pathak, JJ.

At times the language used may be extremely complex and difficult to comprehend. Justice Krishna Iyer in another landmark judgment—Maneka Gandhi's case—wrote the following passage:

Maneka Gandhi v. Union of India[3]
"The Gopalan (supra) verdict, with the cocooning of Article 22 into a self-contained code, has suffered supersession at the hands of R. C. Cooper (1) By way of aside, the fluctuating fortunes of fundamental rights, when the proletarist and the proprietariat have asserted them in Court, partially provoke sociological research and hesitantly project the Cardozo thesis of sub-conscious forces in judicial noesis when the cycloramic review starts from Gopalan, moves on to In re: Kerala Education Bill and then on to All India Bank Employees Union, next to Sakal Newspapers, crowning in Cooper 1973 (3) SCR 530 and followed by Bennet Coleman and Sambu Nath Sarkar. Be that as it may, the law is now settled, as I apprehend it, that no article in Part III is an island but part of a continent, and the conspectus of the whole part gives the directions and correction needed for interpretation of these basic provisions. Man is not dissectible into separate limbs and, likewise, cardinal rights in an organic constitution, which make man human have a synthesis. The proposition is indubitable that Article 21 does not, in a given situation, exclude Article 19 if both rights are breached."

The language used by judges in writing judgments is something very different from what businesspersons can ordinarily use in day-to-day communication while conducting business. The person to whom the communication has been sent cannot be expected to be sitting with dictionaries and linguistic experts to guide him as to what the message means. It is essential that businesspersons do not use legalese in their communication; however, at the same time it is also necessary that the words they use while writing letters or sending any message through electronic communication methods must not be ambiguous. Business leaders have to be careful not to miscommunicate as contractual disputes can arise, and it takes a lot of time, effort and money to resolve them.

[3] Justice Krishna Iyer in Maneka Gandhi v. Union of India 1978 Indlaw SC 212.

Miscommunication Leading to Contractual Disputes and Their Resolution

It is true that communication should be concise, clear and complete. Though business managers are careful while communicating, yet indiscreetness at times may lead to miscommunication. When the receiver understands something different from what the sender wanted to communicate, and acts on this wrong understanding, the end result may be very different from that envisaged by the sender. Disputes arise and in case of disputes of serious nature, the only option available is legal resolution of such disputes. This type of scenario is very unfortunate because both the parties strongly feel that they are correct and, in fact, each party is correct. Yet there is a dispute to be resolved, which could have been very easily avoided by making the communication crystal clear.

One of the universally accepted basic principles of the law of contract is *consensus ad idem* (the common consent for a binding contract). In cases of miscommunication, there is absence of common consent and hence there is no binding contract. The legal ramifications may be disastrous for both the parties to the contract. It may take a very long time to get the matter resolved in a court of law. A lot of valuable time, energy and money are lost in the process.

More business means more contracts. The business parties create rights and liabilities by contracts. The parties agree to fulfil the conditions of a contract. Many times contracts end in a breach when one party or more parties are not able to honour the contract. It creates disputes and often leads to litigation. These disputes need to be resolved as soon as possible to have a viable business atmosphere. There may be different types of disputes which arise because of confusing or ambiguous communication between the parties to the contract. Long ago, the contracts between parties were entered by verbal communication. The most prevalent method of entering into contracts, particularly between business parties, is by writing the terms and conditions of the contract and then getting it signed by the parties. However, it is not possible to always have a written contract. At times, either the trade practice or expediency requires contracts to be entered into on the basis of either telephonic communication or any other modern means of communication, viz., fax, email, SMS and so on. These methods are not only used for domestic contracts but also for the international contracts. Different means of communication, languages, time zones, cultures, perceptions, interpretations and so on make it difficult for the receiver to always have the same understanding of the message received as the sender wished to send. This may result in avoidable disputes. How does the law view such disputes and what would be the obligations of parties in such conditions are interesting questions to be probed.

Indian Contract Law

An agreement enforceable by law is called a contract. Agreements which are not enforceable by law because of certain reasons—illegal, no consideration, against public policy, immoral and so on—are not contracts. Thus, all contracts are agreements, but not all agreements are contracts. A contract starts with an offer. When the offer is accepted for some consideration, it becomes an agreement. In fact, there are two promises. In case of sale–purchase of certain goods, the seller promises to give his goods to the buyer, who promises to pay for the goods purchased. These set of promises form an agreement. One important thing to be remembered is that acceptance of an offer should be unconditional and it must be communicated to the offeror. It is the general principle of law that oral contracts are as good as written contracts, however, businesses prefer to have contracts in writing. The parties should have an intention to create a contractual relationship and the parties should have "identity of mind" called *consensus ad idem* regarding the subject matter of the contract.

Communication, Acceptance and Revocation

Sections 3 and 4 of the Indian Contract Act, 1872, deal with the communication, acceptance and revocation of proposals. By Section 3 the communication of a proposal, acceptance of a proposal, and revocation of a proposal and acceptance, respectively, are deemed to be made by any act or omission of the party proposing, accepting or revoking, by which he intends to communicate such proposal, acceptance or revocation, or which has the effect of communicating it.

Section 4 provides:

> The communication of a proposal is complete when it comes to the knowledge of the person to whom it is made.
>
> The communication of an acceptance is complete,—

as against the proposer, when it is put in a course of transmission to him, so as to be out of the power of the acceptor;
as against the acceptor, when it comes to the knowledge of the proposer.

The communication of a revocation is complete,—

as against the person who makes it, when it is put into a course of transmission to the person to whom it is made, so as to be out of the power of the person who makes it;
as against the person to whom it is made, when it comes to his knowledge.

In terms Section 4 deals not with the place where a contract takes place, but with the completion of communication of a proposal, acceptance and revocation.

Definitions in Section 2 of the Act

Section 2 of the Indian Contract Act, 1872, defines the following terms: a person signifying to another his willingness to do or to abstain from doing anything, with a view to obtaining the assent of that other to such act or abstinence is said to make a proposal: clause (*a*). When the person to whom the proposal is made signifies his assent thereto, the proposal is said to be accepted. A proposal when accepted becomes a promise: clause (*b*). Every promise and every set of promises forming the consideration for each other is an agreement: clause (*e*). An agreement enforceable at law is a contract: clause (*k*).

Binding Contract

Acceptance and intimation of acceptance of offer are therefore both necessary to result in a binding contract. In the case of a contract which consists of mutual promises, the offeror must receive intimation that the offeree has accepted his offer and has signified his willingness to perform his promise. When parties are in the presence of each other, the method of communication will depend upon the nature of the offer and the circumstances in which it is made. When an offer is orally made, acceptance may be expected to be made by an oral reply, but even a nod or other act which indubitably intimates acceptance may suffice. If the offeror receives no such intimation, even if the offeree has resolved to accept the offer, a contract may not result.

Position Abroad

Theory of Consensus Ad Idem

In a large majority of European countries, the rule based on the theory of *consensus ad idem* is that a contract takes place where the acceptance of the offer is communicated to the offeror and no distinction is made between contracts made by post or telegraph and by telephone or Telex. In decisions of the state courts in the United States, conflicting views have been expressed.

The Entores Case[4]

The rules to apply in India are statutory but the Contract Act was drafted in England and the English common law permeates it; however, it is obvious that every new development of the common law in England may not necessarily fit into the scheme and the words of our statute. The Court of Appeal in England in *Entores Ltd. v. Miles Far East Corporation* held that a contract made by telephone is complete only where the acceptance is heard by the proposer (offeror in English common law) because generally an acceptance must be notified to the proposer to make a binding contract and the contract emerges at the place where the acceptance is received and not at the place where it is spoken into the telephone. In so deciding, the Court of Appeal did not apply the rule obtaining in respect of contracts by correspondence or telegrams, namely, that acceptance is complete as soon as a letter of acceptance is put into the post box or a telegram is handed in for despatch, and the place of acceptance is also the place where the contract is made.

Sir William Anson compared the proposal (offer in English common law) to a train of gunpowder and the acceptance to a lighted match. This picturesque description shows that acceptance is the critical fact, even if it may not explain the reason underlying it.

Communicated Acceptance

A contract is an agreement enforceable by law and is the result of a proposal and acceptance of the proposal. The proposal when accepted becomes a promise. As an ordinary rule of law acceptance of an offer made

[4] Entores Limited v. Miles Far East Corporation, May 17, 1955, Court of Appeal, 1955 (2) All E R 493.

ought to be notified to the person who makes an offer, in order that the two minds may come together or, as Anson puts it, acceptance means in general a communicated acceptance. This is the English common law rule and is also accepted in the United States, Germany and France. The communication must be to the proposer himself unless he expressly or impliedly provides that someone else may receive it. According to our law also (Section 7, Indian Contract Act) in order to convert a proposal into a promise the acceptance must be absolute and unqualified and in the manner prescribed or in some usual and reasonable manner. The intention to accept must be expressed by some act or omission of the party accepting. It must not be a mental acceptance though sometimes silence may be treated as acceptance. Section 3 of our Act says that the communication of acceptance is deemed to be made by an act or omission of the party by which he intends to communicate such acceptance or which has the effect of communicating it.

Communication When Parties Are Absent

When parties to a contract are face to face, there is hardly any problem of disturbance, or delay in communication, or any party not being able to follow the communication made by the other party. The problem arises, when they are not face to face, and, hence, physically they cannot see or hear the other party just next to them. These are the situations when parties are physically at a distance and the communication between them is through either letters or telephone or other means of modern communication. The rules applicable to different situations vary. By speech or any other expression, the offer may be accepted and the intention of accepting an offer can be conveyed either expressly or impliedly. Body language, gestures and movements also signify the acceptance or denial of an offer, even if nothing is conveyed by speech. In case of parties being at a distance, the mode of acceptance, if not specified in the offer, shall be determined by the statutory provisions.

The communication is complete when the reply is received by the offeror and it is clear without any ambiguity. It should not be a counter-offer, which is not acceptance. Telephone, in the earlier times, was considered more of a mechanism to talk to another person as if he is sitting next to someone; however, issues like bad transmission lines, broken conversation due to any other technical fault, not able to hear due to any other very loud intermittent noise such as that of an aeroplane flying or taking off or landing, or conversation gets drowned in the loud noise of heavy hammers used for beating metal sheets or breaking buildings and so on created confusion regarding the legal validity of acceptance. The intention of parties, as mentioned by *consensus ad idem*, cannot be taken for granted if the communication has simply been made but not completed due to technical glitches or human problems, such as someone being hard of hearing, being communicated something while he is in conversation with someone else, or is in the process of multitasking. In such cases, there is no acceptance in the legal sense and telephonic conversation will not be deemed to be complete as far as contract formation is concerned.

Supreme Court Cases

Mac Pherson v. Appanna, 1951[5]

The owner of a bungalow lived in England. His agent lived in India and took care of the bungalow. The caretaker got several offers for the bungalow which he communicated to his master in England. Finally, the owner sent a telegram, "Won't accept less than Rs. 10, 000." One of the enquirers (say A) agreed to pay Rs. 10,000 and believed it to be a concluded contract. Later, someone else (say B) offered more than Rs. 10,000, which was accepted by the owner. A asked the owner to honour the contract. The owner refused on the ground that there was no binding contract. A dispute arose.

Ultimately the matter was decided by the Supreme Court. There was no binding contract as the telegram was not an offer. It may be called an invitation to offer. Hence, in the absence of the telegram being an offer, there was no question of accepting it and thus creating a binding contract. Clear and unambiguous communication might have prevented such a dispute.

Tarsem Singh v. Sukhminder Singh, 1998[6]

This dispute arose when the seller and buyer of a piece of land had different units of area in mind. The seller had a smaller unit (say square feet) and the buyer had a bigger unit (say square yards) in mind. The entire deal

[5] Col. D. I. Mac Pherson v. M. N. Appanna and Another, Supreme Court of India, February 9, 1951; AIR 1951 SC 184.

[6] Sri Tarsem Singh v. Sri Sukhminder Singh, Supreme Court of India, February 2, 1998; AIR 1998 SC 1400.

was completed and earnest money was paid. It was decided that the final payment and transfer of deeds would be done sometime later. At that time, calculations were done and both the parties came to a different result, as they followed different units for measurement. They called each other a cheat and matter was taken to the court for resolution. Ultimately, the matter reached the Supreme Court, where it was decided that it was a genuine mistake of fact by both the parties and, hence, there was lack of identity of mind or *consensus ad idem*. Thus, the contract was void and neither of the parties needed to honour it; however, the seller had to refund the earnest money to the buyer.

This is a clear case of miscommunication leading to an avoidable dispute. Had one of the parties bothered to ascertain the rate of the plot of land and compared it with that in the market and displayed his dismay to the other party, it would have been clarified at the very outset. It highlights the importance of completeness of any communication.

John Tinson and Company v. Surjeet Malhan, 1997[7]

The wife held more than a thousand shares in a company. Her husband also held shares in the same company. One day, he handed over his and his wife's shares with blank transfer forms to a person (say A). Wife's shares were transferred in A's name for Re. 1. The wife challenged the transfer in a court of law. She admitted in her evidence that her husband had delivered her shares to A and that she never objected to the transfer. However, she had not given authority by any letter in writing or otherwise to her husband to transfer her shares in favour of A. She pleaded that there was no *consensus ad idem* for a concluded contract and hence it was a void contract.

The Supreme Court held that without any specific authority by the owner of the shares, that is, the wife in favour of the third party, including her husband, he had got no right to transfer her shares; nor A had got any right and title in the shares held by her. There was no communication from her side and it would have been prudent on the part of the husband and A to have written consent and authority letter. Such a step for clear and complete communication would have surely prevented this dispute in reaching a court of law.

[7]John Tinson and Company Private Limited and Others v. Surjeet Malhan (Mrs) and Another, Supreme Court of India, February 3, 1997; AIR 1997 SC 1411.

Bharathi Knitting Company v. DHL Worldwide Express[8]

An Indian manufacturer had an agreement with a German buyer. The former consigned certain goods and documents to latter through DHL, which never reached the destination. The Indian manufacturer suffered a loss of more than $12,000. However, DHL had capped its liability to $100 as per the terms and conditions of the contract with the Indian manufacturer, which raised a plea of lack of *consensus ad idem*, that is, it never agreed to the $100 cap and there was no binding contract.

The dispute went through consumer courts and finally ended at the Supreme Court. It was held that the consignment containing the documents sent in the cover had been accepted by DHL and was subject to the terms and conditions mentioned on the consignment note. The Indian manufacturer had signed the said note at the time of entrusting the consignment and had agreed to and accepted the terms and conditions mentioned therein. Even if it did not bother to read the conditions, it was bound by them. They were very well communicated by DHL along with an advice to purchase insurance cover to ensure that their interests were fully protected in all events. Had the Indian manufacturer paid heed to the entire communication, this dispute could have been avoided.

Avoiding Disputes Due to Miscommunication

Complete Attention to Details

Parties need to pay complete attention to the communication by the other party. In case, a lot of details are in fine print, do not hesitate to ask for a readable copy. By not asking, ultimately, you may suffer. It is better to delay the signing of the contract than to do it hurriedly and later read it properly and repent. Often there may be too many details for any ordinary person of general understanding to really comprehend what is being written in the document. When the stakes are high, it is important for the parties to read the fine print and give their consent only after understanding the finer aspects. Simply looking at a document cursorily may not serve the purpose as certain critical aspects may be hidden somewhere in the detailed text of the document. One must not be shy of asking the other

[8] Bharathi Knitting Company v. DHL Worldwide Express (Courier Division of Airfreight Limited), Supreme Court of India, May 9, 1996; AIR 1996 SC 2508.

party the aspects of the text which have been incomprehensible simply because of lack of confidence or thinking too much about what the other party may feel about him. It's better to clarify at the very beginning rather than face avoidable trouble later on.

Do Not Take Things for Granted

Things should not be taken for granted. In case of confusion, it is better to clarify. Keeping silent at a time when one may ask questions will not help. It will simply complicate the matters. When parties belong to different cultures, the best method is to ask as many questions as possible so as to bridge the gap. Taking things for granted can be suicidal as the basic assumptions for both the parties may be very different according to their strategic position and the need to enter into a business deal. The purpose, and therefore desperation or lack of it, is highly contextual and depends on the aspirations of the parties which themselves are guided by the historical framework coupled with any paradigm shift of late. Cultural differences between the parties can make things extremely complicated and the bottom line while dealing with any business party from a different business culture and legal framework is to doubly ensure the understanding of terms and references of the work to be done and other aspects of the agreement. These things can be taken lightly, and for granted to a certain extent, if the business parties—two or more—are from the same legal and cultural background.

In Writing

Whenever large stakes are involved, it is better to have things in writing rather than in oral form. It is true that oral contracts are as good as written contracts; however, it is very difficult to provide evidence for oral contracts in a court of law. In today's scenario when electronic communication is very easy, it is always prudent to do things in writing, at least electronically, if not using a hard copy. In most of the civilised countries and evolved jurisdictions, electronic communication has been recognised by judicial frameworks, which makes the life of businesspersons easy as they do not have to always rely on a hard copy which is always difficult to store and retrieve. Electronic data can be very easily retrieved and received either on one's personal storage device or on a number of remote servers made available by several service providers, usually without any charge.

There is, however, the inherent danger of getting the data leaked once it is saved on someone else's server while saving electronic documents, yet the ease and convenience are prompting people to use them not only for social and casual communication but also for business communication for matters which are not of very heavy stakes, both in terms of money and confidentiality.

Cross-Check

It is a good strategy to cross-check and check randomly with the other party. There is no harm in calling the other party and telling them what you have understood and ask them whether this is really what they meant. Getting a green signal from the other party is not a reflection on one's lack of confidence or inability to comprehend but provides evidence that he or she is conscientious and is really serious about the work to be done. Periodic interaction with the other party to have a clear understanding as to the expectations in a contract help both the parties to perform the contract in the most satisfactory manner for both the parties, and also to make changes necessary due to certain newer circumstances so that one of the parties is not taken by surprise by a particular action or inaction of the other party to the contract. There is, however, a thin dividing line between clarifying something and repeatedly asking something so that one becomes irritating and a real pain to continue the relationship. No one likes to drag on with an annoying business ally, so one must exercise discretion to understand when cross-checking is acceptable and when it would be considered to be unnecessary intervention and sheer waste of time and energy.

Be Reasonable

Despite all the safeguards, one must not leave common sense behind. It is not possible in any situation to be absolutely fool-proof, and, hence, it is of utmost importance to think in a reasonable manner and behave as a prudent person. Interestingly each party in the contract considers oneself to be the most reasonable person and the other party to the most unreasonable person. This is obviously not possible. There are certain situations when the conduct of a party may not be considered to be reasonable by social and business norms, but due to exigencies of business and low bargaining power, the other party may be left with no option but to continue doing business with the unreasonable party. It doesn't mean that the so-called unreasonable party should continue his conduct in the same fashion; he is expected to change and be in sync with what the norms are. But if it doesn't happen within a reasonable period of time, it is foolhardy to expect that the same relationship between the parties will continue forever. There can be disruption later if not sooner and for such a thing to happen the unreasonable party is to be blamed on two counts: being unreasonable continuously, and not communicating with the other party to make its stand clear and send the message across in strong terms. Conduct on its own may not be sufficient to communicate what a party wishes to convey. Words serve the purpose and one must not avoid using them to portray one's reasonableness.

There is no one best way of entering into a contract. But one thing is certain—if a party is cautious and thinks before acting, it would in all probability do all the necessary things before entering into a contract. There is no need to rush and complicate matters. Interpretations of the same language may be different. Hence, it is important to understand and act. Negotiation between parties prior to the signing of the contract may leave many issues unanswered. Many times, negotiators leave them for future. That is a very dangerous phenomenon. A contract is irreversible until and unless both the parties want to dump it. A contract creates liabilities and, hence, it should be taken in all seriousness and due importance should be given to communication in contract formation.

One case—Bhagwandas v. Girdharilal—decided by the Supreme Court of India in 1966 is worth going through in some detail.

Bhagwandas v. Girdharilal[9]

In this case there was an oral contract made on telephone long ago in 1959 between two parties in the erstwhile Bombay State—which was divided in Maharashtra and Gujarat in 1960. One of the parties, Messrs. Girdharilal Parshottamdas & Company, was from Ahmedabad and the other, Kedia Ginning Factory & Oil Mills represented by Bhagwandas Goverdhandas Kedia, was from Khamgaon. Presently, Ahmedabad is in

[9] Bhagwandas Goverdhandas Kedia v. Messrs. Girdharilal Parshottamdas and Company and Others, Supreme Court of India, August 30, 1965; AIR 1966 SC 543.

Gujarat, and Khamgaon is in Maharashtra. We can call these parties as the Ahmedabad company and the Khamgaon company respectively. During those days, a long-distance phone call was not something very common; however, good business companies used to have telephonic conversations over long-distance and conduct business accordingly. Most of the time the spoken word was later documented to keep a safe record of the conversation made; however, getting the consent of the other party in written form for whatever had been agreed upon orally, especially on telephone, was not simple and easy as a draft document had to be physically sent via post to the other party for its consent in the form of a signature of the authorised person along with the seal of the company. This was always not possible because it would take a few weeks for the physical document to reach from one place to another, and thereafter to be received by the original sender again. More so, due to the norms of different trades—which had evolved over a period of time due to the special nature of the business as well as to take care of the exigencies—a lot of business was conducted over telephone, which was also based on mutual trust between the parties.

The facts of the case are simple. The Ahmedabad company made a phone call to the Khamgaon company and made an offer to purchase goods from the latter. The Khamgaon company accepted the offer on telephone to deliver cottonseed cake to the Ahmedabad company in Ahmedabad, which it failed to do. Aggrieved by the non-performance of the agreement, the Ahmedabad company filed a case in the Ahmedabad court to which the Khamgaon company objected on the ground of jurisdiction. This is a very interesting concept in the contract law and also in the procedural law for civil cases—known as Code of Civil Procedure, CPC in short—to identify the place for jurisdictional issues. On legal procedural issues, the Khamgaon company contended that courts in Khamgaon, and not in Ahmedabad, would have jurisdiction on the agreement between the two parties.

This is very obvious that when businesspersons talk to each other, they are more concerned about the business aspects rather than the legal niceties and intricate legal interpretations. One can very well imagine the state of mind of two business leaders talking to each other over telephone in a long-distance phone call in the late 1950s: at that time they would have been worried about, first, the connectivity of the call, the quality of voice and whether the other party is able to hear them or not, and, second, about the issues related to business such as price, quantity, date of delivery, place of delivery, mode of payment, place of payment and quality of goods supplied. It would be unrealistic to think that any of the parties at that time would have been thinking about the jurisdictional aspects, which a lawyer would be more concerned about.

However, once the dispute had arisen between the two parties due to non-delivery of the goods, and when the Ahmedabad company moved the court in Ahmedabad, the Khamgaon company must have discussed the matter with its lawyer and tried to find out certain legal issues to somehow proceed ahead with litigation on purely technical grounds. Jurisdictional issues are always the first and foremost technical grounds to fight a legal proceeding by striking at the very root of the matter. The other ground is usually drawn from the law of limitation, by trying to prove that the legal action has been barred by time. For a very long time it had been settled law that an offer is deemed to be accepted at the place—in case two different places are involved—where the offeree had made the acceptance, usually in case of letters by post. However, in case of telephonic conversations—which are instantaneous in nature—the offer would be deemed to be accepted at the place where the offeror gets to know about the acceptance, that is, the place from where the offeror made the phone call.

This was also held in this case, and in an appeal to the Supreme Court by the Khamgaon company, the Supreme Court upheld the decision of the trial court that the Ahmedabad court would have jurisdiction as the Ahmedabad company, which had made the offer and thus was the offeror, got to know about the final acceptance in Ahmedabad itself. The matter in the Supreme Court was decided by a bench of three judges, but by a 2–1 majority. The dissenting judge gave a separate opinion and was of the view that courts in Khamgaon would have jurisdiction because the simple rule applicable to the postage of letters would have applied, and the place where acceptance was made—that is, Khamgaon—would be the place deemed to be the place of contract.

It can really be a tricky situation for a business leader when even judges on the Supreme Court can't be unanimous on the certain issue of the place of contract. In such a scenario, is it possible for a business leader to avoid confusion so as not to get embroiled later on in such jurisdictional issues? Yes, it is quite possible. Most of the contracts in our time have a jurisdictional clause in case the parties are from two different places and most importantly when the business parties are from two different countries, which clearly provides for the place of jurisdiction. To have clarity regarding these issues, it is necessary to have the advice of a lawyer at the very beginning. While making the proposal, such jurisdictional clauses are typically incorporated in the draft itself, which give an opportunity to the offeree to either accept the offer or suggest certain changes by making a counter-offer. Business leaders need to do this exercise at least once at the very beginning while preparing a template for making offers to different parties while doing business, and, thereafter, keep on repeating it till the time certain major changes are required, either on the demand made by the other parties, or because of the changes made by external forces, typically the government and the business environment. The way things might be working in a particular legal and business environment might make a business leader think about certain changes required to be made so as to avoid unnecessary disputes in the long run.

How things may change due to technological developments—as currently we are seeing the emergence of multiple means of communication—even more than a century ago technological changes like the development of telex and telephone made it challenging for interpretation of the existing black letter law. The Supreme Court (majority of two judges) observed and held:

> Obviously the draftsman of the Indian Contract Act did not envisage use of the telephone as a means of personal conversation between parties separated in space, and could not have intended to make any rule in that behalf. The question then is whether the ordinary rule which regards a contract as completed only when acceptance is intimated should apply, or whether the exception engrafted upon the rule in respect of offers and acceptances by post and by telegrams is to be accepted. If regard be had to the essential nature of conversation by telephone, it would be reasonable to hold that the parties being in a sense in the presence of each other, and negotiations are concluded by instantaneous communication of speech, communication of acceptance is a necessary part of the formation of contract, and the exception to the rule imposed on grounds of commercial expediency is inapplicable.
>
> The trial court was therefore right in the view which it has taken that a part of the cause of action arose within the jurisdiction of the City Civil Court, Ahmedabad, where acceptance was communicated by telephone to the plaintiffs.
>
> The appeal therefore fails and is dismissed with costs.[10]

[10] Bhagwandas Goverdhandas Kedia v. Girdharilal Parshottamdas and co., and others; Civil Appeal No. 948 of 1964, decided on 30th day of August, 1965; Bench: K.N. Wanchoo, M. Hidayatullah, J.C. Shah, JJ.; majority opinion of K.N. Wanchoo, J.C. Shah, JJ,; and minority opinion of M. Hidayatullah, J.

It is surely intriguing for business leaders as to how to enter into business agreements on the spur of the moment when they have no time to consult their lawyers because sometimes, due to peculiar circumstances, business leaders have to be really proactive and make the decision at lightning speed. In such circumstances, it is advisable that the agreement should be made in principle with keeping it a little open for further fine-tuning and incorporating legal provisions in consultation with respective counsel. However, to get even this much freedom and flexibility may not be possible at times due to enormous bargaining power of the other party in negotiations, and in such a situation, the business leader has to rely on his own wisdom and legal acumen. Such situations really highlight the importance of knowing the intricacies of law, at least for top business leaders, especially related to the jurisdictional issues and the applicability of particular law. These issues are of utmost importance while negotiating international contracts.

The role of lawyers in cases like this and in several other cases, where finer interpretation of words and phrases used in a text—statute or contract—has to be contested, can never be underestimated, but the services of lawyers are not easily available to each and every client simply because most of the sought-after lawyers are quite expensive to be afforded by ordinary businesspersons. This has been a concern since ages.

Expensive Lawyers

In September 2017, the Chairman of the Law Commission of India, Justice B. S. Chauhan—a retired Supreme Court judge—lamented that the lawyers were too expensive and even he would not be able to afford them if the need arose.[11] The question arises as to whether this is true for India or the same is the case in most of the jurisdictions. Another question which deserves to be answered is as to what makes the lawyers command very high fees.

It is undoubtedly true that good lawyers command a very high fee and interestingly it is true in most of the jurisdictions in the world. For the last at least two–three centuries since legal education became formal and the role of educated and trained lawyers gained importance, slowly but surely it became an art to practice law which could have been mastered by a few.

[11] Legal system expensive, big lawyers charge like taxis: Law Commission chairman, ET, 23 Sep 2017, https://economictimes.indiatimes.com/news/politics-and-nation/legal-system-expensive-big-lawyers-charge-like-taxis-law-commission-chairman/articleshow/60806645.cms

It is usually said, particularly in India, about the legal profession that few earn lakhs, and lakhs earn few. Lakh in India means a hundred thousand. Though a lakh in Indian currency is not a big sum of money in today's circumstances, however, the statement means to convey that not all lawyers command such high fee, but it is still high enough, that is, an ordinary person may not be able to afford one. Also, it means to say that the gap between the so-called top lawyers and the other lawyers is so huge that it is not possible for the clients to easily bridge the gap. It is a matter of quantum jump which can very well be explained by the basic principle of economics—demand and supply.

Thus it has always been the position like this where if the legal profession is considered to be a pyramid, then one can easily find that there are a few lawyers at the top who will be earning the maximum, whereas most of the other members in the fraternity would be somewhere either at the bottom of the pyramid or at the middle of the pyramid. In most of the developed world, the legal profession is highly structured and a large number of lawyers get together to form a law firm and bring their expertise together to provide services to the clients. The arguing counsel, however, are the star performers and many a time can be the force which can change the fate of any decision. Most of the senior counsel in several legal systems, particularly following the common law system, are designated by the courts as Senior Advocates or Queen's Counsel and command a huge fee. With the passage of time, individual senior lawyers develop expertise in a particular subject matter and, therefore, are sought after in cases related to such issues. It is, therefore, not surprising that these lawyers become expensive as compared to other average lawyers.

The issue of excessively high fees is not faced only by people in India, but it is a universal phenomenon observed all over the world. In one of the interesting cases when Rajat Gupta from Goldman Sachs was charged for insider trading which resulted in long litigation, Goldman Sachs found itself in a very peculiar position as it had signed a contract with Gupta to indemnify him for litigation costs related to company matters. Ironically, Goldman Sachs reimbursed the lawyer's fees—$30 million charged by Gupta's lawyer Gary Naftalis—to Gupta. Later on, when the company realised the blunder, it filed a suit for recovery against Gupta to recover the indemnified amount. And, in this process, both the parties again paid to the lawyers.

On numerous occasions, especially the time when markets are not doing well—for instance, the period immediately after the subprime mortgage in the United States and the rest of the developed world—the law firms and lawyers were not adversely impacted because they are needed even in times of crisis when the businesses are shutting shop, and bankruptcy, winding up, liquidation, Chapter 11 in the United States and so on are the most often talked about words. There were several articles published in well-known publications discussing the huge business the law firms were doing.

When the going is good, typically during mergers and acquisitions, the companies involved in the process provide tremendous business opportunities to the law firms. It typically depends on the quantum of the deal and the complexity of issues involved which determine the fees commanded by the law firms. There have been several instances when negotiations for mergers and acquisitions, or takeover, fail, but in the process a long legal and financial exercise of due diligence is conducted by lawyers and accountants together. Even with failed negotiations, the lawyers make money. Thus, one can almost say with certainty that the chips are never down for the lawyers, whether the market is bullish or bearish, whether the deal gets through or not.

The pertinent question to be asked at this juncture is as to why it so happens that the lawyers are needed at all the times. To go to the root of the matter, one has to understand that the provisions of the law are not always fully objective and there is usually a little bit of subjectivity in most of the legal provisions which create the opportunity of those provisions to be interpreted in more than one manner. This precise peculiar trait of the laws and regulations makes it possible for polishing the art of using the right thoughts with the right words so as to make the desired impact on the judge. In any case, the facts remain the same, and the law also remains the same for any lawyer. It is the application of the law to the facts and the dexterity to do so that makes all the difference. Choosing the right legal provision and picking up the right time for making the argument are also important aspects of the practice of law.

For a lawyer, making arguments in a court of law is like a "performance." As "timing" is critical for a stage artist, astute lawyers patiently wait for the right time to make a move. Making a decision as to what is the right time is a matter of practice and experience, and till now is beyond the application of artificial learning and machine language. There have been efforts to make the legal profession a bit less dependent on human ingenuity; however, not much success has been achieved in this endeavour. Inroads have been made in making progress in collecting information, which hitherto was considered to be in the domain of the lawyers or their clerks, as digital with options being prompted by the software. Also, there have been efforts to standardise several conveyancing documents and make them freely available so that the masses need not unnecessarily spend money in engaging a lawyer.

These are good moves and will bring more transparency in the legal documentation; still, businesses prefer to have a lawyer as a "retainer." The retainer serves as the first point of contact and takes care of the preliminary issues to be handled. Thereafter, he may decide the future course of action and which other specialist lawyers need to be engaged. Usually, they all work in teams, whether structured and declared or unstructured and undeclared. At times, these teams work on the principle of "you scratch my back, I scratch yours," which makes it obligatory for the firm's retainer to somehow keep the team together, even if there are better specialists available outside the team. This works against the firm's principal interest of getting the best legal counsel to defend its case or align its business and legal strategy in the best possible manner.

Top management in a firm must be aware of this situation and try not to become the retainer's prisoner. This can only be possible by keeping eyes and ears open to the changing situation in the real world and keeping oneself aware of the new shining legal stars emerging in the legal battlefield. Unsurprisingly, some of the young lawyers with updated knowledge on the subject are quite easily available at a much lower fee than that commanded by the established and expensive senior lawyers. It is also natural that with flourishing practice, established lawyers, at times, get complacent and are not ready to invest the requisite time and effort in the preparation of a case. Going for such senior counsel may cost a firm dear.

For a good and effective lawyer, there is no substitute for thorough preparation and truly empathising with the client. Getting briefed and preparing in a mechanical manner is not the desired method for long-term, highly strategised legal battles. A lawyer, like a true professional, should not mix emotions with work, however, he ought to be passionate about the task he is expected to do. While a programmed computer may be working with numbers and the individual supervising it may get paid handsomely to do so, a lawyer commands the high fees largely for the passion he brings in with him.

A businessperson can, after all, engage the best of the lawyers after paying their handsome fees and diligently pursuing the matter. As a true professional, a lawyer can do the best preparation for a particular matter and thereafter argue the matter to the best of his ability. However, after a lawyer has done his best, it is not in his hands to pronounce the decision; it is the prerogative of the judge.

Judges and Their Voice: Lessons for a Businessperson

Judges are supposed to speak through their judgments only. In the courtroom, the seasoned judges ask a few questions to the arguing counsel and again are not supposed to do too much of talking. But, astute practising lawyers often develop the uncanny ability to gauge the mood of any particular judge by keenly observing his body language. Add to that the decibel level of the judge's voice, and the task becomes a little easier. Thus, very often experienced lawyers can quite successfully predict the outcome of a case being heard by a judge.

Court proceedings are not video recorded in most of the jurisdictions of the world, and thus, these proceedings are only witnessed by the persons present in the courtroom at that time. Very few courts allow video recordings and thereafter upload them on the court's website for easy access to anyone interested in watching and analysing them and drawing conclusions from them. The UK Supreme Court has a vibrant website with copious video recordings available. Just like any cricket player—batsman or bowler—would like to watch video recordings of previous matches and learn from the mistakes made earlier, stage performers do the same. Professionals typically take the help of their trainers and coaches to point out their mistakes and suggest corrective measures.

Such corrective techniques are usually not available for lawyers who have to depend on moot-courts during their law school days, but in real professional life a few honest peers, very helpful in nature, may do so. What about businesspersons? They also get hardly any feedback on their business negotiation skills and rely mainly on their gut feeling to understand if something has drastically gone wrong. Most of the business schools have included courses on business communication as mandatory modules, which are designed with the purpose of providing sufficient exposure to written and oral communication. Instructors teaching such courses work pretty hard to give candid and detailed feedback to the participants.

How much a businessperson should speak? And, in what manner—like a lawyer, like a judge, like a salesperson—who usually speak a lot, or like a poet or writer? What can be a typical businessperson-like communication?

For a businessperson, the ultimate goal, ordinarily, is to make profits. Whether it is made by talking or remaining silent, it does not matter. However, for certain businesses, a lot of talking needs to be done whereas for others the businessperson needs to remain silent and let the numbers do the job. For example, for the job of a salesman or a marketing executive one has to talk a lot, but a banker can rely more on the numbers. Nevertheless, a businessperson must appreciate the fact that even if he is supposed to speak a lot, he must refrain from divulging confidential information and trade secrets. At no point in time he can afford to be indiscreet. At the same time, it must be appreciated that even those businesspersons who usually do not have to speak a lot on certain occasions have to engage in a conversation and must not send a wrong signal at that time by keeping quiet when they are supposed to either express themselves categorically or raise certain pertinent queries. It is no one's case that their language and conduct should be either lawyer-like or judge-like while doing business transactions. They need to be themselves.

A lawyer's style of communication is guided by the demands of a certain matter, his own basic nature, the judge before whom he is making the arguments and several other factors, many of them intangible and developed by individual lawyers on their own. For a lawyer, it is like performing on a stage. Not only the judges on the bench are watching him keenly, he is watched with equal keenness by other lawyers and litigants present in the courtroom. Thus, a good lawyer will always try to put his best foot forward and leave a good impression on others. This is not the job of a businessperson, who can afford to not consider a meeting with a client or making a presentation to investors as a performance. Still the businessperson has to bother about being discreet and not leaving any stone unturned in achieving what has been planned. Businesses can ill-afford to have leaders who don't care either about the contents or the manner of their delivery. Both these things matter.

But, judges don't have to perform as the lawyers have to. They have to be avid listeners. And while listening they are expected to maintain stoic silence, not exhibit emotions, remain dispassionate and decide the matter before them on the basis of merits, and purely merits. Strictly speaking, emotions are not supposed to have any place in the decision-making by legally trained judges. Still, one may observe certain judges becoming emotional, at least showing some signs of emotions rather than sitting stone-faced, during court proceedings and sometimes outside the court while meeting members of the legal fraternity and media, in seminars and conferences and so on. An interesting research was conducted using the audio recordings of the US Supreme Court proceedings and the voice modulation of the justices was analysed to come to the conclusion that the pitch of the voice matters and there can be some correlation between the higher pitch of a judge's voice and the possibility of losing the case.[12]

The researches, one can always argue, are microanalysis and in a way somewhat similar to legally hair-splitting. These are not scientifically proven as gravity and cannot be relied on as there are numerous assumptions and several exceptions. Nonetheless, it is interesting to note that the judges are also human beings and each and every individual has a limit to which one can conceal or camouflage one's emotions. This threshold varies from individual to individual, and even for the same individual from situation to situation. Though the judges are expected to make decisions in an objective manner, subjectivity, howsoever small it may be, often creeps in the process of decision-making and may play a critical role in the final outcome.

It is not proper for a judge to lose temper in the courtroom but sometimes it is a matter of a real test of nerves as some of the lawyers may not be leaving any stone unturned to unnerve the judge. Most of the new judges have to go through this ordeal at the hands of some senior lawyers, usually notorious for this craft. Judges are expected to maintain self-restraint and not let the situation go out of control. Seasoned lawyers and hardened judges do not let this happen, and keep their antennae ready to receive even the feeblest signals and act accordingly so as not to give even half an opportunity to the other party to hijack the situation.

Businesspersons while communicating with their partners, customers, clients, vendors, subcontractors, bankers, government officials, suppliers, superiors, subordinates and more use a mix of verbal and non-verbal communication, which often are observed by interested persons. Their body language also communicates a lot. Much higher exposure than yesteryears—due to easy accessibility and affordability of videoconferencing, video calling, uploading video clippings on social networking sites and far greater exposure given by the electronic media with hundreds of channels telecasting thousands of minutes of video footage—have pushed even the most

[12] Supreme Court justices may give away their votes with their voices, Economist, 21 Dec 2017, https://www.economist.com/blogs/democracyinamerica/2017/12/pitch-perfect?cid1=cust/ddnew/email/n/n/20171221n/owned/n/n/ddnew/n/n/n/nap/Daily_Dispatch/email&etear=dailydispatch

introvert business leaders, though unwillingly, onto the centre-stage. Today, every place is a stage and every move is a performance. Like movie stars, top business leaders are also followed—physically and virtually—every minute. Their every move is analysed deeply, sometimes resulting in unquestionably avoidable exercise, and, thus, raising serious issues about drawing the thin line between their personal and private lives.

Conclusion

Business leaders, like judges of superior courts, can possibly train themselves not to show emotions and thereby avoid the chances of getting their strategic and tactical business moves anticipated by business commentators, competitors, regulators, media and others. There's a small problem, however. Business leaders—usually highly successful ones—are truly passionate about their work and usually for them there is no difference between shop and home; they are always at work and always tuned to the unending demands of the work. For most of them, work is not work simpliciter; it is life. And, in such circumstances it is very difficult for a passionate businessperson to restrain himself, be stiff as a cardboard, not exhibit emotions and not explain passionately to a curious knowledge-seeker about the subject of his work.

Where to draw the line between being passionate and not showing feelings is a matter of individual choice and preference, which cannot be scientifically determined. Science, mathematics and statistical analysis have their limitations. Being fully devoid of emotions is neither possible nor desirable for human beings, more so in the world which is moving in the direction of incorporating more and more of artificial intelligence—leading to emotions—in robots. It can, thus, be said that businesspersons should not always force themselves to micromanage the language they use; however, broadly speaking there must be a subtle control and a particular bandwidth within which they must communicate to possibly avoid sending ambiguous signals and unnecessarily getting into legal problems.

CHAPTER 4

It's All Greek to Me

Graecum est; non legitur.

It means "it is Greek, it cannot be read." This phrase, though, is in the Latin language.

The idiom "it's all Greek to me" means that something is beyond comprehension. Usually, it is said for self, and not for others. It is used maybe for a foreign language which a person is unable to understand, or for some very complex written work full of jargon and technical language, or verbal message loaded with extremely difficult words, pompous and circuitous arguments. It may be even a drawing or a design or certain symbols which the user is not able to understand. It is not at all necessary that the message itself is so difficult and complex, but it also reflects on the ability of the person who is not able to grasp. Thus, the same message or piece of information may be Greek to someone, but to someone else it may be something very easy to understand.

The phrase became popular from Shakespeare's 1599 play *The Tragedy of Julius Caesar*. In Act 1 Scene 2, this was what Casca had said to Cassius.

> *Cassius: Did Cicero say anything?*
> *Casca: Ay, he spoke Greek.*
> *Cassius: To what effect?*
> *Casca: Nay, an I tell you that, I'll ne'er look you i' the face again: but those that understood him smiled at one another and shook their heads; but, for mine own part, it was Greek to me....*

A. K. Agarwal, *Legal Language and Business Communication*,
https://doi.org/10.1007/978-981-13-7534-7_4

For an aristocrat Roman in those days, it was expected to know the Greek language; however, with the passage of time the use of this language declined and fewer people were able to understand it, and, hence, the saying "it's all Greek to me."

Nevertheless, there are a number of words in the English language which have Greek origin and some of these words are very commonly used in our day-to-day life. For instance, music, cinema, democracy, plastic, air, Galaxy, Marathon, marmalade, narcissism, panic, planet, sarcasm, schizophrenia and telephone are all Greek words which are routinely used in colloquial language all over the world. According to experts, there are more than 150,000 English words of Greek origin. It is next to impossible to engage in any meaningful conversation in the English language without using Greek words. However, these words have so very well been adopted in the English language and are so very often used that there is hardly any feeling of these words being non-English words. It is not the purpose of this chapter to discuss Greek words and how they have become an integral part of the English language. The purpose is to discuss and think about various issues which arise before a business leader while reading any legal text or trying to have a reasonable and well-comprehensible conversation with a person who typically uses foreign words and phrases which may appear to be not too familiar. Add to it the problem of legal words, phrases and maxims which surely makes it even more difficult to understand. It is very common to experience lawyers and others in the legal fraternity to use a lot many difficult words, phrases and maxims at a great frequency.

Business leaders have to very often interact with legal professionals who, purposely or unconsciously, use several foreign words, phrases and maxims. There are a few reasons for legal professionals to conduct themselves in this manner. First, they are trained in such a manner that such foreign words on their own roll off the tongue. Second, while practising law for a substantial number of years, use of such words and phrases becomes a habit, and it is said that old habits die hard. Third, and a very important reason, is the concise and precise meaning which can easily be conveyed to someone who is expected to be fully aware of them. It can be said that when computer software experts talk to each other they also use a lot of technical jargon and simply do not communicate with each other in running text in the English language, or for that matter in any other language of the world. Similarly, when medical professionals wish to convey to each other something about a particular ailment, they just use the technical words required for that very purpose rather than writing a note in running text format. The same applies to legal professionals; however, there is one unique problem that it is not only the people in the legal fraternity who have to use these words and phrases, but the common man on the street is also concerned and impacted by decisions of various courts, which willy-nilly use a good number of such words and phrases and maxims. Thus, the problem is not confined to a select group of people in the legal profession, but everyone, including the business leaders, is directly or indirectly affected.

Very often legal maxims, foreign words and phrases are used by courts in their judgments all over the world, particularly in common law countries. It however depends on the judges on the bench and their preference to use maxims to drive their point home. It is surely not at all necessary to use maxims in judgments as knowledge of these maxims is usually limited to lawyers and other scholars. Common people in general do not know these maxims and hence it is undoubtedly difficult for them to get a good understanding of the judgment by a plain and simple reading; however, the maxims embellish a judgment and give it a scholarly touch. Let us go through two judgments I have picked up—one from the European Court of Human Rights and the other from the Supreme Court of India—where the judges have liberally used maxims, foreign words and phrases.

The Regner Case[1]

The judgment by the Grand Chamber of the European Court of Human Rights was delivered in September 2017 and dealt with the issue of fair trial rights. The importance of this decision is due to the controversial question of fair trial in cases of not sharing the information on which the proceedings had initiated with the accused on grounds of national security. The facts of the case are as follows.

Regner was born in 1962 and used to live in Prague. He got employment with the Ministry of Defence in 2004 and sometime later was given access to state-classified "secret" information. He was appointed as the director of the department of administration of the Ministry's property and also appointed as deputy to the first Vice-Minister of Defence. On the

[1] Case of Regner v. The Czech Republic (Application no. 35289/11), European Court of Human Rights, Strasbourg, 19 September 2017, pdf version accessed and downloaded, August 11, 2018, pp. 1–95, https://hudoc.echr.coe.int/eng#{%22appno%22:[%2235289/11%22],%22itemid%22:[%22001-177299%22]}

basis of certain classified "restricted" information, his security clearance was revoked. It was done primarily due to two reasons: that Regner had not disclosed at the time of applying for the position that he had foreign bank accounts and had been director in a number of companies, and that he was considered to be a national security risk. The basis of this decision was not communicated to him as that piece of information was considered to be restricted and by law could not be shared with him. The inference was drawn that he was not trustworthy. He appealed against the decision which he lost on the ground that the classified documents could be relied on and thus he could not be trusted; however, it was held in that appeal that he did not fail to disclose pertinent information at the time of applying. While the proceedings were going on, he had applied to be relieved from his duties on the ground of not keeping good health, which was accepted the same day; however, technically, the date for terminating the contract was after about hundred days.

Before that date, he moved the Prague Municipal Court to get the decision of his removal reviewed judicially. He was allowed to have a look at the contents of the file, except the classified documents. The court, nonetheless, had the complete record for perusal. During public hearing, Regner stated that the action against him was revengeful as he had denied cooperating for something which he believed was beyond his duties. The court did not agree with the review application and dismissed it primarily on the ground that classified information cannot be made public and as the decision is based on such information, the court's hands were tied behind its back, though it had access to the classified information and had gone through it and evaluated it. There was no need, and the law did not allow, public disclosure of that information, not even to Regner. He appealed in the Supreme Administrative Court, where also he lost. The appeal was dismissed on the ground that the court was convinced on the basis of classified documents that he could not be trusted with keeping secrets, and thus, his credibility had eroded. Also, the disclosure about the method of working of intelligence was not desirable as it would have been very risky for the country. As the nature of proceedings was special due to the involvement of secrecy, confidentiality, classified and restricted documents and the like, ordinary and routine method of procedure could not be followed. Thus, the precise reasons for his removal could not be unveiled to him, though the administrative courts had access to unlimited classified documents, and observed that the reasons were in no way connected with his denial to cooperate with the intelligence service.

A few years later, in 2010, Regner moved the Constitutional Court on the ground that the proceedings of the termination of his services were unfair. The complaint was dismissed, and the reason for the decision was simply given as the special nature of the duties, and in such cases, fairness of proceedings as understood in normal circumstances for routine cases cannot be assured. It was held that the lower courts were fully justified and their decisions were as per the Constitutional norms. Thus, there was no reason for the Constitutional Court to intervene. A year later, in 2011, Regner, among others, was indicted on charges of manipulating public contracts at the Ministry of Defence—where he had served for about two years—and also abusing position of public power, and related issues. He was found guilty in 2014 by the České Budějovice regional court and was imprisoned for three years. The Prague High Court upheld his conviction but prison sentence was suspended for two years. This decision was challenged in the Grand Chamber of the European Court of Human Rights on the ground of violation of Article 6 § 1 of the European Convention on Human Rights. This article protects the "right to a fair hearing." It is reproduced for ready reference.

Article 6. Right to a Fair Trial[2]

1. In the determination of his civil rights and obligations or of any criminal charge against him, everyone is entitled to a fair and public hearing within a reasonable time by an independent and impartial tribunal established by law. Judgment shall be pronounced publicly but the press and public may be excluded from all or part of the trial in the interest of morals, public order or national security in a democratic society, where the interests of juveniles or the protection of the private life of the parties so require, or the extent strictly necessary in the opinion of the court in special circumstances where publicity would prejudice the interests of justice.
2. Everyone charged with a criminal offence shall be presumed innocent until proved guilty according to law.
3. Everyone charged with a criminal offence has the following minimum rights:

(*continued*)

[2] https://www.echr.coe.int/Documents/Convention_ENG.pdf

(continued)

(a) to be informed promptly, in a language which he understands and in detail, of the nature and cause of the accusation against him;
(b) to have adequate time and the facilities for the preparation of his defence;
(c) to defend himself in person or through legal assistance of his own choosing or, if he has not sufficient means to pay for legal assistance, to be given it free when the interests of justice so require;
(d) to examine or have examined witnesses against him and to obtain the attendance and examination of witnesses on his behalf under the same conditions as witnesses against him;
(e) to have the free assistance of an interpreter if he cannot understand or speak the language used in court.

On the whole, the court by majority decided that Regner's right to a fair trial was not violated and due to the nature of proceedings on the basis of national security and interest, there were some restrictions imposed, as compared to any other case, which were reasonable and justified. The judgment was not unanimous. It was held by ten votes to seven that there was no violation of Article 6 § 1 of the Convention. There were dissenting opinions which merit reading and attention. The primary ground for the majority decision is that the Czech courts had gone through the confidential documents which can satisfactorily be considered to be adequate assurance that the proceedings in the domestic courts were fair and just. Another important reasoning on which the decision is based is that the Article 6 § 1 of the Convention does not in any way give absolute right, but this right has to be interpreted in the light of public interest. And, by any yardstick, public interest prevails when compared with individual's interest.

The main points raised by dissenting judges are regarding the adequacy, sufficiency and appropriateness of the proceedings followed in the Czech courts, which did not allow either the accused or his lawyer to get a copy of the confidential report on the basis of which Regner was prosecuted. Though the courts had access to the classified documents, yet the accused never ever got a chance to have a look at it. Prima facie, it violates the principle of natural justice of giving an opportunity of being heard. In the dissenting judgment, the judges have cited various Latin legal maxims which bring out the issues being discussed very clearly and in the right perspective.

Partly Dissenting Opinion of Judge Serghides

Put another way, the absolute prohibition of access by the applicant to the classified information on which the withdrawal of his clearance certificate was based, which was the subject of his application to the administrative courts, amounted to a violation of the principle *audi alteram partem*, which literally means "hear the other party or side" and of course the principle of equality of arms, as has been said above. Of relevance also is the ancient Greek rule of fairness and equality "*μηδενί δίκην δικάσεις, πριν αμφοίν μύθον ακούσεις*", which can be translated into English as "you cannot judge before you hear what both parties have to say". As Bennion observes, "Coke took from Seneca's *Medea* the saying that *qui aliquid statuerit parte inaudita altera, aequum licet dixerit, haud aequum fecerit* (he who decides a thing without the other side having been heard, although he may have said what is right, will not have done what is right)". From this Latin maxim, and especially the words *haud aequum fecerit*, one can see how important it is for the judge to hear both sides even if what that judge says is right.

...

The procedural injustice that occurred as a result of the deprivation of the applicant's rights to equality of arms and adversarial proceedings was exacerbated by the ineffective procedure used by the domestic courts to examine the evidence before them and which was not compatible with the principle of adversarial proceedings. The rule *affirmanti, non neganti, incumbit probatio*, meaning he who affirms, not he who denies, must bear the burden of proof, which is used in several instances in the case-law of the Court, found no application in the present case, since this maxim applies only in adversarial proceedings.

...

(*continued*)

(continued)

I believe that if the procedural means to pursue a right are taken away, this unavoidably destroys the end result, namely, the protection of its essence—*qui adimit medium dirimit finem*, meaning "he who takes away the means destroys the end".

...

Two legal Latin maxims are relevant in this respect: *exceptio probat regulam*, meaning "an exception proves the rule"; *exceptio quæ firmat legem, exponit legem*, meaning "an exception which confirms the law, expounds the law". On the other hand, an absolute or blanket exception or restriction or ban goes right to the core of a right. So it cannot be said that it confirms or expounds the right, but it merely annihilates it and renders it ineffective by removing the foundation on which it lies. Here the general Latin maxim *sublato fundamento cadit opus*, meaning "remove the foundation, the work falls" may also be relevant. Were the proceedings criminal rather than civil or administrative, such a blanket and absolute restriction would probably violate the presumption of a person's innocence.

...

Article 26 of the Vienna Convention on the Law of Treaties of 1969 (VCLT), headed by the Latin maxim *pacta sunt servanda*, provides that: "Every treaty in force is binding upon the parties to it and must be performed by them in good faith".

...

But in my view the national authorities' failure to inform the applicant even summarily of the accusations against him can only be described as arbitrary and unjust. With due respect, in my humble opinion, in examining whether there has been a fair hearing under art.6(1) of the Convention there is no room for distinctions similar to those made between *de lege lata* and *de lege ferenda* legislation, referring to what is or what is not desirable for future legislation. The notion of fairness and the mechanism of the balancing test under the Convention provision are concerned only about what is just and logical and exclude what is unjust and arbitrary, and they do not have to be concerned with what is desirable or not. In the present case, however, what has been described by the majority as "would

(*continued*)

(continued)
have been desirable" was in fact what was not done by the national court, in breach of the right of applicant to a fair trial, and was therefore both arbitrary and unjust.

...

Hence, whatever the outcome of a subsequent set of proceedings, one should avoid the **post hoc** *ergo propter hoc* fallacy, meaning "after this therefore because of this".

...

If security considerations were able to provide a blanket or an absolute restriction on the right to a fair trial, as has been decided in the present case, I am afraid to say that such a finding would be catastrophic for human rights. This could be the opening of Pandora's box and the protection of every human right—not only the right to fair trial—would be bankrupt. To borrow an expression used by then Justice Benjamin N. Cardozo (though in another context), such an approach "would carry us to lengths that have never yet been dreamed of".[3]

Comments and Questions

This judgment, rather the dissenting portion by Judge Serghides is full of maxims. One of the basic principles of natural justice "***audi alteram partem***" means that the other side has to be heard and that no one should be condemned unheard. Thus, every accused has to be given a reasonable opportunity to defend himself. In the instant case, the dissenting judgment stresses the point that without getting to know the charges against oneself, how can one effectively defend oneself. Thus, not disclosing the confidential report to the accused amounts to violation of the principle of natural justice. Similar thoughts are conveyed by the maxim, "you cannot judge before you hear what both parties have to say." Another way of expressing the same thought is, "***qui aliquid statuerit parte inaudita altera, aequum licet dixerit, haud aequum fecerit,***" that is, "he who decides

[3] Partly dissenting opinion of Judge Serghides. Footnotes in the cited passage not included, pp. 49–82 of the ECHR judgment, Case of Regner v. The Czech Republic (Application no. 35289/11).

a thing without the other side having been heard, although he may have said what is right, will not have done what is right." Such is the importance of giving an opportunity to the other side to be heard. These are fundamental principles followed in any evolved jurisdiction and go to the root of the matter in the present case. Had the confidential report been shared with Regner and his lawyer, there is a chance that they might have found inconsistencies and lapses in the report and it might have been dumped by the courts, without taking any action on its basis.

Another fundamental maxim is "*affirmanti, non neganti, incumbit probatio.*" The person who affirms, not he who denies, must bear the burden of proof. It is reasonable and fair. Practically, if this is not the case, and is otherwise, it would be so simple for anyone to make allegations against someone and then sit back and relax, and watch the fun as the other party is now supposed to prove his innocence. This is ridiculous and amounts to misuse of judicial process. That is why the person who makes allegations is under an obligation by law to prove the veracity of allegations. This is the founding principle of adversarial proceeding.

Also, making it difficult or impossible by removing the means to achieve something will tantamount to denying the end result. The maxim "*qui adimit medium dirimit finem*" conveys this meaning, "he who takes away the means destroys the end." Thus, it is not only by making the end result elusive for someone, but by simply making the means to reach to the end difficult or unmanageable, one is guilty of depriving the other party and can be liable under the law.

The other maxim used is "*exceptio probat regulam,*" which is short for "*exceptio probat regulam in casibus non exceptis.*" It means that the exception confirms the rule in cases not excepted. This is also based on simple common sense that why would any exception be made if there is no general rule; however, it has been used and misused on various occasions to interpret something the way a party wishes. But, it is plain and simple that exceptions whenever made prove the existence of a general rule.

A natural corollary is the maxim "*exceptio quæ firmat legem, exponit legem,*" which means that an exception whenever made and which confirms the law typically explains and illustrates the law. Thus, absolute exception does not make sense and attracts the application of the maxim "*sublato fundamento cadit opus,*" which means that if the foundation is removed, the work will fall and cannot survive.

"*Pacta sunt servanda,*" a very popularly used maxim in international law and relations, means that treaties are entered into good faith and must be honoured by the parties. Promises must be kept. Typically, all the international treaties are based on this maxim and the intention of the parties to the treaty is assumed to be honest and based on trust and confidence. At that moment, it is not to be asked that if a party does not perform according to the treaty, then what would be the course of action as the founding principle is good faith and trust.

There is an important difference between "*de lege lata*" and "*de lege ferenda*" legislation. The former is the law as it is at present, and the latter signifies what the law ought to be and refers to future. It is not proper to impose the *de lege ferenda* on existing problems. What the law ought to be is an ideal situation and should not be used to resolve the current matters.

The logical fallacy "*post hoc ergo propter hoc*" means "after this therefore because of this," which directly suggests a sequence of events and therefore causality. It is not at all necessary that there is a correlation between the two events, and there may be many other factors which might be responsible for the latter event. Hence, conclusion should not be drawn merely because of the sequence of events. Such a belief often gives rise to superstitions but is not explainable on the basis of logic and reasoning. In the application of law and interpretation to legal text, one has to be wary of this fallacy.

The second case is from the Supreme Court of India.

The Indore Development Authority Case[4]

The case is related to land acquisition and payment of fair compensation to the landowners. Land has been a serious issue in the infrastructure development of late and since the independence of India, in general, for the big landlords and the government. All sorts of legal technicalities have been used to either obfuscate the process of land acquisition or at least cause as much delay as possible. Even once land has been acquired, its compensation—as far as fair market value is concerned—has been a highly contentious issue for one simple reason that the governments, both at centre and in provinces, have not been open to pay true value to the owner. Often, matters have dragged in courts, right from the lowest to the highest court, for decades. The cases have usually been dependent on the

[4] Indore Development Authority and another v. Shailendra (dead), through Lrs. and another; Supreme Court of India; 8 February 2018; Bench: Arun Mishra, Mohan M. Shantanagoudar, Adarsh Kumar Goel, JJ.

interpretation of a few words or phrases. Typically, either there are no major disputes about the facts, or if there are any such disputes, those ordinarily get settled at the trial court level.

The instant case is one in which the Supreme Court of India has referred to dozens of legal maxims. Citing these maxims bring in the age-old worldly wisdom associated with the vindication by decided cases. The government and the landowner are not very much interested in the legal maxims, as their primary concern is the decision of the court. Legal language laced with these maxims makes the reading of the cases often a pleasure for voracious readers and linguistic experts, but for litigants the maxims are irritants and clutter in an otherwise simple and easy-to-follow judgment. Both these perspectives have their values as maxims cannot be just avoided but too much use also is undesirable.

Some of those maxims and phrases in this judgment are highlighted.

Should a litigant suffer due to the delay in the court proceedings or due to any other act of court? Definitely not, and that is what is mentioned in the maxim *"actus curiae neminem gravabit,"* which means that act of court should not prejudice anyone. The Supreme Court wrote in the judgment:

> In the book titled "Selection of Legal Maxims" by Herbert Broom, the author about the said maxim has observed:
>
> *"This maxim "is founded upon justice and good sense; and affords a safe and certain guide for the administration of the law" (b). In virtue of it, where a case stands over for argument on account of the multiplicity of business in the Court, or for judgment from the intricacy of the question, the party ought not to be prejudiced by that delay, but should be allowed to enter up his judgment retrospectively to meet the justice of the case (c); and, therefore, if one party to an action die during a curia advisari vult, judgment may be entered nunc pro tunc, for the delay is the act of the Court, for which neither party should suffer(d)."*
>
> It is settled proposition of law that no litigant can derive the benefit of pendency of a case in a court of law. In case any interim order is passed during the pendency of litigation it merges in the final order. In case the case is dismissed the interim order passed during its pendency is nullified automatically. It is also settled that a party cannot be allowed to take benefit of his own wrong as 'commodum ex injuria sua nemo habere debet' i.e. convenience cannot accrue to a party from his own wrong. "No person ought

> to have advantage of his own wrong." In case litigation has been filed without any basis and interim order is passed it would be giving illegal benefit or wrongful gain for filing untenable claim.

So, any party to litigation should not get any benefit due to pendency of a case in a court. This sounds good, however, is not practical, as one party typically suffers due to delay in proceedings in the court. Even in this cited portion, we find foreign words and phrases—*"curia advisari vult"* and *"nunc pro tunc."*

"Curia advisari vult" means the court wishes to reserve the decision and would like to consider the matter. Now, at the time of reserving a decision, courts generally do not specify the date when the judgment shall be pronounced. This time gap may be very short, of a few days, or very long, of several months and unbelievably of even years. Should a litigant suffer as the judgment has been reserved? The answer obviously is no.

"Nunc pro tunc" literally means "now for then" and is used by courts for retroactive action—for some correction to be made from an earlier date. It may be to rectify certain clerical errors or other defects from the previous applicable date so that no party is prejudiced. Thus, the basic purpose is to correct any errors and give it effect from the time of initial decision.

Another maxim used in the reproduced portion is *"commodum ex injuria sua nemo habere debet,"* which means that a person cannot be allowed to benefit from his own fault.

There are different words in which the same meaning is conveyed and understood by common persons, without resorting to legal language or any maxim. It is often said that one cannot benefit from his own fault or no one should be allowed to take advantage of his own mistake. These are basic norms of living in a civilised society, and in case of any dispute, these are followed as fundamental decisive principles of equity and justice. So, how does a Latin maxim help? The greatest help a person can get from such maxims in any argument is the authoritative value and universal acceptance of these maxims. As these maxims have a certain set language, like "*commodum ex injuria sua nemo habere debet*," there are no two versions to create any confusion. There is usually acceptance of the same meaning of the maxim, which helps tremendously in bringing any argument to a closure with only facts to be put in the right perspective of the maxim. Thus, it is the application of the "right" maxim to a set of facts. The other party is surely free to argue that a particular maxim will not be applicable in a specific case as there may be distinguishing factors to be taken care of. However, on most of the occasions, even if the facts and a particular maxim do not fit inch by inch, still there is usually agreement between the parties in principle on the fundamental aspect of the maxim. And, that itself is a great starting point in bringing the parties together, and makes the difficult job of convincing them a bit easy.

At another place in the judgment, while mentioning about interpretation of statutes, it has been observed, *"A Verbis Legis Non Est Recedendum,"* which means that a court cannot add or subtract a word from the enacted law, or in other words, it means that no word can be treated as superfluous in the written law and in similar fashion word cannot be added to the written law to give a new meaning to it. Thus, it simply means that whatever is written as the black letter law has to be interpreted as it is, and not as it ought to be, or not the way the judge or the lawyers would like it to be written. This makes the job of the judge while interpreting any statute quite difficult and the scope very narrow as the freedom to interpret the written statute is not too much and must be done within the limited boundaries. This has been a very well-settled position in law and has been documented in a number of books on interpretation, including one of the treatises in India, the *Principles of Statutory Interpretation* by G. P. Singh.[5] Literally, it means, from the words of the law, there should not be any departure. For instance, in this case there was an interpretation to be made for the expression "compensation has not been paid," which cannot be interpreted to mean "paid and deposited." The same has been the view of the Privy Council for more than one and a half centuries, and later on cited in several judgments including the House of Lords decision in 1948, where the passage was cited verbatim:

> ... (a) Avoiding addition or substitution of words.
>
> As stated by the Privy Council: "We cannot aid the Legislature's defective phrasing of an Act, we cannot add or mend and, by construction makeup deficiencies which are left there". "It is contrary to all rules of construction to read words into an Act unless it is absolutely necessary to do so." Similarly, it is wrong and dangerous to proceed by substituting some other words for words of the statute. Speaking briefly the court cannot reframe the legislation for the very good reason that it has no power to legislate.[6]

[5] Principles Of Statutory Interpretation (Also Including General Clauses Act, 1897 With Notes); G. P. Singh; 14th Edition, Revised by Justice A. K. Patnaik, LexisNexis, 2016.

[6] Lord Howard de Walden v. Inland Revenue Commissioners (No.2); also known as Inland Revenue Commissioners v. Scott-Ellis; House of Lords, 29 October 1948; [1948] 2 All E.R. 825; 41 R. & I.T. 526; 30 T.C. 345; [1948] T.R. 321; [1948] W.N. 419.

It has been reiterated by the House of Lords that the courts do not have legislative power and it would not be proper for them to reframe the law which has been made by the legislature. It is the duty and power of the court to only interpret the law which has been made by the legislature.

Discussing the matter of omission of a word, the court observed:

> ...When the legislature has used different expressions with respect to past events – the word "paid" is used in a discernibly distinctive sense than the sense conveyed by the word "deposited" occurring in the proviso – both are required to be given different meanings. There is casus omissus, i.e. conscious omission made by the Legislature....[7]

The phrase *"casus omissus"* is often used in legal texts and literally means "case omitted." While enacting a statute, or writing a contract, or any other legal text, it is not possible for the persons drafting the document to anticipate each and every situation which may arise. One may, with better understanding and the ability to analyse the situation, come up with more and more possible scenarios; however, we're not dealing with people who can see the future and thereby write about it while drafting the document. Thus, it is quite natural that there may be a number of situations which might not have been talked about or even mentioned in passing in statutes, or contracts, or any other document. Now, here is the difficult situation for the courts to handle: in certain circumstances which have not been mentioned in the statute or other legal documents, should the courts read something which has not been provided? That would not be the correct approach as the courts are not supposed to fill the gaps in statutes and, hence, should not try to bridge the gap as the job of the courts are primarily is to interpret, and not legislate. There is, however, an important function which the courts have necessarily to perform whenever there is *casus omissus* and that is to try to gauge to the best of its ability the intention of the legislature. The rule of harmonious construction has to be applied to get the best possible interpretation, which can be reasonable and not absurd.

At another place the court used the maxim *"Omnis Innovatio Plus Novitate Perturbat Quam Utilitate Prodest,"* which means the results from an innovation may not be beneficial eventually as the problems caused by it might dwarf the advantages arising from it. The court used it

[7] Indore Development Authority v. Shailendra, *supra*.

to explain that "Every innovation made has to be, ultimately, adjudged from stand point of the events that follow it" in the perspective of a decision made earlier and thereafter applied to the practical situation at the ground level. The court explained that it is the bounden duty of the courts to be extremely careful to prevent misuse of provisions of law and also somehow bypass the legal technicalities so as to arrive at the real purpose of the legislature, the land acquisition law in this instant matter. Purposive interpretation of any statute has to take into account the previous decisions of the courts along with legislative amendments and applicable executive orders so that newer innovative methods are not legally allowed by the courts to create chaos in the name of effort made to make it more orderly and streamlined. It should never be allowed that the "remedy is worse than the malady."

The court used another maxim, *"nemo debet bis vexari pro una et eadem causa,"* and wrote:

> In relation to the maxim 'nemo debet bis vexari pro una et eadem causa', which means that it is a rule of law that a man should not be twice vexed for one and the same cause, Broom, in Legal Maxims, has discussed thus:
>
> *When a party to litigation seeks improperly to raise again the identical question which has been decided by a competent Court, a summary remedy may be found in the inherent jurisdiction which our Courts possess of preventing an abuse of process.*

The maxim is based on fundamental principle of reasoning that a person should not be penalised twice for the same cause, and it surely makes sense if the formerly aggrieved party raises the issue again—after it has been decided—that the courts treat it summarily and may even impose a penalty on the petitioner or complainant. There is a companion maxim, *"interest reipublicae ut sit finis litium,"* which means that it is in the interest of the society that there should be an end to litigation. Along with this the principle of *"res judicata"* is applicable that once a matter has been decided by a competent court, it cannot be raised again on the same grounds and without any change in the factual position; however, an appeal is a different matter altogether, which is often a matter of right to be made in appellate courts.

One more maxim used in this judgment is *"expressio unius est exclusio alterius,"* which simply means that the expression of one thing is the exclusion of the other. It usually means that if certain persons or things are specified in a statute or a contract or any other legal document, it implies the intention of the legislature in case of the statute or the person preparing the other documents to exclude all other persons or things, as the case may be, from the application of the concerned document. It can also be said to be having a negative implication by getting the interpretation in a manner providing for implied exclusion. Therefore, one of the most important arguments against persons or things not mentioned in a particular list, whereas others have been mentioned in that list and the list is not blank, is that the names of the persons or things were intentionally not included, and thereby deliberately excluded. Thus, implied exclusion is inferred from inclusion of some other names. This is a very old maxim and has been applied very often in legal matters for centuries; however, there have been serious challenges made to the universal applicability of this maxim. In the present case, the Supreme Court cited several previous decisions in which a decision of Court of Appeal of more than a 100-year-old has been quoted repeatedly regarding this maxim:

> The maxim "Expressio unius, exclusio alterius," has been pressed upon us. I agree with what is said in the Court below by Wills, J., about this maxim. It is often a valuable servant, but a dangerous master to follow in the construction of statutes or documents. The exclusio is often the result of inadvertence or accident, and the maxim ought not to be applied, when its application, having regard to the subject-matter to which it is to be applied, leads to inconsistency or injustice.
>
> I think a rigid observance of the maxim in this case would make other provisions of the statute inconsistent and absurd, and result in injustice. I cannot, therefore, permit it to govern my decision.
>
> The judgment, therefore, in the Court below in my opinion was wrong and must be reversed.[8]

It is, therefore, enlightening to know that the applicability of legal maxims is not to be done in a mechanical manner and the exercise of discretion is of utmost importance. Context cannot be simply overlooked while using the legal maxim to the facts of the case lest it should create an absurd situation. Interpretation of any written legal text is done for a purpose and not for the sake of proving a maxim correct. If a maxim results in impractical

[8] Colquhoun v. Brooks, Court of Appeal, 28 April 1888; (1888) 21 Q.B.D. 52; Lord Esher, M.R., Fry and Lopes, L. JJ.

and illogical situation, it cannot and should not be used for interpretation. There should not be any miscarriage of justice because of relying on maxims blindly.

Further, the court used the maxim *"lex non cogit ad impossibilia,"* which means the law does not compel a person to do something impossible. It is also read in conjunction with another maxim conveying almost the same meaning, *"impossibilium nulla obligatio est,"* which means there is no obligation to do the impossible. The court mentioned the arguments made by one of the counsel:

> Shri Patwalia has pressed into service the doctrine of *'lex non cogit ad impossibilia'* and has urged us to consider the scope and application of the same. He argued that a law does not expect the State authorities to do what cannot possibly be performed by owing to the adamant attitude and conduct of such landowners; it is a settled proposition of law that law does not expect a party to do the impossible. It was urged that the maxim *'impossibilium nulla obligatio est'* would come to the rescue of State authorities in such cases.

Thereafter, the court cited from a 1999 judgment of the Supreme Court giving interesting discussion and application of the maxim to an election petition:

> It is a well-settled salutary principle that if a statute provides for a thing to be done in a particular manner, then it has to be done in that manner and in no other manner...An election petition under the Rules could only have been presented in the open Court upto 16.5.1995 till 4.15 P.M. (working hours of the Court) in the manner prescribed by Rule 6 (supra) either to the Judge or the Bench as the case may be to save the period of limitation. That, however, was not done. However, we cannot ignore that the situation in the present case was not of the making of the appellant. Neither the designated election Judge before whom the election petition could be formally presented in the open Court nor the Bench hearing civil applications and motions was admittedly available on 16.5.1995 after 3.15 P.M., after the Obituary Reference since admittedly the Chief Justice of the High Court had declared that "the Court shall not sit for the rest of the day" after 3.15 P.M. Law does not expect a party to do the impossible – *Impossible nulla obligation est* – As in the instant case, the election petition could not be filed on 16.5.1995 during the Court hours, as far all intent and purposes, the Court was closed on 16.5.1995 after 3.15 P.M.[9]

[9] Chander Kishore Jha v. Mahabir Prasad (1999) 8 SCC 266; 1999 Indlaw SC 737.

It is, therefore, settled that whenever the law creates a duty and the party cannot perform it due to any disability—that is, it is not possible for the party to perform it, without any intention not to perform it even though able to perform it—the law will not compel him to perform it, and he shall be excused from doing it. There shall be no legal repercussion from non-performance of any such duty. The party does not have to justify in any manner the non-performance. In contracts also the same principle is applied which does not cast any duty on a party to perform impossible tasks; however, the impossibility should be due to law or anything due to nature, not because of personal reason. The contractual conditions, which are voluntary, will take into consideration the ability of any party to the performance of a promise made, if it is a personal performance. In case of changed circumstances, which render performance impossible—but not due to commercial difficulty—there is no duty to perform.

Another interesting maxim is *"ex dolo malo non oritur actio,"* which means no right of action can have its origin in fraud or fraud does not give a right for legal action. Therefore, any legal action cannot be based on fraud, immorality or any illegality. It is sheer common sense and has been the principle of public policy for ages. Related maxim is *"frustra legis auxilium quaerit qui in legem committit,"* which means one who offends against the law vainly seeks the help of the law. Simply put, these maxims convey the sense that one cannot misuse the provisions of law and also seek shelter under it. One has to be on the right side of the law to take the benefit of legal protection.

The court cited a short passage from a 2014 Supreme Court judgment which used two maxims to explain the object of criminal law—*"nullum tempus aut locus occurrit regi"* and *"vigilantibus et non dormientibus, jura subveniunt."*

> As we have already noted in reaching this conclusion, light can be drawn from legal maxims… The object of the criminal law is to punish perpetrators of crime. This is in tune with the well-known legal maxim *'nullum tempus aut locus occurrit regi'*, which means that a crime never dies. At the same time, it is also the policy of law to assist the vigilant and not the sleepy. This is expressed in the Latin maxim *'vigilantibus et non dormientibus, jura subveniunt'*.[10]

[10] Sarah Mathew v. Institute of Cardio Vascular Diseases, (2014) 2 SCC 62; 2013 Indlaw SC 762, Constitution Bench.

The maxim ***nullum tempus aut locus occurrit regi*** means no time or place affects the Crown, that is, lapse of time is no bar to the King in proceeding against offenders. It has also been said in other words to mean crime never dies. Thus, the maxim is a powerful doctrine promising action against offenders any time without the constraints of the law of limitation. Though the statutory law provides time periods within which legal proceedings must be initiated, however, for the King—or the State in modern democratic systems—there is no such restriction, which can surely be interpreted by the courts in exceptional circumstances with special reasons for delay. The courts, therefore, have the power of discretion to condone the delay.

The other maxim ***vigilantibus et non dormientibus, jura subveniunt*** means that the law helps the vigilant. In other words, if a person is seeking the help of the law, he must be vigilant and not sleeping on his rights. Eternal vigilance is essential for any freedom and the rights granted by the law must be protected well in time. A person who sleeps on his rights and does not take timely legal recourse is not supposed to get due protection from the law. One has to be careful and move the court within the prescribed statutory limits of time. In the absence of any compelling circumstances, if a person has not taken the legal action for enforcement of his rights within the limitation period, he, generally, will not be allowed by the court to initiate legal proceedings for recognition of his rights.

Comments and Questions

Thought-provoking questions arise due to the use of the maxims, phrases and other foreign words. Is it necessary to use them in the judgment? Are they used for better clarity and comprehension? Or, it is the opposite. Does the use impede understanding and simplicity? Can these be avoided totally for brevity and ease?

A number of such questions arise. Often the use of maxims is to convey the message emphatically and unequivocally. It is a forceful method to embellish the language and like the icing on the cake. The reader is pulled along in a particular direction of thoughts by the use of maxims and established phrases. Classifying thoughts in different categories or segments is done very nicely by them. Rather than simply deciding this way or that way, the judge prefers to blend the judgment with maxims and phrases to make the decision more lucid, readable, oozing with wisdom and very difficult to refute. It is not a good idea to avoid them; however, excessive use is also not appreciated. It has to be very well balanced. Maxims, phrases and the like should be used to enhance the meaning and value of a judgment rather than to exhibit one's knowledge about them.

Some of the foreign words, phrases and maxims have been in use routinely and thereby have become popular with general readers and not only legal scholars. Also these maxims have been able to convey the meaning in a pithy manner and applicable in a number of situations which make it easy for the law-abiding persons to remember and follow them. In case of a dilemma, these maxims can provide good guidance to select the right option and not get into unnecessary confrontation and argument. But, the usage of the maxims depends on the circumstances of the case. For instance, the Royal Opera House in London lost a case against a musician despite the maxim *volenti non fit injuria*, which means if a person does something voluntarily and in the process get injured or hurt, he has no claim.

The Royal Opera House Case: *Volenti Non Fit Injuria*

In March 2018, a musician won a historic judgment against the Royal Opera House London for getting permanent loss of hearing due to extremely high levels of sound during rehearsals.[11] The court decided on the ground that the musicians should have been provided with protective equipment and should have been forced to use the equipment. The court made a distinction between voluntary use of equipment and mandatory use of equipment according to interpretation of law.

Though it may sound quite ironical that music itself can be noise and at times so loud that it can cause loss of hearing to the musicians. These problems have often been discussed and litigated for factory workers and other people working in areas with very high levels of noise such as places near aircraft at airports, at construction sites, shipbreaking units and car racing tracks. The problem is genuine and/or the musicians who rehearse repeatedly positioned near high decibel musical instruments have to seriously face the problem of continuous very high levels of noise.

The Royal Opera House argued that noise was not a by-product of its activities, but it was the product. It also relied on the basic idea advanced in law that one who voluntarily accepts a known risk cannot ask for

[11] Diminuendo? A hearing-loss lawsuit raises questions about orchestras' duty to protect musicians; *While hearing loss is a real risk for members, the existing safeguards are clunky and undesirable;* The Economist; 13 Apr 2018; https://www.economist.com/prospero/2018/04/13/a-hearing-loss-lawsuit-raises-questions-about-orchestras-duty-to-protect-musicians

compensation in case of any damage. This is best known by the Latin maxim, *volenti non fit injuria*—to a willing person, injury is not done—and this is the basic principle applied in a number of situations where a participant in a bout of wrestling, boxing, fencing, bullfighting and the like on his own waives the right to be compensated in the case of injury. It goes without saying that the event should be conducted in a fair manner. The same applies when spectators gather to watch an event, for instance, cricket matches. In case the ball hit by the batsman for a six injures a spectator, there cannot be a case against the batsman as the spectator has chosen on his own to sit in the stadium and watch the match.

The Royal Opera House Issued a Statement[12]
We have been at the forefront of industry-wide attempts to protect musicians from the dangers of exposure to significant levels of performance sound, in collaboration with our staff, the Musicians' Union, acoustic engineers and the Health and Safety Executive... Although this judgment is restricted to our obligations as an employer under the Noise Regulations, it has potentially far-reaching implications for the Royal Opera House and the wider music industry... We do not believe that the Noise Regulations can be applied in an artistic institution in the same manner as in a factory, not least because in the case of the Royal Opera House, sound is not a by-product of an industrial process but is an essential part of the product itself... This has been a complex case and we will consider carefully whether to appeal the judgment.

The expansion and development of law has slowly but surely shifted the burden more and more on the employer to take all the measures for protection of the employees, which must be updated with the developments of technology, and force the employees to use all the measures of protection. It is quite common and understandable that in most of the construction sites anyone is not allowed to enter without the protective hat. In the same way no one is allowed to enter even hospitals, particularly intensive-care units, without protective masks which serve the dual purpose of protecting the patients from being infected by the visitors, and vice versa.

[12] Musician wins landmark case against Royal Opera House for causing damage to his hearing; Classicfm.com; 28 March 2018; https://www.classicfm.com/music-news/musician-wins-landmark-case-royal-opera-house/

The government has a role to play with the evolution of administrative law to force the citizens to do a lot many things which hitherto were left to them as a matter of choice. For instance, wearing a helmet while driving a two-wheeler and the seat belt while driving a four-wheeler are not a matter of choice for the driver but are mandated by law.

Similarly, tough enforcement and realistic interpretation of the laws related to noise levels is the need of the hour to make the society a better place to live in. The noise level during music concerts is often so high that it is quite damaging for the audience close to the speakers, which in most of the cases are like a small wall of multiple speakers arranged together. Not only the level of noise but the vibrations along with the noise are of very high levels. Not only the human beings, the nearby buildings can also get damaged due to these vibrations.

Very often good music can be appreciated at low decibel levels and there is no need to always amplify fine music to such loud levels that it doesn't remain music but becomes noise. There is, however, a major difference between this type of amplification of sound and certain musical instruments which have been designed to create music at a high decibel level. Historically, in the absence of any amplification system, musical instruments were designed to produce high levels of sound so as to reach the farthest person sitting in the audience. This is no more needed. With fantastic amplification systems available easily, loud sound producing musical instruments may be technologically modified to produce acceptable levels of sound. Till then it is for the law to mandatorily enforce the use of protective equipment.

The limits of the age-old maxim have been tested. According to the changed circumstances in a welfare state, where welfare of the people and public interest are paramount, literal interpretation and sticking to the maxim while deciding a case, it can be expected today that the courts would shift the burden of mandatorily using protective gear on the government or the employer. Thus, the legal maxim gets a new meaning. The meaning given through newer interpretations exhibits dynamism in the usage and adaptation according to the changed aspirations and context.

In a welfare state, undoubtedly public interest has to be given topmost priority. For this purpose, the administration must not leave any stone unturned. But, when unfortunate incidents do happen, blame game starts, and in legal proceedings, one of the most cherished principles of "guilty mind" or "intention" contained in the maxim *"actus reus non facit reum nisi mens sit rea,"* meaning any physical act without a guilty mind is not a crime, protects government officers and others from prosecution. However, it has to be read with another maxim, *"res ipsa loquitur,"* which means the thing speaks for itself, that is, the act is so clear and vivid that it requires no evidence, as there could not be any other inference drawn except that the defendant is guilty. Unfortunately, several such incidents keep happening throughout the world.

Gross Negligence: *Res Ipsa Loquitur*

April 2016 had been very disturbing in India because of fire at Kollam temple[13] in Kerala in which more than a hundred persons lost life and demolition drive in Ahmedabad[14] where four persons lost life. Both cases are the worst examples of gross negligence. Both were avoidable. There were no uncontrollable factors.

One is completely at a loss to understand the indifference of the concerned authorities in decision-making. The lackadaisical attitude—*chalta hai* (it's fine) syndrome—is to be blamed in general for creating a system in which the decision-making individuals become so casual and take things so lightly that mishaps are bound to happen. By not acting prudently, these accidents had rather been planned to happen.

But, can we call them "accidents"?

Accident by its very definition and meaning is unexpected, unintentional and without any deliberate cause. True, one can always prove that there was no intention on the part of the concerned persons, neither in Kerala nor in Ahmedabad. However, simply absence of intention cannot make an individual go scot free. Criminal law emphasises on the presence of intention or *mens rea*—the guilty mind—for being penalised; however, gross negligence is deemed to be almost equivalent to intention, particularly in cases involving human life.

How can one call the fire at Kollam temple accident? There were huge quantities of fireworks stored without proper monitoring. The storage of fireworks was known to the temple authorities and local administration; or rather, it was with their permission and active involvement that the fireworks show was organised. Were adequate preventive measures taken? No.

[13] Kollam fire accident: 100 dead; at least 383 injured; The Financial Express; 10 Apr 2016; https://www.financialexpress.com/india-news/63-killed-during-fireworks-display-at-kerala-paravoor-temple/234572/

[14] AMC demolition drive claims four lives; The Hindu; 13 April 2016; https://www.thehindu.com/todays-paper/tp-miscellaneous/tp-others/amc-demolition-drive-claims-four-lives/article8469375.ece

There was even a complaint made earlier, which had fallen on deaf ears and was rubbished. Could the temple and local administration not foresee the safety measures needed? The activities of storage, use and demonstration of fireworks are not new and are done all over the country. Norms for them have been well established. For several years, even during *Diwali* (festival of lights in India), sale of fireworks is strictly controlled by the local administration and anyone and everyone is not allowed to do so. Licences are issued for this purpose, which carry detailed guidelines to be followed.

Did the administration not know that large number of persons would have congregated at the temple for watching the fireworks show? Why permission should be granted for such shows in the heart of the town with huge crowds gathering within close proximity to the show? Human life is too precious to be lost due to callousness of a few individuals making critical decisions.

After the incident, the Kerala High Court had banned such shows from sunset to sunrise. But, it is difficult to comprehend as to why the High Court had to make a decision, which simply is an executive matter and did not require any legal interpretation. Also, the High Court order didn't make sense. This was a knee-jerk reaction by the High Court and practically banned fireworks totally. Who would like to watch fireworks during day time? There is no fun. It is only the dark background of night which makes fireworks glow and spread light, sparkles and joy. But, all this needs to be done in a controlled manner with a little more than usual precautions required for the purpose.

Coming to Ahmedabad, four persons had lost their lives when the demolition squad for widening a road did not note that they were still inside the buildings to be demolished. This didn't require anything to be proved. As the maxim goes, *res ipsa loquitur*—the thing speaks for itself. This was gross negligence, not less than intentional killing. Of course, it would be absolutely wrong to call it an accident. How could the demolition squad even start the proceedings without confirming it doubly or triply that there was no one inside? And, if someone was still there, it was undoubtedly the responsibility of the demolition squad directly and of the top administrators indirectly. Under the concept of vicarious liability, they were bound to be prosecuted.

But the problem is not simple to be resolved as there are a number of statutes, particularly in a federal democratic structure like India, with the central laws and state laws often providing provisions which may have to be interpreted in harmonious manner depending on the context. At times, for a particular act there are so many laws to be considered while making a decision that it becomes extremely difficult to pinpoint the application of a particular law as multiple interpretations appear to be possible, sometimes nullifying the impact of the most potent law enacted for the purpose. In such a scenario it is incumbent on the court seized of the matter that it takes into consideration all the laws available, that is, statutes in *pari materia*.

Statutes in *Pari Materia*

It is a well-settled principle of interpretation that any statute must be read as a whole and the other statutes dealing with the same subject matter should be considered together while deciding a contentious issue. Whenever different statutes are available which may be applicable to the issue at hand, all of them must be considered together even though they might have been enacted at different points in time and some of them might have already been repealed. It is usually helpful to put them together and try to understand through their statement of objects and reasons the intention of the legislature at the time of making the particular law. It is also important that the statutes which are not in *pari materia* should not be considered together and there lies the fine distinction between the statutes which are in *pari materia* and which are not in *pari materia*, which truly depends on the discretionary power exercised by the judges hearing the matter.

It is something similar to scientific principles where application of a particular formula while trying to solve problem is contested by different scientists on the grounds of the applicability or non-applicability of a formula to a set of facts. In simple cases there may not be any difference of opinion between the experts; however, as the matters become ticklish and more sophisticated when assumptions themselves may be questioned, identifying the proper formula for application is in itself a problem which needs to be tackled first. Similarly, arguments by leading lawyers regarding statutes in *pari materia* for a case usually hit at the root of the matter by insisting on the application of a favourable statute, and at the same time non-application of an unfavourable statute.

The problem of interpretation is further aggravated because the meaning of words may change with the passage of time and it is the duty of the judge to give meaning to a certain statute according to the meaning of words understood at the time of the meeting of that law. It is also important that the meaning of any particular time is determined from the meaning generally understood by the experts. These are the two principles according to the following maxims.

Contemporanea expositio *and* Communis opinio

The first maxim, *contemporanea expositio*, states that words of any statute must be interpreted according to the meaning given to those words at the time of making the statute. It is quite logical as the meaning of words may expand or shrink, or may become something very different, with the passage of time and usage. As the basic purpose of interpretation of any statute is to find the intention of the legislature at the time of making the statute, it is quite fair to find out what the legislature intended when the law was made. Once it has been ascertained, extrapolation of the statute to the case at hand by making it applicable to the subject matter and the particular time zone can be done, but it should not result in something which was not intended by the legislature.

The second maxim, *communis opinio*, emphasises the importance of using the general professional opinion rather than picking up the opinion of an expert who may be at the far end of the spectrum in divided opinions on certain subject matter. Very often, while deciding subjective issues—which are heavily dependent on the opinion of experts—the courts have to rely on expert advice and opinion. For instance, in cases of medical negligence, judges, obviously, have to seek the opinion of medical experts. At times there are certain super-specialists who may be having a style and opinion of their own, which might be working for patients, but is not approved by the larger medical community, and that is why it cannot be called the general opinion of experts. The courts usually avoid relying on that opinion, which can at best be called an individual's view but not the general professional opinion.

Conclusion

For international commerce to happen, and also for domestic business to take place in large countries with diversity and multiple languages being used, a common language can be a great unifying factor; however, plurality of languages can never be denied as language is an essential part of society and culture in different parts of the world. With regard to scientific languages—for instance, mathematics, physics and chemistry—the members of that particular fraternity do not have problems because of language being used as a medium for communication, but there is no single, uniform, globally accepted legal language which can be used by members of the legal fraternity across the globe, irrespective of differences of local language and culture. To a large extent, Latin played an important role in at least unifying several jurisdictions in Europe as being the common language for legal proceedings. Expansion of the British Empire globally in form of colonies all over the world made it possible to spread the use of Latin for legal matters; however, with the passage of time, medium of communication in general, and also in courts, became English, but the usage of Latin maxims to convey certain well-settled principles of law continued. With the decline in Roman Empire—which had patronised Latin as legal language and even for writing historical documents—the rich cultural and literary heritage could only be used as guiding principles and establishing higher aspirational standards.

It is important to have a common language for lawyers all over the world, which appears to be an impossibility due to differences in legal systems, culture, language as medium, differences in the law itself, and, therefore, for anyone to try to achieve that impossible goal is not prudent. The second-best can be to liberally use whatever is commonly understood by members of the legal profession and try to incorporate the common understandings in law school curriculum. Foreign words and phrases—particularly Latin and French—have very often been used in day-to-day working. Students and law schools are encouraged to understand and memorise Latin legal maxims so that they are able to distinguish between two very close maxims and also take care of seemingly conflicting maxims at times. Application of the right maxim to a particular situation is an art and can be mastered with regular practice.

The same applies to a large extent to businesspersons who are very often supposed to deal with legal texts and lawyers. They would in all probability cut a sorry figure if they have zero understanding of commonly used legal maxims and foreign words and phrases. An effective business leader could not abhor them; rather he would try to make himself familiar with them. Their knowledge will pay rich dividends in the long run. International business, in today's scenario, is dominated by the English language, but there is a sense among global business leaders that knowledge of the English language per se is not sufficient to interact with the lawyers; hence, some orientation to legal language can prove to be investment of time and effort in the right direction. The legal language embellished with maxims and foreign words can be considered to be a separate language in itself demanding familiarity and usage, and thereby developing expertise.

It can safely be said that business communication becomes complete only with proper understanding of legal language.

CHAPTER 5

Read My Lips!

Lip-reading is the ability to understand what a person has said by minutely observing the movement of lips and mouth. Hearing-impaired persons are usually trained to lip-read. However, "read my lips" has a very different connotation from lip-reading. It is an idiom which means that the speaker tells the listeners in a rather impolite manner to listen sensibly as to what he is saying. The speaker demands full attention from the listeners. It also conveys that the speaker is naturally in a commanding position vis-à-vis the audience. It has been in use for several decades; however, it was noticed and gained popularity when George W. Bush in his presidential campaign in 1988 stated, "Read my lips: no new taxes." This statement got a lot of attention from the people and the media and after being elected as the President of the United States, Bush had to eat crow when he raised taxes. He had made a very bold and categorical statement, leaving no room for any other interpretation, and that too while using the idiom, "read my lips," which conveyed unequivocally that he wanted everyone to consider whatever he had stated with due seriousness. This statement boomeranged. Bill Clinton, the presidential candidate in the 1992 US elections, got an opportunity on the platter. He attacked Bush using inter alia this statement made by Bush, which could not be honoured by Bush. Thus, it became very easy for Clinton to prove that Bush was not serious enough and did not keep his promise.

A. K. Agarwal, *Legal Language and Business Communication*,
https://doi.org/10.1007/978-981-13-7534-7_5

While picking up the "top 10 unfortunate political one-liners," the *Time* rated Bush's statement, "Read my lips: no new taxes,"[1] as the third from the top, with the first being, "I am not a crook," a statement made by Richard M. Nixon in 1973 at the height of the Watergate scandal. It is quite common for political leaders to make a statement, and once they receive brickbats for that, they very easily blame it entirely on the media and the people that they have been wrongly understood, and that they did not mean it that way. The statement "I didn't mean it that way" is oft-repeated by individuals in public life, sometimes due to a genuine mistake of misinterpretation, but usually as an after-thought and as a damage-control exercise. It may happen that the words uttered by public figures are quoted out of context, or not in full, or with a slight twist, so as to give a very different meaning from what the speaker had intended. Sometimes, the speaker might have made an innocuous statement which was taken as offending by someone for whom the message was not directly meant for. These can be the unintended consequences of communication, which may have the possibility of being interpreted in more than one way. Such reactions eventually put the speaker in a defensive position, without any intention of hurting or harming anyone, with the obvious reflex action being making the statement, "I didn't mean it that way."

Honest feedback, positive criticism and challenging messages test the ability of a business leader to walk the tight rope—convey the real message to the receiver without creating heat and friction. Though the intention of the business leader may be to communicate the difficult message, without mincing words, the tone and tenor are critical to keep the meeting pleasant and congenial. If it is not possible, or a bit too much to expect to keep the meeting amiable, at least the effort can be made not to create distastefulness by keeping the communication straight, simple and unequivocal. This thought process helps in planning the manner in which the communication has to be made so that the business leader does not have to state after obnoxiousness has crept into the deliberation, "I didn't mean it that way." In the case of written communication, things are somewhat easier. There is ample time to review, edit, discard and modify, among others, a written text, and hence, it is expected that written communication is, as far as possible, unambiguous and the sender has gone through it to take care of any possible anomalies. For the receiver also, there is usually sufficient

[1] Top 10 Unfortunate Political One-liners, The Time, http://content.time.com/time/specials/packages/article/0,28804,1859513_1859526_1859516,00.html

time to read the message, assimilate and thereafter think of a proper reply. Care can be taken by the writers to avoid sneering and condescending words and language. Unless the primary aim of the sender is to be spiteful, it is not a good idea to be vitriolic. Crossing the thin dividing line between honest feedback and being venomous can bring legal trouble for the sender.

There can possibly be a difference of understanding between two parties to a business agreement, and in case of dispute, the courts interpret the contractual clauses on the basis of the applicable law, context and background. A large number of cases reach the doors of the court all over the world for this very purpose. One such case is that of the legally acceptable interpretation of the health care benefits clause.

The Health Care Benefits Case[2]

This case sealed the fate of many retirees and left them high and dry with respect to their health benefits. The Supreme Court justices favoured with an interpretation of the contract which was against the retirees who had high hopes of getting a sympathetic decision. The issue was primarily of the contract not mentioning a particular clause, which could have easily been decided by the parties—whether in favour of the retirees or the company—at the time of formation of the contract. The judges had earlier even expressed their displeasure on the way the contract had been drafted—both sides knew about the issue but left it unaddressed—which had forced the matter to reach the court of law. The facts of the case are as follows.

It was in 1992 that the Goodyear Tire & Rubber Company sold a polyester plant, located in West Virginia, to Shell Chemical Company, which later sold it to M&G Polymers in the year 2000. There were various agreements negotiated between labour union, representing the employees, and the companies as owners. All these were collectively bargained agreements (CBAs) as the union had represented the employees, and instead of individual agreements, collective agreements were negotiated. One of the important clauses of the CBAs was that senior employees would receive full company contribution towards health care, whereas employees who were not senior enough—based on a point system—would receive reduced

[2] M&G Polymers USA, LLC, et al. v. Tackett et al., (2015), No. 13-1010, Argued: November 10, 2014; Decided: January 26, 2015, U.S. Supreme Court.

company contribution, with the balance to be paid by such employees themselves. The retirees were to get the benefits on retirement.

There were certain side letters—also known as side agreement, which is not an integral part of the main agreement and usually deals with issues which have not been addressed in the main contract—which stipulated a cap on the maximum average retiree cost for the company on an annual basis. The side agreement in the case was the related agreement to CBA and was known as the "Pension, Insurance, and Service Award Agreement" (P & I agreement). It was also specified that if the cost was more than the capped amount, the extra amount would have to be contributed equally by all retirees. This arrangement for extra cost was to be put into effect from a certain specified date. M&G Polymers decided that date to be December 2006 and informed the retirees.

Some of the retirees and the former union took strong objection to the company's communication and challenged it in a court of law by filing a class action suit in the District Court in Ohio in February 2007. Their challenge was based on the ground that the company had promised full contribution in the CBAs and, hence, they were not under any legal obligation to contribute to the health care plan, even if the costs were more than the capped amount. The company averred that its liability was limited to the capped amount as per the side agreement and the extra amount had to be borne by the retirees.

The District Court decided in favour of the company, and the retirees appealed in the Court of Appeals for the Sixth Circuit. The Sixth Circuit court reversed and remanded to the District Court and after some back and forth between the District Court and the Sixth Circuit, due to issues of legal procedure and the right to appeal, the Circuit Court decided in favour of the retirees and interpreted that the CBAs assured health care to the retirees. The Sixth Circuit's inference was based on the reasoning that the benefits were vested and hence would have continued for an unlimited period. However, some courts hearing appellate matters have preferred to take the interpretative approach while resolving such issues, which depend more on the interpretation and explanation of the contractual clauses. In such cases, it is not necessary that the decision will be tilted in favour of the employees, the weaker and vulnerable party in most of the employer-employee agreements, even if it is a CBA.

The company M&G Polymers appealed in the US Supreme Court. The Supreme Court admitted the matter and framed the primary issue inter alia as determining the duration of a contractual obligation—whether indefinitely or synchronous with the contract, that is, expiring with the contract coming to an end—in cases when the contract is silent about it. The company argued that the health care benefits terminated when the CBAs ended and that these benefits could be accepted to have been agreed for perpetuity only if there had been an explicit statement in the agreement to such effect. In the absence of any such clear and unambiguous provision, silence could not be deemed to be acceptance to continue the benefits forever. The P & I Agreement on which the entire case is based is reproduced.

The Contentious P & I Agreement[3]

"Employees who retire on or after January 1, 1996 and who are eligible for and receiving a monthly pension under the 1993 pension plan... Whose full years of attained age and full years of attained continuous service... At the time of retirement equals 95 or more points will receive a full company contribution towards the cost of [health care] benefits described in this exhibit B-1.... Employees who have less than 95 points at the time of retirement will receive a reduced company contribution. The company contribution will be reduced by 2% for every point less than 95. Employees will be required to pay the balance of the health care contribution, as estimated by the company annually in advance, for the [health care] benefits described in this exhibit B-1. Failure to pay the required medical contribution will result in cancellation of coverage." app. 415–416.

The most important and highly contentious portion of the agreement was "…receive a full Company contribution towards the cost of [health care] benefits…" and it was because of this sentence that the entire interpretation exercise had to be done.

The Supreme Court followed the oft-quoted Aristotle's famous phrase, "the law is reason free from passion," and took the difficult path of choosing reason and not the passion. It is widely believed that when the issues are related to retired employees and their health benefits, the judges in any court get a bit sentimental and passionate and usually have a soft corner for them. However, in this case the Supreme Court unanimously followed the

[3] From the judgment, M&G Polymers v. Tackett.

basic principles of contract law and interpreted the P & I Agreement, without bringing in emotions. The American federal law and the state law in different states protect the rights of the employees, during employment and post-employment, to a certain level which is quite high as compared to so many other countries but may not be as high as in Germany or France; however, the employees are generally given a free choice of entering into agreements with the employer to protect their self-interest and it is usually done for a large group of employees collectively. As unity is strength, the collective bargaining power of the employees is surely higher than that of individual employees. The Supreme Court made it very clear in the beginning of the judgment that it was following the principles of contract law to the extent there was no clash with the labour policy. So, any agreement has to be within the framework established by the law of the land, both federal and state, and, thus, cannot bring in clauses which take away the rights and benefits given by the labour policy formulated for the welfare of employees.

A contract is merely an agreement between the parties with an intention to create a contractual relationship for something which is lawful and signifies the identity of minds of the parties. It is of utmost importance that the parties to a contract understand the terms and conditions very clearly and have no ambiguity in their mind regarding the performance of a contract. The Supreme Court laid a great deal of emphasis on the intention of the parties which, unfortunately, was not obviously seen in the written agreement. While highlighting the importance of the intention of the parties, the Supreme Court cited from a 2010 judgment:

> In this endeavor, as with any other contract, the parties' intentions control.[4]

One of the most important methods of interpreting the language of statutes or contracts is the literal meaning of the written text. If on a plain reading that text gives simple and straightforward meaning then there is no reason not to follow that meaning and look for some other meaning in the text. It is important to find that the literal meaning of any text should not be absurd and impractical so as to signify that the parties could never have decided to go with that meaning and possibly never ever intended to mean that. It is only under such circumstances that the passage needs to be understood and interpreted in a manner which can practically give reasonable and comprehensible meaning so that the parties and not put to

[4] Stolt-Nielsen S. A. v. AnimalFeeds Int'l Corp., 559 US 662, 682(2010).

impractical and impossible situations to be faced. This has been stated by the US Supreme Court and various other courts in different jurisdictions in a number of judgments. The US Supreme Court cited the following:

> Where the words of a contract in writing are clear and unambiguous, its meaning is to be ascertained in accordance with its plainly expressed intent.[5]

The Court of Appeals had relied on its 1983 judgment—Yard-Man[6]—and had clarified in that judgment that it was based on traditional rules for contractual interpretation. The court had found that there was certain ambiguity with the words that the employer "will provide" and to take care of that ambiguity the court had looked at the contract as a whole by considering other provisions of the agreement. There was no provision regarding the duration for providing and terminating the benefits. Absence of any such provision was taken by the court as making an illusory promise, making it difficult to be enforced. The court had also looked at the context of the entire employer and employee negotiations, which in the CBA is different from that of an individually reached agreement. There was a clause mentioning about the general termination of the contract; however, the court had interpreted that because of the context and after looking at the agreement as a whole the benefits to the employees would continue for life.

In 1985, the Court of Appeals had interpreted "will continue to provide at its expense, supplemental medicare and major medical benefits for Pensioners aged 65 and over" to mean lifetime benefits and had underscored that the meaning was unambiguous.[7] But, in Yard-Man, the words "will provide" were said to be ambiguous. In several other cases, it has been found that the Court of Appeals relied on the Yard-Man that though rights were not vested forever, yet the courts had been inclined to do so.

According to the Supreme Court, this is contrary to the plain and simple reading and interpretation of contractual provisions and that it did not agree with the Court of Appeals that it had relied on contract interpretation in arriving at the decision. With the ordinary principles of contract law applied to the facts of any of the cases mentioned above, it would not have been possible to reach to the decision that the rights were vested for

[5] As cited in the judgment M&G Polymers; 11 R. Lord, Williston on Contracts §30:6, p. 108 (4th ed. 2012).

[6] International Union, United Auto, Aerospace, & Agricultural Implement Workers of Am. v. Yard-Man, Inc., 716 F. 2d 1476, 1479 (1983).

[7] Policy v. Powell Pressed Steel Co., 770 F. 2d 609, 615 (CA6 1985).

all time to come. The way things have been interpreted simply means a distorted way of looking at the written text with probable behaviour of the parties, rather than trying to find the intention of the parties, imagined and used in the analysis of the contractual terms. This approach can be highly hypothetical and far away from the realistic approach of finding the intention of the parties.

Comments and Questions

This case has been in the public eye since its filing and when it was argued in the court there had been wide reporting in the media with several of the observations made by the justices cited and commented upon. As the case pertained to retired persons and their health benefits, there has been interest across the sections in the society and as the circuit courts had earlier favoured the decision usually in favour of the retired people, it has been expected that the Supreme Court might uphold the view of the circuit courts, but there had also been apprehension because the justices had asked uncomfortable questions in the court and also made unfavourable comments about the contract which had been made between the company and the union. It would be enlightening to have a look at some of those comments.

Comments by Justices During Arguments[8]

"This is an important benefit and an expensive one," said Justice Samuel A. Alito Jr. He would have expected, he said, that the issue would have been resolved in the company's contract with the union.

"Why is it that in this collective bargaining agreement and apparently many others," he asked, "there isn't anything explicit one way or the other?"

The upshot of the contract's failure to address the matter in so many words, Justice Antonin Scalia said, was that one side or the other would soon be unhappy.

"Both sides knew it was left unaddressed, so, you know, whoever loses deserves to lose for casting this upon us when it could have

(*continued*)

[8] Supreme Court Weighs Case Over Cuts to Retirees' Health Benefits, New York Time, Nov. 10, 2014 https://www.nytimes.com/2014/11/11/business/supreme-court-to-hear-retiree-benefits-case.html

(continued)
been said very clearly in the contract," Justice Scalia said. "Such an important feature. So I hope we'll get it right, but, you know, I can't feel bad about it."

Justice Stephen G. Breyer responded that "the workers who discover they've been retired for five years and don't have any health benefits might feel a little bad about it."

...

But other justices seemed ready to rule, and several seemed prepared to side with the retired workers. "There are all these indicia that vesting was intended," Justice Ruth Bader Ginsburg said.

Justice Scalia seemed to agree. "It is a reasonable assumption, call it a presumption if you like, that any promise to pay those benefits continues after the termination of the union contract," he said.

Justice Elena Kagan, citing a friend-of-the-court brief, said about 60 percent of collective bargaining agreements say that health benefits for retirees do not go on indefinitely.

"Yours doesn't do that," Justice Kagan told Allyson N. Ho, a lawyer for the company. "So there we are. We're left with this ambiguity, and you have some language and they have some language and some judge has to figure it out."

...

Justice Ginsburg seemed to find the point persuasive. "Doesn't that sound like as long as they're getting the pension, they will get health benefits?" she asked."

(*from the NYT, 10 Nov 2014*)

Unsurprisingly this case had evoked great interest and all the justices were involved in the proceedings without being indifferent. Factually, in a good number of cases there is a possibility that all the judges do not apply their minds and remain unresponsive and unconcerned with the proceedings in the matter. Despite the justices asking different questions and from different perspective which also exhibited their tilt—whether in favour of the company or the retirees—it is quite remarkable that the final decision of the court was unanimous and all the justices favoured interpretation of the contract using the basic principles and thereby deciding that the right is not vested for life.

The Supreme Court, while giving reasons for its decision, commented that for proper interpretation of contract the context has to be kept in mind like the customs and usages in a specific industry; however, these have to be proved with sufficient affirmative evidence. In the instant case, it was never proved that vesting the health care rights for life is customarily followed, and ironically the Court of Appeals had applied it across industries. Further, the decisions of the Court of appeals "... distort the text of the agreement and conflict with the principle of contract law that the written agreement is presumed to encompass the whole agreement of the parties."[9]

Another reason given by the Supreme Court was that the Court of Appeals did not apply properly the "illusory promises doctrine," it says that contract should not be interpreted in a manner which would make promises illusory as these cannot be taken as a part of the consideration for the contract. Consideration in a contract technically is reciprocal promises, and if one of the promises is illusory, definitely it will result in only promise by one party, which goes to the root of the matter in a contract making it either voidable or void, depending on the facts and circumstances of the case.

The Supreme Court also found fault with the Court of Appeals on the ground of failure to abide by the "traditional principle that courts should not construe ambiguous writings to create lifetime promises." It has been quite well established that any contract which is silent regarding the term of the contract will, in ordinary circumstances, not be interpreted as meant for perpetuity but only for a reasonable period of time. Also the court failed to apply the traditional principle that "contractual obligations will cease, in the ordinary course, upon termination of the bargaining agreement."[10] It is true that any of the contractual obligations may continue for any period of time, but it has to be explicitly mentioned in the contract. Silence does not mean perpetuity.

The Supreme Court remanded the case to the Court of Appeals with the direction that the case may be resolved by applying the basic principles of contract law.

Significantly, four of the justices, out of nine, wrote a different concurring opinion. They heavily emphasised on the cardinal principle of contract

[9] Cited by the Supreme Court: 1 W. Story, Law of Contracts §780 (M. Bigelow ed., 5th ed. 1874); also 11 Williston §31:5.

[10] Litton Financial Printing Div., Litton Business Systems, Inc. v. NLRB, 501 U. S. 190, 207 (1991).

interpretation to be based on the intention of the parties which has to be understood by reading the whole document, rather than any portion of it. Whenever unambiguous expressions have been made in the contract, the court need not explore anything but just go with what has been written.

Once the judgment was pronounced, it was duly noticed in the media and a few of the notable quotes are as follows:

Gist of the Judgment[11]

"Courts should not construe ambiguous writings to create lifetime promises," Justice Clarence Thomas wrote for the court, adding that "retiree health care benefits are not a form of deferred compensation."

...

The appeals court erred, Justice Thomas wrote, "by placing a thumb on the scale in favor of vested retiree benefits in all collective bargaining agreements."

(*from the NYT, 26 Jan 2015*)

The judgment in this case is a stern reminder to all the persons who might be relying too much on the goodness of human beings and the emotional perspective of contractual relationships. The understanding of the contract and relationship is typically purely legal, mechanical and cold. Usually one should not mix the warmth of personal relationships in contractual obligations. These are two different things—strict legality and human passion. It is important for employees, in particular, to understand that they should not live in fool's paradise with a belief that their needs and demands would be taken care of by the employer. Similarly, business leaders should be extremely careful about the political-legal environment for doing business in a country with different provinces where local leaders have great influence over the people and may not allow a particular business activity to be continued, despite the existence of a properly executed legal contract between the company and the government.

[11] Supreme Court Rules Against Retirees in Union Health Benefits Case, New York Times, Jan. 26, 2015 https://www.nytimes.com/2015/01/27/business/supreme-court-rules-against-retirees-in-health-benefits-case.html

Tata: Open Letter

Tata Motors—one of the prominent companies in India—experienced the same in 2008 in the state of West Bengal when the company wanted to make the cheapest car, Nano. There was stiff opposition from certain political quarters, which forced the company to move its manufacturing base to the state of Gujarat in West India. At that time Ratan Tata, the head of the Tata group of companies, wrote an open letter to the people of West Bengal. The letter has been written with emotion and passion, and with hard cold facts. It is one of those business communications by the head of a company directly with the people—consumers, workers, prospective employees, people in general—which definitely touches a chord with readers. The message is loud and clear.

Tata Motors: Open Letter to the Citizens of West Bengal[12]
Over the past three weeks there have been statements by vested interests criticising the decision taken by Tata Motors to move the NANO car project out of Singur claiming that this decision was easy and politically motivated. I therefore feel compelled to address this letter to the people of West Bengal, to explain how our dream of contributing to the industrial revival of West Bengal has been shattered by an environment of politically-motivated agitation and hostility that finally left us with no option but to withdraw the Nano project from West Bengal.

Two years ago, when Tata Motors decided to locate the Nano car project in West Bengal, it reflected the tremendous faith and confidence we had, and still have, in the investor-friendly policies of Mr. Buddhadeb Bhattacharjee's government. All through the two years that we have been constructing the plant at Singur, this feeling of faith and confidence in the vision and objectives of the State Government has been reinforced. All our interactions with the Chief Minister and the Industries Minister in particular, as also with several other officers, have been exemplary. We had therefore hope that this project would reinstate confidence for further investments in West Bengal and would create a large number of jobs for the younger

(*continued*)

[12] The Telegraph, Kolkata, 17 Oct 2008.

(continued)
citizens, directly in the Company and its suppliers, as also foster a large number of small enterprises in the Singur area which would provide livelihood to the citizens of that area. We had also undertaken medical and other community services in the Singur region. Our fervent desire has always been to be a good, contributing corporate citizen, enhancing the quality of life of the people around the plant.

Unfortunately, the confrontative actions by the Trinamool Congress led by Ms. Mamata Banerjee and supported by vested interests and certain political parties, opposing the acquisition of land by the State Government, have caused serious disruption to the progress of the Nano plant. The land acquired by the State Government at Singur and leased to Tata Motors has been, we believe, through a transparent process with fair compensation. The Trinamool Congress's position has been that this land acquisition by the State Government is illegal. In response to public interest litigation, the Hon'ble Calcutta High Court has ruled that the land acquisition is totally legal but the same plaintiffs have filed against this judgment in the Supreme Court, which is pending a hearing.

Throughout the construction of the plant, the Company has had to endure constant acts of open aggression on the site, occasional acts of violence, breakage of the compound perimeter walls, theft of construction material from within the project area, as well as intimidation and even physical assault of employees, contract labour and residents of the area to be absorbed in the project. Country bombs have been lobbed into the premises, obstructing the movement of material and personnel into and out of the plant.

Various attempts at finding solutions were thwarted by the Trinamool Congress's consistent demand that land acquired by the Nano plant and/or its integrated vendor park be returned to the segment of the land owners which the Trinamool Congress party claims to represent. Tata Motors has always maintained that this project has been conceived of as an integrated campus of manufacturing facilities and suppliers, so as to maximise integration and minimise logistics

(*continued*)

(continued)

and material flow costs. Disruption of this integrated campus would make it extremely difficult for the Company to meet strict product price and productivity goals.

On August 22nd, I addressed a Press Conference in Kolkata, generally referring to the hostility and difficult environment we were facing and appealing for a more congenial environment, failing which we would have no option but to consider taking the project out of West Bengal. Unfortunately, the response to this appeal was an escalation of hostilities through a dharna on the highway in front of the plant, some more incidents of physical assault and considerable amount of intimidation of personnel working at the site, which finally resulted in the suspension of the completion work on the plant for almost a month. All of you will therefore appreciated the final and painful decision to move the project out of West Bengal has not been a decision taken in haste, but a decision taken with great regret after a great deal of deliberation and a final assessment that it was unlikely that a sustainable, peaceful environment would develop in which our project could operate.

We are conscious of the disappointment and despondency that may be felt by some of the residents of Singur who may have hoped for an improvement in their quality of life after the plant was operational. We believe the responsibility for this would lie with the Trinamool Congress, which has created the hostile environment that has obliged the Company to move the project from Singur.

In the future, in the state of West Bengal many Tata Motors-type projects may come and go, many political ideologies may come and go, but the future of the state of West Bengal will depend on the path its leaders and citizens take in developing and retaining an environment which will result in the prosperity of the state in the years to come. Many may have forgotten that West Bengal was a major centre for heavy industry and steel fabrication. Agitation and violence drove away many industries around 30 years ago, and it has only been in recent times that the present government has been able to rebuild the confidence of investors to invest in the state.

(*continued*)

(continued)

It is therefore ironic that, at this crucial time and moment of hope for the state, history appears to be repeating itself. Agitation, violence and terror are overtaking the state in the name of agricultural community, to serve political goals – stalling progress and destroying the new-found confidence in the state, while doing nothing for the rural poor, other than making promises. West Bengal's agriculture was a success story in the 1970s and 1980s but the farm sector's growth has slowed in the recent past. It is self-evident that industrial growth and agricultural growth must happen together in peace and harmony, and not through agitation and activism.

The people of West Bengal – particularly the younger citizens – will need to express their views and aspirations as to what they would like to see West Bengal become in the years ahead. Would they like to support the present Government of Mr. Buddhadeb Bhattacharjee to build a prosperous state with the rule of law, modern infrastructure and industrial growth, supporting a harmonious investment in the agricultural sector to give the people in the state a better life? Or would they like to see the state consumed by a destructive political environment of confrontation, agitation, violence and lawlessness? Do they want education and jobs in the industrial and high-tech sectors or does the future generation see the future prosperity achieved on a "stay as we are" basis?

The future destiny of West Bengal lies with its citizens. They will need to decide whether they wish to stand still and let growth take place elsewhere, or move forward with the present Government's progressive policy, so that West Bengal can take its rightful place with other states – sharing in the future prosperity of India.

Ratan N. Tata

Comments and Questions

The question which arises is about the need for writing this open letter to the people of West Bengal. Usually, political leaders address the people directly to sway them in their favour and eventually get their support in elections through commitment of their votes. What could a business leader have achieved by such direct communication with the people?

At that time the issue had become very hot and contentious. There were all sorts of stories—most of them fabricated—being circulated at that time by disruptors to malign the otherwise clean image of a highly regarded business leader like Ratan Tata. Also, the future prospects of the Tata group of companies were under clouds of doubt with great uncertainty due to political opposition at the site itself in the name of the cultivators and local unemployed youth. Tata had the easy option of not clearing the air and moving ahead with business in Gujarat. But, he chose to speak out in clear terms so as to send the message directly to the people and indirectly to the political masters, bureaucrats and competitors. There was some speculation that the protests taking place at the Nano factory site were funded by competitors who never wanted Tata to make and sell the cheapest car. Nano was the "dream come true" for Ratan Tata, who wanted to make the "Rupees One Lakh"—100,000—car by using innovative methods in designing and manufacturing. Though the car did not succeed commercially, yet it surely created a buzz in the automobile industry in India and abroad.

There were numerous issues related to shifting the Nano plant to Gujarat, most of them were fuelled by political aspirations as the ideology of the ruling political parties in West Bengal and Gujarat was very different. West Bengal, for a very long time, had been ruled by political parties fully tilted in favour of socialism and communism, whereas Gujarat had been more of providing opportunities to big businesses, and thus could have been tilted towards free enterprise and entrepreneurship. These could have been different ideologies and thus different paths followed—however, the goal was public good and public interest. Creation of jobs was the main plank on which the Tatas had convinced the West Bengal government to hand over the big chunk of land for constructing the car factory. It was all done with the approval and overt support of the state government, and, thus, it was important for the Tatas to come out clear on this aspect to the public at large. Several petitions were filed in the Calcutta High Court, and even in the Gujarat High Court. In the former set of petitions transfer of land to the Tatas was challenged, which finally reached the Supreme Court, and after a long legal battle, the Supreme Court decided against the propriety of transfer of land to the Tatas. Petitions in the Gujarat High Court had challenged the transfer of land, at a very short notice, and setting up of the manufacturing facility at Sanand in Gujarat. These petitions were dismissed as it was held that establishment of a factory would, in general, be good for the people of the state by creating new jobs, and making the place—Sanand, not very far from Ahmedabad—a hub for the automobile industry.

The open letter was, therefore, very well thought and written to let everyone know straight from the horse's mouth as to what the position was. Also, the purpose was to convey certainty about the financial and strategic strength of the company. The letter can also be analysed as a damage-control exercise, as breaking of relations with any one state, which hitherto had been the major business centre for the company, could have caused a negative domino effect for automobile and other business interests of the company. The letter, in unequivocal terms, blamed one political party—Trinamool Congress—and its leader—Mamata Banerjee—for the entire fiasco. As luck would have it, the party came to power in West Bengal after a few years in 2011, and forcing the Tatas out of Singur apparently helped the party in electoral gains. But, in 2008, the Tatas did not wish to sour their relations with the government of the day. It is debatable whether the Tatas would have written the open letter had they anticipated that there might have been a change in the government in the near future. Probably not. But, taking risk by venting one's feelings at times is the best option to live in peace, and be true to oneself. For the same car, Tata had promised to the people that the company would make the "Rupees One Lakh" car. Till the time of launching the car, it was known to the world only as the "Rupees One Lakh" car, and the name "Nano" was only made public at the launch. At that time, Ratan Tata had said, "a promise is a promise."[13] It was the sight of a family of four riding a scooter on a rainy day that had inspired him to make such a car.

> "Today's story started some years ago when I observed families riding on two wheelers, the father driving a scooter, his young kid standing in front of him, his wife sitting behind him holding a baby and I asked myself whether one could conceive of a safe, affordable, all weather form of transport for such a family", Tata said while unveiling Nano in New Delhi. He said, "This is been referred to as one man's dream and indeed it was."[14]

[13] Tata walks the big promise; rediff.com, 11 Jan 2008; http://www.rediff.com/money/2008/jan/11tata.htm.

[14] How a scooter on a rainy day turned into Ratan Tata's dream project Nano; Business Today, 14 April 2017, https://www.businesstoday.in/current/economy-politics/how-a-scooter-on-a-rainy-day-turned-into-ratan-tatas-dream-project-nano/story/239035.html

So, while dreaming to make the car which almost everyone could afford, it was befitting for him to write the letter and connect directly with the people. After all, it was the people's car, and the people were at the focus of his entire plan.

There had been exciting moments during the launch of the car, including the naming of the car. As it was quite a small car, and also with the lowest price tag, there was a frantic search for a suitable name, which could easily convey these characteristics and also go along with the Tata values and philosophy. As the company was deeply indebted to the then Chief Minister of West Bengal, Buddhadeb Bhattacharjee, for letting the project see the light of the day, some suggested to name the car "Buddha," which would have gone well with the Indian history and philosophy of non-violence propagated by Gautam Buddha. Some suggested naming it "Mamata" as she had been eyeing the project since its inception as a wonderful political opportunity to grind her axe, and she surely exploited it to the fullest. Some suggested naming it "Despite Mamata," as the company was able to launch the car *despite* the opposition of Mamata. It was a joke, as Tata clarified in a press meet; however, Mamata Banerjee and Trinamool Congress were not amused. She neither forgot nor forgave. She forced the Tatas out of Singur. It was written:

> At the Nano launch during the 2008 Auto Expo in Delhi, Tata remarked in a lighter vein that before the company decided on the new car's name, suggestions had included "Mamata" and "Despite Mamata". The anti-land acquisition campaign led by Mamata Banerjee forced the Nano project to move out of West Bengal to Gujarat.[15]

None of these was finally chosen. The company eventually named the car "Nano," which means too small. There were other connotations also as *nano* means the younger one or the smaller one in the Gujarati language.

But, does a name make much of a difference?

Not much!

As Shakespeare wrote about a rose in the play *Romeo and Juliet*, "a rose by any other name would smell as sweet."

[15] Behind Ratan Tata's reserved façade, LiveMint, 20 Dec 2012, https://www.livemint.com/Companies/faM3h1lrDnOyV5e0kqyO0I/Behind-Ratan-Tatas-reserved-facade.html

Juliet:
'Tis but thy name that is my enemy;
Thou art thyself, though not a Montague.
What's Montague? It is nor hand, nor foot,
Nor arm, nor face, nor any other part.
Belonging to a man. O, be some other name!
What's in a name? That which we call a rose.
By any other word would smell as sweet;
So Romeo would, were he not Romeo call'd,
Retain that dear perfection which he owes.
Without that title. Romeo, doff thy name,
And for that name which is no part of thee.
Take all myself.[16]

Trying to Understand the Veiled Meaning

The deep understanding that the name itself doesn't mean anything has been illustrated in a delightful manner by Shakespeare as a dialogue between Romeo and Juliet. Such has been the impact of Shakespeare's works that a lot many intricate and complex relationships and situations have been dealt with finesse. One such difficult situation, so many of us face in life, arises when one has to really criticise the other person; however, the situation so demands that the criticism has to be veiled and coated with praise. This is an extremely difficult task and requires a very high level of expertise and deftness. Dexterity of a master orator and communicator is often at its most difficult test when the situation may result eventually in severe and grave punishment to the speaker, which may even be death. Business leaders, among other people who need to communicate with each other, do require the expertise to say what they want to say but camouflaged in such a language which may appear to be really praising the other party. In the play *Julius Caesar*, the speech by Marc Antony is one of the finest depictions of the quality of the speaker who can truly have the audience glued to him and make them listen to his train of thoughts patiently, with several twists and turns in between. The communication is not straightforward and literal but has to be absorbed and assimilated by the audience to get the real meaning and somehow compel them to ask pointed questions. Masked answers by the speaker lead the audience to take some crucial decisions and act upon them.

[16] Shakespeare, Romeo and Juliet, Act II, Scene II.

Friends, Romans, Countrymen, Lend Me Your Ears[17]

ANTONY
Friends, Romans, countrymen, lend me your ears;
I come to bury Caesar, not to praise him.
The evil that men do lives after them;
The good is oft interred with their bones;
So let it be with Caesar. The noble Brutus
Hath told you Caesar was ambitious:
If it were so, it was a grievous fault,
And grievously hath Caesar answer'd it.
Here, under leave of Brutus and the rest--
For Brutus is an honourable man;
So are they all, all honourable men--
Come I to speak in Caesar's funeral.
He was my friend, faithful and just to me:
But Brutus says he was ambitious;
And Brutus is an honourable man.
He hath brought many captives home to Rome
Whose ransoms did the general coffers fill:
Did this in Caesar seem ambitious?
When that the poor have cried, Caesar hath wept:
Ambition should be made of sterner stuff:
Yet Brutus says he was ambitious;
And Brutus is an honourable man.
You all did see that on the Lupercal
I thrice presented him a kingly crown,
Which he did thrice refuse: was this ambition?
Yet Brutus says he was ambitious;
And, sure, he is an honourable man.
I speak not to disprove what Brutus spoke,
But here I am to speak what I do know.
You all did love him once, not without cause:
What cause withholds you then, to mourn for him?
O judgment! thou art fled to brutish beasts,

(*continued*)

[17] Julius Caesar, by William Shakespeare. Act III, scene II.

(continued)

And men have lost their reason. Bear with me;
My heart is in the coffin there with Caesar,
And I must pause till it come back to me.
....
ANTONY
But yesterday the word of Caesar might
Have stood against the world; now lies he there.
And none so poor to do him reverence.
O masters, if I were disposed to stir
Your hearts and minds to mutiny and rage,
I should do Brutus wrong, and Cassius wrong,
Who, you all know, are honourable men:
I will not do them wrong; I rather choose
To wrong the dead, to wrong myself and you,
Than I will wrong such honourable men.
...

All of us, either in school or college or otherwise, must have read the speech made by Antony, and also watched it in several plays and movies. Still, there is merit in refreshing our memory.

In the play, Brutus murdered Caesar and thereafter spoke to the people of Rome that he had to do it to save Rome from the ambitious Caesar's evil plans. But, it was all untrue. Caesar's friend, Antony, was allowed by Brutus to speak to the people of Rome, and it was the sheer tact and the wonderful choice of words that Antony managed to convey very effectively to the people that it was Brutus, not Caesar, who was not good at heart and that Brutus was to be blamed for the entire conspiracy and Caesar's killing. It led the people to revolt against Brutus. In his address to the people, Antony repeatedly mentioned, "And Brutus is an honourable man." The use of this statement after every few sentences signifies the sarcasm hitting the audience again and again. In the beginning, anyone who listens to Antony saying "and Brutus is an honourable man" takes the words at face value and comprehends the related sentences in the same fashion; however, slowly but surely as the message goes deep and the people start realising the real and hidden meaning. The message conveyed by this sentence starts deviating from its literal meaning, and in the latter half, it fully conveys the disdain and therefore the real character of Brutus. By that time, it was too late for Brutus to control the damage. The penny had dropped. People could not be befooled any longer. The harsh truth was out, though clandestinely. That is the real beauty of the afore-cited passage.

This passage is a masterpiece and so many people–particularly leaders—have taken inspiration from it to convey to their competitors, enemies, superiors, bosses and so on in a very subtle manner what they would have liked to say directly, but as the relationship between the two of them does not permit them to do the same openly. Often, experienced persons have called it as *sophisticated overt behaviour*—sob—which helps in public life not to hit directly, keep the things decent, make them cryptic and equivocal, keep alive the possibility of being interpreted differently; but at the same time dropping enough hints and references in the communication that people, who read between the lines, are able to understand the real meaning, may be with a little bit of effort, or may be with absolute ease. It all depends on the context—the persons involved, the place, the time, uniqueness of the situation, what is needed to be done at that hour, what is to be achieved, purpose, urgency and so forth. It can be very close to *innuendo*, which is obliquely referring to someone, never directly, but with adequate clues so that only the uninitiated are not able to understand. These are "high context" communications, which require the audience or reader to have sufficient background knowledge and understanding. It can be innuendo in certain cases, which is legally actionable in most of the evolved jurisdictions under the law of defamation or some other equivalent legal action stipulated by the legislature. However, the effectiveness of any such proceedings depends on the legal environment in which the legal action is envisaged.

Frenemy is a person with whom one is friendly though an enemy in real sense. There may be occasions when the person is treated like a friend and at times like an enemy. In politics and business it is very common to be friendly in public and in personal relationship with your competitors. However, professionally they are enemies with ruthless competition and an inner desire to stab the person, in professional sense, if given even half an opportunity. The word has been in vogue for a long time—since the 1950s—when it was used in an article to describe the relationship of Americans with Russians. In evolved business environments, where sophistication requires that parties do not resort to base and savage behaviour, it is prudent for business leaders to mind their words and convey their thoughts—howsoever honest, candid, known openly, backed by evidence, truthful, can withstand scrutiny in a court of law, obvious, reactionary after being hurt emotionally or commercially and so on—in a properly packaged form, highlighting the importance of style over substance. It is typically self-defeating to be straightforward and too frank in these communications. One has to be diplomatic and discreet. Lowering the guards may result in souring of personal relationships, and even initiation of legal action. Until and unless one is hell-bent on doing it, without bothering about the personal relationships and professional reputation, it is quite common and acceptable to heap praise on your frenemy.

A thought-provoking article was written in 2016 by one of the highly regarded corporate leaders in India—N. R. Narayana Murthy—about his rival Azim Premji.

The Azim Premji I Know: Narayana Murthy on the Wipro Legend's Extraordinary Legacy[18]

The first time I met Azim, I was working at Patni Computer Systems as head of the Software Group. My boss, Ashok Patni, is the best boss I have ever had.

Due to some personal reason in 1979–80, he had decided to spend some of his time in Pune. Since I was reporting to him, I would go to Pune once a week and update him on my Key Performance Indicators.

While I was 100% happy with my relationship with Ashok, I felt somewhat uncomfortable with this arrangement and wanted a shift in my job before jumping back to my entrepreneurial journey.

My friend, Prasanna, who was the head of human resources at Wipro, asked me to consider heading the Software Group at the yet-to-be-started technology group at Wipro and arranged a meeting with Azim.

Grateful for a 'No'

Azim took me to Willington Club in Mumbai for a discussion. He was very courteous and very easy to transact with. Apparently, I did not come up to his satisfaction and I did not come up to his satisfaction and I did not get the job. I am grateful to Azim that he rejected me, else my founding of Infosys would have been delayed by a few years. What struck me during the entire conversation was his deep desire to understand the market and the competitors.

(*continued*)

[18]The Economic Times, 17 August 2016, https://economictimes.indiatimes.com/magazines/panache/the-azim-premji-i-know-narayana-murthy-on-the-wipro-legends-extraordinary-legacy/articleshow/53732147.cms

(continued)

Once Infosys started operating in the post-liberalisation era, Azim realised that we were on to something good and his respect for Infosys and me multiplied several times. He would call me several times a year to find out about our progress and our market strategies. I was very open with him and did not hide anything from him since I knew that our superiority with our competitors came only from how quickly we came out with new ideas and how well and quickly we executed them.

He was shy about coming many times to our office in Electronics City and would nudge me to visit him in his isolated turret on the Wipro campus in Sarjapur. While most of the time I went alone to his office, a couple of times I took Nandan Nilekani, Kris Gopalakrishnan and Mohandas Pai with me. We would go into detailed discussions of how we were managing Infosys. Azim and his CEOs, Vivek Paul and Chandrashekaran, would ask a barrage of questions. We truthfully answered them.

Azim and his wife, Yasmeen, are simple people with very good values. My wife, Sudha, and Yasmeen are good friends and share their interest in literary activities. Azim has always led by example in hard work and austerity. He travelled by economy in India and it was a joy to meet him on flights and continue our conversations.

He and I were the only two members of the Indo-French Business Forum who travelled by taxis or subway and stayed in three-star hotels when we went to Paris for meetings. His son, Rishad, and daughter-in-law, Aditi, are chips off the old block in honesty, simplicity, frugality and hard work. I have worked with Aditi in my work with Embrace, a socially relevant startup that she was involved in.

Azim is an honest person. He would accept his or Wipro's mistakes openly and make an effort to correct them. In 2001, Nandan and Phaneesh Murthy came to me and informed me about how a Wipro salesperson had plagiarised our presentation in Europe verbatim and made a presentation to a prospect. The prospect was amused and he brought it to Phaneesh's attention. I spoke to Azim about this and requested him to issue an instruction to his staff not to repeat it. He apologised on behalf of Wipro and did what was necessary.

(*continued*)

(continued)

Manage, Don't Control

Azim is one of the finest exponents of good governance in India. He is the best example for separating management from control. For him, like for us, compliance with the laws of the country always came first. He stands for honesty, decency, fairness and courtesy in every decision he takes.

Azim goes into deep details of an issue and wants to be on top of everything under his control. I use a principle called the Degree of Optimal Ignorance (DOI) in every decision I take. This principle states that your knowledge for any decision should be strategic and not be as much as your subordinate and not as little as your boss. You learn to arrive at the optimality through experience. My conversations with Azim give me the impression that many times he errs on the side of too much of information. He is aware of it and tries (to) avoid it.

One area where Azim and I have agreed to disagree is in our view on tax exemption for exports. I believe that businessmen operating in the Indian market are doing as much value addition to India as us in the export market. Second, we charge our customers in hard currency and are generally insulated from dips in profits due to exchange rate variations and, finally, we are a profitable industry.

Therefore, I do not believe in any tax exemption for our industry. But my conversations with him indicate that Azim favours continuation of tax exemption.

It has been a pleasure knowing Azim, Yasmin, Rishad and Aditi. Every one of them is a role model for us Indians in honesty, simplicity, courtesy, hard work, fairness and decency. Azim is taking a leading role in philanthropy in India. His focus area is improvement of primary education. I wish there were more people like Azim in business in this country.

Azim completes 50 successful years as the leader of Wipro on August 17. I wish him many more years of a happy, healthy, productive and prosperous life as the leader of Wipro, as a patriotic Indian that he has always been, and as a leading philanthropist.

(*The Economic Times, 17 Aug 2016*)

In the entire article, Murthy has talked about the sterling qualities of Azim Premji. Not once, but several times he has written that Premji was courteous, honest, decent, fair, believed in simplicity, had an eye for details, believed in complying with the laws of the country, hard-working, austere and so on. While mentioning all these things, Murthy has beautifully blended a couple of bitter truths he wanted to convey to the reader. The fact that Wipro was involved in plagiarising the presentation made by Infosys has been very nicely written in the article without any rancour, giving the impression to the reader that apology for plagiarising really absolved Wipro, but remembering the incident and mentioning it in the article itself show that the apology was not commensurate with the act of plagiarism and that the apology did not erase the wrongdoing. At a couple of other places in the article, it can easily be understood that people at Wipro were not truly open either in their interactions with Infosys team or in sharing details about business, which Infosys was doing to the best of its intention and ability. Reading between the lines tells a reader that there were occasions when the writer did not feel comfortable with the way business was being conducted by the leader, yet words of praise have been written. Only an uninitiated will not be able to see that they are laced with subtle reproach. This is truly the elegant manner in which a cultured business leader would write about his competitor.

Conclusion

The problem of conveying difficult messages is manifold. First, the message itself is challenging and obviously is not liked by the receiver, so the sender has to be extra careful that the message is received in a constructive manner without hurting the feelings of the receiver, and also without being bitter. Second, a well-balanced message by a seasoned business leader, whether it is a routine message or a rare piece of communication written or spoken on a certain memorable day, reflects the class of the business leader and tells how different perspectives have been moulded so as to be presented as a rounded message without sharp edges and abrasive surface. Third, there is an inherent danger, while trying to smoothen the sharp edges and file the abrasive surface, that there is extra sweetness rubbed into the message which may eventually take away the real and necessary sting as envisaged by the sender, defeating the very purpose of the message. Thus, the message need not be either extra sweet or extra stingy. Balancing has to be done depending on the context. In no case the communication should be condescending or accusing. At the same time, it must draw the attention of the target audience sufficiently and for an adequate period of time so that the entire message is read and assimilated. Often smaller parts of a complete message may not truly convey the meaning of the entire message and therefore it is essential that the sender somehow is able to hold the reader or audience captive for the minimum required period of time, otherwise some wrong meaning may be inferred by reading and listening to small portions.

Avoiding unnecessary conflict in messages by the sender and receiver may also depend on the level of confidence of both the parties in each other. If the level of confidence is very high, there are very low chances of the message to be misinterpreted as the receiver usually takes that message literally, and if it has to be understood in a different manner depending on the context, the receiver will usually understand that as it has been sent by a particular sender. On the other hand, if the level of confidence between the parties is very low, there are very high chances that the message may be misinterpreted by the receiver as there is always a sense of suspicion in what is written or spoken, and what the real meaning could be. Others, who are not directly impacted by the communication, may also interpret the communication in a number of ways according to their own convenience, liking and vested interest. One need not be defensive so as to always avoid sharp and terse communication as it is for the sender to exercise discretion while drafting—either in a fraction of a second or with the luxury of more than necessary time—the piece of communication according to the context and the definite purpose at that moment.

The motive has to be clear and thereafter it can be achieved as tactfully as possible without ruffling feathers unnecessarily.

Being on the right side of the law is equally important while conveying messages with a hidden meaning.

CHAPTER 6

Man Is a Social Animal

Man—the word is being used for human beings, irrespective of the gender—loves to live with others, and not in isolation. Community and society fulfil the needs of a man and typically make the life worth living. Aristotle, the Greek philosopher, had strongly stated about the social nature of the man:

> Man is by nature a social animal; an individual who is unsocial naturally and not accidentally is either beneath our notice or more than human. Society is something that precedes the individual. Anyone who either cannot lead the common life or is so self-sufficient as not to need to, and therefore does not partake of society, is either a beast or a god.[1]

Strong words indeed! There is merit in living in a society rather than in isolation. Thoughts of the father-son duo, James and John Stuart Mill, the British philosophers in the nineteenth century, were directed towards social thinking and primacy to society as compared to an individual. Jeremy Bentham's thoughts about social good and collective good also strengthened the thoughts of a man living in a society and not in solitude.

The pain, the sorrow and the suffering of an individual living in forced isolation are unfathomable by someone who has never experienced such isolation. Daniel Defoe in his famous work *Robinson Crusoe* imaginatively

[1] Aristotle, Politics; https://www.goodreads.com/quotes/183896-man-is-by-nature-a-social-animal-an-individual-who

A. K. Agarwal, *Legal Language and Business Communication*,
https://doi.org/10.1007/978-981-13-7534-7_6

created the character that had been cast away on an uninhabited island. It is believed that the story was inspired by the Scottish sailor Alexander Selkirk, who was cast away on a small island in the Pacific for four years and four months from 1704 to 1709. Poet William Cowper very nicely brought out the feelings of a person so isolated—at times feeling like a monarch of the entire such territory, and the very next moment longing for society and company.

> I am monarch of all I survey,
> My right there is none to dispute;
> From the centre all round to the sea,
> I am lord of the fowl and the brute.
> …
> Society, Friendship, and Love
> Divinely bestow'd upon man,
> Oh had I the wings of a dove
> How soon would I taste you again![2]

It is difficult, nigh impossible, for a man to live alone. Selkirk did not live in isolation on the marooned island as a matter of choice. He was forced to do that as punishment by the captain of his ship and no one could have imagined that he would survive. He was destined to survive and his courage and resourcefulness helped him in enduring. Given a choice he would have chosen to live in a society, mingling with other human beings.

Though there have been several researches which highlight the significance of connecting with others, rather than living in seclusion, it has been known and is very obvious since times immemorial that man likes to live in groups, with some exceptions in seeking truth and self-salvation choose to live in total remoteness. The entire discipline of sociology aims at studying the relationship of individuals with the society, how the society is impacted by individuals and how individuals are impacted by the society. These interactions bring change in society, maybe slowly but surely.

Social interactions, social institutions, social phenomena, social relationships, social actions and inter-relations are at the root of the study of sociology. Considered to be the founding father of sociology, Auguste

[2] William Cowper, "The Solitude of Alexander Selkirk."

Comte preferred to call sociology the "science of social phenomena."[3] At the fulcrum of all these studies and investigations is the man—the human being—who is supposed to conduct himself in a certain manner in the company of other human beings. How things change with the change in his conduct and how the external factors have an effect on his behaviour are the curious and interesting topics of study. With the passage of time and evolution of society, new issues crop up which obviously impact the behaviour. Technology has a tremendous influence on the way human beings behave. Some influence can be observed directly and some indirectly. For instance, the invention of the steam engine in the eighteenth century, and thereafter industrial revolution in the eighteenth and nineteenth centuries had a direct influence on the manner in which individuals led their lives. Also, it started influencing the manner in which people got educated and searched for jobs, leading to migration and living in nuclear families. In brief, the steam engine and the industrial revolution left an indelible mark on the social aspects of human beings. Impact of the same level, or arguably even more than that, can be observed by the invention of computers and thereafter the internet. The way smartphones, since the early twenty-first century, have merged the computer and the mobile phone and have created innumerable options for the user is unprecedented.

The legal challenge is of pushing the frontier of society from face-to-face interaction to more and more interaction in digital form, where parties are not able to be physically in each other's presence, but it is very easy to enter into someone's personal and private space, unsolicited and without any hindrance. The courts are faced with the problem of determining the extent to one's private space in which others cannot encroach, even if technology permits. The role of the government is expanding in most of the developing and developed world due to expansion of public services and ever-growing demands of the people. Technology is a great enabler and helps the government in performing its job in a better manner; however, there are often difficult questions of law to be decided regarding a proper balance to be achieved between government, technology and law. One such case got prominence in the United States and the rest of the

[3] Principles of Sociology, Lester F. Ward, The Annals of the American Academy of Political and Social Science, Vol. 8 (Jul., 1896), pp. 1–31, Published by Sage Publications, Inc., in association with the American Academy of Political and Social Science, https://www.jstor.org/stable/pdf/1009590.pdf

world due to the possibility of recording the exact location of a person, who is carrying a smartphone, with great accuracy and without taking permission from the person, or even informing him.

Carpenter's Case[4]

With the developments in smartphone technology and such phones becoming ubiquitous, it has become very easy to find the location of the user. This information is recorded in the computer servers of the mobile phone companies, internet service providers, and also different web browsers used for web surfing and multiple other uses made practically possible by a large number of applications, which have become integral to using a smartphone. The locational information of any subscriber can be used as evidence in legal proceedings, typically minimising, if not completely eliminating, the importance of alibi in several investigations. It has now become realistically impossible for a person to negate his presence at a particular place which is clearly being indicated in the information retrieved from the locational data made accessible by the cellular service provider. The only excuse which can be made is that the user and the phone were not together, and for that excuse to be made it is essential that the phone was either lost or stolen. In either of the cases, the user is under a sort of legal obligation to report the matter to the police and the cellular service provider. If neither has been done, the assumption can easily be made that the subscriber and the smartphone were together and the presence of the smartphone at a particular place can reasonably be deemed to be the presence of the person at that place. Such has been the indispensability associated with the smartphones in the recent years that any reasonable and prudent person, in today's world, will probably refrain from making a statement that he does not carry a smartphone.

In a fascinating judgment pronounced by the US Supreme Court in June 2018, the court dealt with the issue of locational data information being used by the investigating agencies against a person without prior permission of a magistrate or a court. The court decided that the government cannot use such information in normal course without a warrant issued for that purpose. The court was not unanimous in its decision, and it was by a razor-thin majority of 5–4, with five judges including the Chief

[4] United States Supreme Court, Carpenter v. United States, (2018), No. 16–402, Argued: November 29, 2017; Decided: June 22, 2018.

Justice John Roberts Jr. deciding in favour of privacy in the fast-changing technological world. The minority, of four justices, wrote a dissenting opinion emphasising on the newer challenges faced by the government and the fact that the latest technological tools and innovations should be used for public welfare and preventing criminal activities in the country. There has been a strong voice of the dissenting judges that the expanding frontiers of law should allow the use of technology to make the society a better place to live in, and the hands of the government should not be tied behind its back as multiple challenges of internal security and prevention from external aggression can be faced in a better way by technological upgradation and by legally permitting its application to practical problems. The majority, however, vigorously pursued the arguments in favour of privacy of a person and not giving the government unfettered rights.

The facts of the case, in brief, are as follows.

In typical movie style, four persons were involved in robbing stores, and they used to do it in a professional manner with different roles performed rotationally. These roles were primarily of doing the actual job of robbing, being on the lookout for any signals of danger such as police, armed people and onlookers who could inform the police, and also the drivers, whose job was to get away; so they had to be ready with a proper vehicle. All the team members were supposed to work in close coordination and take directives from the leader, and the leader's role can also be rotational. This team of four persons had been quite successful in robbing stores in Michigan and Ohio. There were more than a dozen accomplices who had been active in the robberies. The police arrested four persons in 2011 on suspicion of robbing several RadioShack and T-Mobile stores in Detroit. On the confession made by one of them, the police collected a lot of information regarding the accomplices, their cell phones and their roles in the robberies and the heists. The information regarding the cell phones, the location of the persons and their roles centred on a number of calls made by them were to be verified by the cell phone companies based on the locational data recorded by the companies. For this, the prosecution filed an application in the court so that an order can be passed by the court to the cell phone companies to share the data with them regarding these persons—particularly Timothy Carpenter, the alleged leader—and about the veracity of the information provided by them regarding the calls made and the places visited.

The court allowed the application on the basis of the relevant law which provides for compelling disclosure in cases when the records could possibly offer specific facts germane to criminal investigation. The two cellular companies—MetroPCS and Sprint—were ordered to share the details of calls made and cell-site information—the locational data—for Carpenter's phones. The companies provided these details along with data for the time the phones were on "roaming" in different states. With about hundred data points per day, the government prepared a chronological sheet detailing Carpenter's movement during the period of time when a string of robberies had taken place and could easily strengthen its case in the court against him. Carpenter opposed the reliance on this piece of evidence being used against him on the ground of being in violation of the Fourth Amendment to the US Constitution, as the records had been obtained by the prosecution without a warrant issued upon probable cause.

The Fourth Amendment[5]

The Fourth Amendment to the U.S. Constitution reads as follows:

> The right of the people to be secure in their persons, houses, papers, and effects, against unreasonable searches and seizures, shall not be violated, and no Warrants shall issue, but upon probable cause, supported by Oath or affirmation, and particularly describing the place to be searched, and the persons or things to be seized.

It was introduced in the U.S. Congress in 1789 by James Madison and Thomas Jefferson, the Secretary of State, announced its adoption in 1792.

It is a part of the Bill of Rights and its importance lies in the fact that individual privacy has been recognised, protected and remedy provided for its violation in the form of judicial intervention. Thus, the right to privacy has been truly established and very strongly anchored by this amendment. Government can conduct searches and seizures but only upon issuance of a warrant by a competent judicial authority, which is also constitutionally bound to exercise discretion to weigh properly the probable cause. Also the warrant for search and seizure shall be very specific about the person and the place. It cannot be a general order sanctioning

(*continued*)

[5]The U.S. Constitution, Fourth Amendment, 1792.

(continued)

blanket permission. In a catena of judgments, the three contentious issues raised by the Fourth Amendment have been explained and interpreted. The three main issues are: first, meaning of search and seizure; second, meaning of probable cause; and, third, remedies for violation of the rights under this amendment. With the passage of time and development of technology, protection has been enhanced from physical presence to violation of an individual's privacy. Digital technology, and the manner in which it is spreading its wings, is far more damaging in breach of privacy than physical intervention. Thus, the courts have to deal with the question of finding a justified balance in use of technology and the privacy of an individual.

This is the dynamic nature of law which is exhibited in the newer and changing interpretation of the existing black-letter law. It is the role of the courts to give new and apt meaning as the aspirations of the persons change with changing times. The purpose of the Fourth Amendment to the U.S. Constitution was to stop the misuse of general search warrants being used under the British government, which was not in line with the fundamental rights – as enshrined in the Bill of Rights – which were envisaged in the American Constitution. Because of the very strong federal character of the United States, investigations were rarely carried on under the federal law. It was only in the 20th century that the Fourth Amendment also found application to the States. Thus, as of now, the Fourth Amendment is one of the strongest pillars, along with the First Amendment – assuring free speech, of the American Constitution which guarantees the right to privacy, both physical and digital, and in any other way it can be conceived and executed. Therefore, the interpretation of the Fourth Amendment is quite wide and the courts have refrained from accepting a narrow interpretation limited only to physical intrusion.

Carpenter could not convince the District Court and the trial started. According to the experts on cell phones and wireless networks related to cell site and locational data, there was no doubt that almost every time and every place of robbery Carpenter was right there as could be ascertained from the records received from the cellular companies. The data provided clinching evidence which was difficult, well-nigh impossible, to be refuted.

Carpenter was convicted on the basis of this evidence. At the outset, Carpenter had strongly opposed the use of this evidence against him on the basis of the Fourth Amendment rights as mentioned above. So, he appealed in the Court of Appeals for the Sixth Circuit, which decided against Carpenter with the reason that he himself—or for that matter any subscriber—had shared his locational information with the cellular company voluntarily. This is one of the important aspects because the moment any user wishes to make full use of the services provided by the cellular companies, one has to switch on the feature in the smartphone which captures the present location of the person. So, by simply using the feature one is deemed to have accepted to all the terms and conditions of the contract between the cellular company and the subscriber, which necessarily includes a clause that the subscriber is using the services voluntarily and provides access to the cellular company to almost all the data saved on the smartphone and also saved somewhere on the server managed by the way browsers and internet service providers. This is a tricky situation which transfers the onus on the subscriber regarding voluntarily accepting to share his current location with the company to be recorded for all times to come. And, as this is being done voluntarily, there is no protection under the Fourth Amendment.

The US Supreme Court reversed the decision of the Court of Appeals and remanded it back. The discussion of the case of the majority is quite interesting and enlightens a reader about the importance of the right to privacy and how it is to be interpreted today and tomorrow. A few portions are worth reproducing.

Majority Discussion[6]

"The question we confront today is how to apply the Fourth Amendment to a new phenomenon: the ability to chronicle a person's past movements through the record of his cell phone signals… Much like GPS tracking of a vehicle, cell phone location information is detailed, encyclopedic, and effortlessly compiled… in 1979, few

(*continued*)

[6] Roberts, C. J., delivered the opinion of the Court, in which Ginsburg, Breyer, Sotomayor, and Kagan, JJ., joined. Kennedy, J., filed a dissenting opinion, in which Thomas and Alito, JJ., joined. Thomas, J., filed a dissenting opinion. Alito, J., filed a dissenting opinion, in which Thomas, J., joined. Gorsuch, J., filed a dissenting opinion.

(continued)

could have imagined a society in which a phone goes wherever its owner goes, conveying to the wireless carrier not just dialed digits, but a detailed and comprehensive record of the person's movements... we hold that an individual maintains a legitimate expectation of privacy in the record of his physical movements as captured through CSLI. The location information obtained from Carpenter's wireless carriers was the product of a search.

...

A person does not surrender all Fourth Amendment protection by venturing into the public sphere... A majority of this Court has already recognized[7] that individuals have a reasonable expectation of privacy in the whole of their physical movements...Prior to the digital age, law enforcement might have pursued a suspect for a brief stretch, but doing so "for any extended period of time was difficult and costly and therefore rarely undertaken."... For that reason, "society's expectation has been that law enforcement agents and others would not--and indeed, in the main, simply could not--secretly monitor and catalogue every single movement of an individual's car for a very long period."

...

Allowing government access to cell-site records contravenes that expectation. Although such records are generated for commercial purposes, that distinction does not negate Carpenter's anticipation of privacy in his physical location. Mapping a cell phone's location over the course of 127 days provides an all-encompassing record of the holder's whereabouts... cell phone tracking is remarkably easy, cheap, and efficient compared to traditional investigative tools. With just the click of a button, the Government can access each carrier's deep repository of historical location information at practically no expense.

...

(*continued*)

[7]United States v. Jones, 565 U.S. 400 (2012). The case involved the installation of a global positioning system (GPS) tracking device on a car, which was challenged in the court on the basis of the Fourth Amendment, and the Supreme Court held that it was *search*.

(continued)

While individuals regularly leave their vehicles, they compulsively carry cell phones with them all the time. A cell phone faithfully follows its owner beyond public thoroughfares and into private residences, doctor's offices, political headquarters, and other potentially revealing locales... Accordingly, when the Government tracks the location of a cell phone it achieves near perfect surveillance, as if it had attached an ankle monitor to the phone's user.

...

Only the few without cell phones could escape this tireless and absolute surveillance."

(*From the Carpenter's case, US SC, 2018*)

After the discussion, the majority of five justices ordered:

> We decline to grant the state unrestricted access to a wireless carrier's database of physical location information. In light of the deeply revealing nature of CSLI, its depth, breadth, and comprehensive reach, and the inescapable and automatic nature of its collection, the fact that such information is gathered by a third party does not make it any less deserving of Fourth Amendment protection. The Government's acquisition of the cell-site records here was a search under that Amendment. The judgment of the Court of Appeals is reversed, and the case is remanded for further proceedings consistent with this opinion.[8]

Comments and Questions

The technology comes first, and then the law follows. The instant case is a wonderful example to illustrate and vindicate it. The cell phone technology started to be used commercially by ordinary people about a quarter of a century ago. Since then, the technology frontier has been pushed forward at a lightning speed, often creating a product capable of providing such services which could have never even been dreamt of, simply like fairy tales, or a magician using a magic wand. In the early twenty-first century, newer developments made it possible to connect the cell phone to the

[8] Roberts, C. J., Ginsburg, Breyer, Sotomayor, and Kagan, JJ.

internet and thereafter gave more power to that phone, which resulted in the launch of smartphones. They had three important features: first, huge memory; second, connection with the internet; and third, advanced computing ability. With these features, the smartphones, within a short period of time became a constant companion of almost everyone who could afford them. With the passage of time, the prices also had fallen dramatically, and with many new players entering the market, competition became very tough. The technological advances, coupled with falling prices, brought the smartphone in every hand—particularly in the first world countries like the United States where the number of smartphones being used is more than the population (developing countries like India have a long way to go and still are far from being saturated)—irrespective of the economic and social strata to which a person belongs.

The individual and his smartphone have almost become inseparable. Social scientists are worried about the heavy dependence on smartphones for almost everything in life, and researches are being conducted throughout the world to study the impact of smartphone association for too long on physical, mental, psychological, social and other aspects of the health of a person. One of the most important reasons for the deeper penetration and ubiquitous use of smartphones has been the ability to seamlessly use it while travelling, which has been made possible by the "cell sites" connectivity. These are divisional radio antennas which are mounted on cell towers and various other places. The more the cell sites, the better the reception. Thus, more number of cell sites indicate smaller area designated to a particular site, which is identifiable by an accepted method in the cellular telecom industry. The signals from several adjacent cell sites overlap and, quite obviously, the strength of the signal from a particular cell site weakens with distance from the core. Smartphones keep on connecting with the best signal available and leaving the previous signal, thus changing the cell site frequently, which the user does not even get to know. Every time, a cell site is connected and disconnected, a record is maintained, which easily tells the position of the user, with a great deal of accuracy. This record is called the "cell-site location information" (CSLI) which is at the root of the dispute. In thickly populated areas, with a very high number of users, the cellular companies have created a highly dense network of cell sites, which makes precise locational information possible.

This judgment includes dissenting opinion of four judges with the major difference of opinion being that the majority decision will defeat the very purpose of the application of the Fourth Amendment in many regular and routine law enforcement operations. Basically, the purpose of the Fourth Amendment was not to intervene in the routine activities of administration, especially the police, and with the development of technology, the police have been making themselves contemporary and adept with the newer possibilities being opened up with advancements in technology. By not allowing the police to use these advancements in a legal manner protected by the Constitution, it would be a disservice to the people and would not be in the interest of the public. With the cell-site records, it would be precise and easy for the police to catch hold of highly dangerous criminals, who otherwise are quite smart not to leave tell-tale signs. The dissenting opinion also included the view that the majority of you would in all probability deny a legitimate enforcement of the hard work done during investigation and can probably open the floodgates of litigation, making it extremely difficult for the investigating agencies to prove even genuine cases.

A question arises regarding certain matters of great national and public importance like terror threats and imminent harm to vulnerable people and the issue of the use of the locational data to nab the culprits, and if possible to avoid the occurrence of any such unfortunate event. The majority opinion made it clear that such exigencies will be treated as exceptions to the protection provided by the Fourth Amendment. Thus, a great deal of subjectivity has been injected into the decision-making process and is treating different happenings according to their merits.

One very interesting and profound observation has been made by the majority decision:

> Only the few without cell phones could escape this tireless and absolute surveillance.[9]

This one sentence speaks volumes about the age we live in. Today, the norm is that each and every person is carrying a smartphone, and in emerging economies people who cannot afford to have one do aspire to have one of these modern gadgets at the earliest. Sometime back these smartphones were considered to be *luxury*, then they became a *convenience*, and now for sure they have become a *necessity*. Presently, it is important for most of the people to remain socially connected and the

[9] Roberts, C. J., Ginsburg, Breyer, Sotomayor, and Kagan, JJ.

easiest way to do that is through a smartphone. A large part of the global population spends several hours daily on a smartphone to remain connected with friends, relatives, colleagues, well-wishers, business associates, prospective customers and clients and many others. Business organisations necessarily have to have their digital presence in the social media lest they may get severe lashing and bashing by customers as feedback not on their designated and dedicated website but on various social media platforms, which is extremely damaging. Thus, it is next to impossible for any person to remain isolated from the social media, which willy-nilly means that almost no one is immune from tireless and absolute surveillance as observed by the US Supreme Court.

The smartphone manufacturing companies and cellular service providers along with companies providing social media platforms submitted a brief in this case to protect themselves from being forced to divulge the locational information and other details about subscribers.

> Technology companies including Apple, Facebook and Google filed a brief urging the Supreme Court to continue to bring Fourth Amendment law into the modern era. "No constitutional doctrine should presume," the brief said, "that consumers assume the risk of warrantless government surveillance simply by using technologies that are beneficial and increasingly integrated into modern life."[10]

It is commercially useful for the service providers to have very strong legal protection for their subscribers as it ensures the privacy of data, and in case of a breach, guaranteed legal action. Several companies providing these services have strong data protection policies which help them attract subscribers to share their thoughts with their friends, relatives, colleagues and others using voice, text, video and any other possible method without the fear of being tapped or tracked. Companies have been going to the extent of coding and encrypting data which cannot be accessed by anyone, and even when the government wants it for national security, there is strong resistance in sharing it. Apple got the support of many of top technology companies in early 2016 when there was a demand by the American government for giving access to a particular subscriber's data.

[10] In Ruling on Cellphone Location Data, Supreme Court Makes Statement on Digital Privacy; NYT, 22 June 2018 https://www.nytimes.com/2018/06/22/us/politics/supreme-court-warrants-cell-phone-privacy.html

Frenemies, Business Niceties and Social Media

February and March 2016 witnessed unprecedented support for Apple in its legal battle with the American government for the sanctity of the security code of its products. Unfortunately, the support is guided by commercial interests and lacks a principled stand.

In brief, the government authorities in the United States asked Apple to decode one of its devices used by an alleged terrorist a year before to enable them to get more information and leads. Apple refused by citing privacy laws and its rights to maintain secrecy and provide protection to clients' and subscribers' personal data and communication details. The government got an order from the lowest court of competent jurisdiction to reveal the said information keeping in mind the national security and public interest. Apple defied. The matter was later appealed in the appellate court. Several electronic, software and communication giants had filed *amicus*—as a friend of the court—briefs in support of Apple.

This is not surprising. Companies having cut-throat competition with each other and conducting themselves as sworn "enemies" often join hands when they have to fight an outsider—often the government, regulatory institutions and legislators—and appear as bosom "friends." For such businesses, the term "frenemies" had been coined several decades ago. It can be seen in action all over the world, irrespective of geographical differences and differences in business sectors. Facebook, Google, Microsoft, Box, Amazon and several others are together and the phenomenon can be studied as one of the latest examples of frenemies in action.

It can't be more ironical than happening in a country which takes pride in democratic values and public interest. The country belongs to the people of the United States, as is true for our own country—the Republic of India belongs to the people of India. How can a business entity even think that its products' security code is more important than the security of the people of the country where it is incorporated? This is preposterous. Nothing can be more absurd than saying that a company will not share a piece of information it is privy to, or can get access to with some effort, to the legitimate and democratically elected government of the day.

With terror organisations getting access to the latest technology by hook or by crook, it is the duty of every nationalist to come forward and provide every piece of information he knows to the government voluntarily. And there should not be even an iota of doubt that once that information is sought by the government, how that person must conduct himself. Without any demur, he must extend his full support. Taking legal recourse not to divulge the contents can only be inferred that the person or the company doesn't care two hoots about national security as long as its cash registers keep ringing.

But, the same persons and business companies must keep it in mind that they are able to survive and thrive only when there is peace and tranquillity in the society. Of course, a counter-argument can be by gun manufacturers and sellers that for selling their products, they don't need either of the two prerequisites. For them, more the chaos and disorder, better the sales will be. But, even for them, it is necessary that they are able to continue to sell their products in a legal manner and keep the proceeds with themselves without worrying about it being looted and plundered.

Friendly business environment needs to be nurtured by trust-building and sharing information, not the trade secrets and confidential information, but information necessary for buttressing and bolstering national security and general security for doing business for everyone. There can be no case for not sharing vital information for this very purpose with the security agencies. Greatest good of the greatest number—the fundamental Benthamite principle—governs the greatest democracies. For the profit-making interest of a few, security of the majority can't be and shouldn't be ignored.

Privacy laws in most of the evolved jurisdictions—and the United States leads the pack—never ever hold commercial interest on a higher pedestal than national security and public interest.

Sometime later the Federal Bureau of Investigation was able to unlock the Apple iPhone code and the matter had become infructuous.

Of late companies in India are showing publicly their admiration for competitors, which sometime back was unheard of and if something of that sort had happened it would usually be considered abnormal. In the recent past, business analysts and even the public would have tried to find out the real intention of any business entity saying good things about any of its competitor. However, there has been a definite impact of social media, which is bringing a lot many people together in cohesive groups. These groups publicly show displeasure, discontentment, disappointment, and make disparaging remarks. Expressions of similar sentiments are looked down upon. Blurting out something deplorable on the social media in a fit of anger is not taken kindly. Though there are people looking out for certain clashes on the social media either between two individual giants or between businesses and such happenings provide juicy material for gossip columns and numerous television shows and radio programmes. But, despite getting attracted towards acrimonious debates and arguments, most of the people in general like to go through warm, cordial, amiable, friendly and good-natured messages. A number of experts advocating the practice of remaining away from social media for at least a definite period of time every day without fail instruct to remain away from negativity. Messages with positive vibes get attraction and help in creating a progressive and forward-looking image for a company in the minds of consumers. This surely helps in getting loyal customers and more business in the long run. In an article, *The Economic Times* wrote:

> Urban Ladder makes a nice gesture to rival Ikea, Parle to Britannia, Mother Dairy to Patanjali. And not just in FMCG. There's Mahindra & Mahindra teaming up with Ford, Tata Motors cozying up with Chrysler, Maruti with Toyota… "May you find the Melody to many more Little Hearts". Nice touch, since Melody is a Parle brand, and Little Hearts, Britannia's. Britannia responded almost immediately with a "Thanks for the love, Parle" tweet. Both tweets went viral, attracting plenty of positive comment. When Baba Ramdev-promoted Patanjali announced its dairy foray, milk behemoth Mother Dairy promptly released a statement "welcoming" Patanjali. Online furniture store Urban Ladder welcomed Swedish furniture and home accessories giant Ikea with a namaste through an Instagram video. Ikea's near-immediate response was "Tack (Thank you in Swedish)… we are very happy to be here with you". Companies have not only sent welcome notes, but also remained unaffected by spoof ads from rivals.[11]

Carpenter's case in 2018, while giving protection under the Fourth Amendment, gave exceptions in cases of exigency, which may arise due to terror, crime and other compelling reasons.

Technology is wonderful and emerging uses of technology for bringing people together have resulted in a lot of interaction in the digital world with the machines becoming more powerful and at times a little bit intelligent given the extremely fast developments in the field of artificial intelligence and machine learning. Sometimes it may result in a certain embarrassing

[11] Changing consumer preference and cost pressures bringing rivals closer in FMCG & automobile sectors; The Economic Times, 22 Sep 2018; https://economictimes.indiatimes.com/industry/cons-products/fmcg/changing-consumer-preference-and-cost-pressures-bringing-rivals-closer-in-fmcg-automobile-sectors/articleshow/65907856.cms

and awkward situations which had not been anticipated. Translation from one language to another has always been quite a complex exercise as literal translation of individual words may not, and often does not, convey the real meaning. There are often shades of grey in choosing a proper word in the language in which the original work is being translated and it may not be very different, though may not be the perfect communication and most apt meaning, from what is being tried to be conveyed. The problem arises when mechanical translation results in something absolutely absurd. Something of this sort happened when YouTube mechanically and wrongly translated this speech by the Polish Prime Minister.

Lost in Translation

In February 2018, the Polish Prime Minister had a tough time facing issues of translation done by YouTube using automatic translator. The Polish Prime Minister Mateusz Morawiecki had made a public address on the television with reference to a new law being made at that time in Poland known as the *Holocaust law*. From the very beginning this law had been controversial and its passage by the national legislative body was expected to create tension not only in Poland but also in other places as the law was being made with the primary purpose of distancing Poland from Germany's action in the Nazi death camps.

Germany has a common border with Poland and during the Second World War several death camps were set up in Germany as well as in Poland. During that time about 6 million Jews were killed by the Nazis. Most of them met their death in the camp of Auschwitz and other death camps in Poland. Poland's view is that during that time it all happened in the German-occupied Poland and hence Poles could not rightly be blamed for the atrocities committed during that time. However, it has been common, and naturally so, for the people to talk about the concentration camps situated in Poland as whatever one may say, geographically these camps were surely located and are still located in Poland. Such type of mention in conversations, news reporting, literature and artistic work, among others, very often deeply hurts the people in Poland—as they consider that they had no role—and hence, rather than changing the perception of the people, which is truly a very long-term and uncertain affair, or just allowing them to talk whatever they want to, following the spirit of free speech and expression, the Polish government made up its mind to stop all this simply with a stroke of the pen, that is, by making a new law.

Such a move has been criticised by the Polish Jews, Israel and several other countries with a substantial Jewish population. This law has also been opposed by several countries championing free speech, though in guarded language. The law makes it punishable for anyone saying that Poles were responsible for the crimes against humanity which were committed by Nazi Germany on its soil by imposition of fine and jail for about three years.

The Polish Prime Minister had mentioned the new law in his television address; however, the online translation done by YouTube mentioned that the Polish Prime Minister had said that the Nazi German death camps were Polish. This is ironical as the law had prohibited use of even phrases such as "Polish death camps." By automatic translator, the meaning had been lost and in fact given exactly opposite picture of what the speaker wanted to say.

Legally the question arises as to who should bear the responsibility for such a mistake done by an automatic translator. Though YouTube categorically and unconditionally apologised[12] for the mistake it made, for a good number of people and for a substantial period of time the mistake had been made, as today we are living in a world where messages move very fast and on social media information can move in seconds to a very large number of people all over the world. It is equally important that there are reactionary messages resulting in a spate of hate messages pouring in from different parts of the world making it extremely difficult, if not impossible, to control the damage caused.

It is quite obvious from this particular incident that the social media platform provider—YouTube—apparently did not have any ulterior motive; however, there is a possibility that sometimes any mischievous person can initiate a discussion thread by posting a message on the social media network—which the sender very well knows to be damaging and untrue—and after instigating feelings of hatred and distrust and thereby causing tension, unrest and disharmony simply withdraws the statement and apologises.

Business leaders have to be quite cautious about such a trend as there are a large number of people—dissatisfied customers, disgruntled employees,

[12] YouTube Apologizes for Translation Error in Polish Leader's Video About Holocaust Bill. By Maciej Martewicz and Adrian Krajewski, February 2, 2018, Bloomberg, https://www.bloomberg.com/news/articles/2018-02-02/translation-mix-up-dents-polish-efforts-to-defend-holocaust-bill

competitors, mischievous elements, extortionists and others—who are just waiting for an opportunity to malign a company's image in whatever manner they can. Social media provide them a fitting platform for doing so without being physically present anywhere near the company, by simply typing a few keys on the laptop. This is really threatening for businesses as it becomes important for any business concern not to ignore such a development.

Uncontrolled use of technology and social networking platforms, whether for sharing one's thoughts or messages or audio and video clippings or any other relevant material, may not be approved by the legal framework in different jurisdictions until and unless there is a legislative sanction against such use of technology. Social networking platforms have been widely used in the last several years, and as their use is increasing day by day, there is a need felt by regulators to have some control over them so that the people are not able to misuse them. Not only the common masses but also individuals in public positions of responsibility have been mixing the use of social media for their personal and official communication. Innovative use of the existing technology, which can be permitted by the frontiers which the existing technology has reached, maybe a fantastic idea; however, discretion is to be exercised by people in authoritative positions to push that frontier in such a manner which keeps them on the right side of the law. An interesting matter happened in a court in India where the presiding officer used a WhatsApp call to conduct a trial.

Technology as Courts' Friend: Trial Through WhatsApp Call

In September 2018, the Supreme Court of India took up a case of a court in Jharkhand—a province in India—which had pronounced an order to the accused through a WhatsApp call. The Supreme Court took note of it and criticised it heavily by calling it a joke. The frontiers of technology have been pushed by the court to unrealistic and unacceptable limits, not due to any limitation of technology, but due to non-approval of such a method either by legislature or by judiciary.

The brief facts are thought-provoking. In the state of Jharkhand, a former minister Yogendra Sao and his wife Nirmala Devi had been accused in a riot case. They were granted bail and the Supreme Court had imposed a condition that they should stay in Bhopal, capital of Madhya Pradesh, another state in India and close to Jharkhand. They were not allowed by the court to enter the state of Jharkhand. Only for the purpose of court proceedings, they could have entered into Jharkhand. They were not supposed to go out anywhere from Bhopal and the trial was to be conducted through videoconferencing from the district court in Bhopal and district court in Hazaribagh, Jharkhand. It was argued by the lawyers that the connectivity of videoconferencing facility was very low and that might have been the reason as to why the trial judge used a WhatsApp call.

It is undoubtedly true that there are a large number of cases pending in the country due to the problems of not being able to serve the summons, or the accused not turning up in the court on the stipulated dates, etc. Due to a variety of reasons, many of them get legal sanction when an application is made to the judge on numerous grounds, some of them being genuine and most of them being fake. Such a practice results in delay in the system, particularly in criminal matters, which may linger on for years and years.

With the advancement in technology, there have been changes in the evidence law in the country making it possible for videoconferencing to be legally admissible as evidence; however, it has to be done in an approved manner which promoted the use of this technology typically for prisoners. This was the case about a decade ago, but today, inexpensive and easily accessible technology has made it possible for almost every person to make a video call without the need of having expensive videoconferencing equipment and establishing the entire setup. A simple hand-held device like an easily available and inexpensive smartphone, powered by a 4G connection and with reasonable signal strength, is more than enough for making a video call to anyone in the world. Thus, practically it is much more convenient and public friendly to be able to communicate with the court from anywhere in the world.

There are, however, legal issues primarily of identifying the person ensuring that it is the same person on the other end who is supposed to communicate, and also that there is no tapping of the phone or breach of data or hacking of the entire system, and that there is no tutoring of the person and doctoring of message. These are difficult to be ensured in uncontrolled circumstances, and that's the reason why the law cannot allow such communication between the people and the court to the time most of the above mentioned concerns are taken care of technologically and legally. Another important issue is that the person with whom the court wishes to communicate should be on the right side of the law and willing to help to take the process of law forward. The technology cannot be allowed to be used by someone who is running away from the legal system.

Sao and his wife had been violating the bail conditions frequently and could not be allowed by the courts to be treated sympathetically. This is a very different case in which the accused are themselves at fault; however, there are practical problems of videoconferencing connectivity—some might have been intentionally created by vested interests—so as to make that facility defunct. The Supreme Court strongly condemned the conduct of the trial court and the accused. It was reported:

> A bench comprising Justices S A Bobde and L N Rao took serious note of the submissions and said, "What is happening in Jharkhand. This process cannot be allowed, and we cannot allow administration of justice to be brought into disrepute".
>
> "We are here on the way of trial being conducted through WhatsApp. This cannot be done. What kind of a trial is this? Is this a kind of joke?" the bench asked the counsel appearing for Jharkhand.
>
> The bench issued notice to Jharkhand on the plea by both the accused, who have sought transfer of their cases from Hazaribagh to New Delhi, and asked the state to respond to it within two weeks. Jharkhand's counsel told the top court that Sao has been violating the bail condition and had been out of Bhopal most of the time due to which proceedings in the case were delayed.
>
> To this, the bench observed, "That is a different thing. If you have a problem with violation of bail conditions by the accused, you can file a separate application seeking cancellation of bail. We make it clear that we have no sympathy with those who have violated bail condition."[13]

The courts in India have their own websites and mobile applications, and it would be in the interest of litigants and the public at large that these mobile apps provide a court-approved video calling facility.

Technology, if used properly, will prove to be courts' friend. In the times to come it would be desirable that the use of the latest technology is made legally permissible. Social media platforms do have a fantastic role in bringing people together and certain legal issues can be effectively handled through such platforms. Businesses have now for a long time been using the latest means of communication including videoconferencing and other methods of talking to each other face to face in a digital form, despite being thousands of miles away, and thus saving money and travel time.

[13]'Is this a joke?': SC blasts lower court for delivering order through WhatsApp; The Times of India, 9 Sep 2018; https://timesofindia.indiatimes.com/india/is-this-a-joke-sc-blasts-lower-court-for-delivering-order-through-whatsapp/articleshow/65739971.cms

One of the problems faced by people regarding the digital world is that whatever one posts on social platforms, it remains there almost forever and, despite the changing circumstances, others are able to dig out old information which might not be relevant and correct at the given moment. The digital world has a huge memory, unlike society where people tend to forget quite fast and move on with their lives. Businesspersons and everyone in general need to be cautious in sharing details on social media platforms as legal recourse to remove the details, once in the control of the service provider, is extremely difficult, time-consuming, uncertain and expensive. One such matter was heard in a British court where the complainant was lucky enough to get an order in his favour.

The Right to Be Forgotten in the Digital World

In April 2018, a UK court ruled in favour of a person who had filed a legal action against Google claiming his right to be forgotten. This is a curious case in which the British court relied on a legal precedent set by the European Court of Justice in 2014.[14] However, for another person, the High Court did not allow a similar request on the ground that this person had continued to mislead the public whereas the other person had shown remorse.

Which huge amounts of data available on Google, which can be retrieved at a lightning speed, it may be quite damaging to the reputation of any person who might have changed the course of his life—from bad deeds to good deeds or at least neutral—to be constantly reminded of his past in the digital forum. This information is available to everyone having access to the internet and that is precisely the reason why there have been issues related to a person's past.

For forward-looking persons, it has always been said to follow the fundamental policy of "forgive and forget" so as not to continue to wallow in grief and either get labelled oneself or label others as a wrongdoer or offender or criminal. Sometimes, in certain circumstances, in life someone might have done something wrong, or someone might be habitual wrongdoer but

[14] Google Spain SL, Google Inc. v. Agencia Española de Protección de Datos (AEPD), Mario Costeja González; The Court of Justice of the European Union (Grand Chamber); composed of V. Skouris, President, K. Lenaerts, Vice President, M. Ilešič (Rapporteur), L. Bay Larsen, T. von Danwitz, M. Safjan, Presidents of Chambers, J. Malenovský, E. Levits, A. Ó Caoimh, A. Arabadjiev, M. Berger, A. Prechal and E. Jarašiūnas Judges; Case C-131/12; 13 May 2014; http://curia.europa.eu/juris/document/document_print.jsf?doclang=EN&text=&pageIndex=0&docid=152065&cid=244711

wishes to reform himself, it becomes important for society to allow such reformation and even facilitate that. The past should not come haunting the person trying to reform and this basic idea has been at the foundation of one of the important theories of punishment—reformative theory—which is practised in a majority of the jurisdictions.

With ever-increasing access to unlimited data and with the usage of simple data mining tools available to almost any internet user, all sort of information—facts, opinions, fabricated facts, doctored opinions, real and fiction, and so on—is available within a fraction of seconds. The world is grappling with the problem of the so-called fake news and it is truly a nightmare, particularly for celebrities, to deny the damaging information available on various digital platforms. Social media, though a fantastic method of disseminating information and views, can and is being used by mischievous and unscrupulous persons to easily disseminate wrongful and disparaging information about individuals, institutions and so on. This problem can easily be anticipated to aggravate in future.

Can there be an easy technical solution? Of course, yes. It is for the companies managing digital information to take proactive measures to remove such links from their websites and filter the contents from the digital platform. But, the companies providing such services are usually not open to this idea as filtering data can easily be inferred as a blow to the neutrality of information available all the otherwise "neutral" digital platforms.

The European Court of Justice had earlier ruled that if a request is made to Google, irrelevant and outdated data should be erased. In today's world, it is quite common for anyone meeting a person for the first time to find about that person on the internet using a search engine, and Google is the most widely used search engine. Thus, it becomes Google's responsibility, unarguably in ethical terms, to accede to such a request. However, legally it is a question of rights of Google as a business entity to do business without too many restrictions which are based on the judgment of an individual. Hence, this is a tussle between an individual's right to privacy and a firm's right to do business.

In the British case, the judge observed,

> "There is not [a] plausible suggestion ... that there is a risk that this wrongdoing will be repeated by the claimant. The information is of scant if any apparent relevance to any business activities that he seems likely to engage in," the judge added. He said his key conclusion in relation to NT2's claim

> was that "the crime and punishment information has become out of date, irrelevant and of no sufficient legitimate interest to users of Google search to justify its continued availability".[15]

The European Union and the British courts have often been quite stringent as far as individuals' rights are concerned. In the current scenario of the ongoing debate regarding unauthorised and illegal use of personal data, shredding privacy rights to pieces, the instant judgment can prove to be a landmark judgment showing the way for the proper and desired balance between personal rights of individuals and the rights of firms to do business.

It is not going to be easy for the courts and law enforcing agencies to control the strides of the technology, as it is very well known that technology comes first, and the law follows. The courts in most of the countries committed to the rule of law try their best to interpret the black letter law to promote personal freedom and uphold the dignity of individuals. Hopefully, the digital world will not forget to take note of this development. But, the role of governments in different jurisdictioyens is not uniform and business leaders find it quite a challenge to deal with varied regulations—from very liberal to very strict—while formulating strategies to take their business to digital platforms. In India, the situation has been somewhere in between with a lot of freedom given to businesses in general, but restrictions can be imposed under compelling circumstances. These situations are principally related to security of the nation, maintenance of law and order, and public interest. Specific situations may demand special treatment depending on the circumstances and the need of the hour, for which sufficient discretionary powers are given to the executive arm of the government. However, there was an idea of creating a "social media hub" to regulate the misuse of wide and very fast dissemination of information, specifically fake information. But, it did not see the light of the day.

Social Media Hub, Government and Business

In early August 2018, the central government in India withdrew its proposal to create a social media communications hub, which was envisaged to monitor social media in the country. Their apparent reason was to

[15] Google loses landmark 'right to be forgotten' case, The Guardian, 13 Apr 2018; https://www.theguardian.com/technology/2018/apr/13/google-loses-right-to-be-forgotten-case

review and improve the reach of social welfare schemes through social media campaigns. However, opposition and social activists opposed the project and termed it surveillance under the pretext of evaluation of welfare schemes. Remarkably, a month earlier in July 2018, the Supreme Court, in a petition filed to challenge the project, had made the observation that if the State can be legally allowed to go through each and every message on social media, it would be nothing else but living in a surveillance state, which surely hadn't been the goal of the founding fathers of the constitution of India. Fundamental rights, especially the right to free speech and expression, would be directly hit. *The Indian Express* wrote:

> The court was hearing a petition by Trinamool Congress legislator Mahua Moitra who contended that the project was intended "to monitor social media content". When the matter came up for hearing first on July 13, Justice D Y Chandrachud had observed that "we will be moving to a surveillance state" if every tweet and WhatsApp message was going to be monitored…"Such intrusive action on the part of the Government, is not only without the authority of law, but brazenly infringes her fundamental right to freedom of speech under Article 19(1)(a) of the Constitution. Such action of the Government also violates her right of privacy", the petition contended. The "entire scheme/scope of the (Hub) as sought to be set up through the impugned RFP is violative of Articles 14, 19(1)(a) and 21", Moitra submitted and prayed that the RFP be "quashed and set aside as being arbitrary, illegal and unconstitutional".[16]

Better sense prevailed with the government, and following a non-confrontationist approach, the idea of such a centre or hub was shelved. Political reasons, particularly in the approaching election year in 2019, might have dominated the decision-making process. The government might not have mustered enough courage to take it forward and get it truly tested for its constitutional validity under judicial review. Moreover, the relationship between the government and the higher judiciary at that time was anything but cordial and amiable. Though there was a valid reason—of national security and maintaining law and order—with the government to be able to monitor innumerable messages on social media, the legal framework as interpreted by the judiciary had to be honoured.

[16] Facing flak over surveillance fears, govt drops its plan for social media hub; The Indian Express; 4 Aug 2018; https://indianexpress.com/article/india/facing-flak-over-surveillance-fears-govt-drops-its-plan-for-social-media-hub-5291034/

Mass surveillance is not desirable in real democracies. It is only on reasonable suspicion that investigation can be carried out and the State has to build up a case. Big data and strong tools of data analysis have made it a child's play to dig out relevant data and arrange that data in any format. Profiling of persons on the basis of data so collected is a direct infringement of one's privacy and can in no way be allowed legally in a country like India, which is committed to the rule of law. The government had already issued a request for proposal (RFP) to invite tenders for setting up social media communication hub and also reviewing welfare programmes. All this was done using a public sector unit, Broadcast Engineering Consultants India Limited, very closely connected with the Information and Broadcasting Ministry at the centre.

This relationship, by its very nature, was incestuous and smacked of protectionism and some hidden agenda. Transparency, faith and trust were evidently absent. It might have been the hobby-horse of a few individuals manning the show. But, it was not believed by avid watchers that something really would be initiated to implement the idea of the social media hub. It can be said to be the failure of the bureaucracy and the legal advisors who could not see the writing on the wall. It could have been easily anticipated that such a centre would have attracted criticism not only from the opposition but also from the public in general. How could it have gone through the strict judicial scrutiny?

The Supreme Court on several occasions had struck down laws passed by the legislature, like the National Tax Tribunal in 2014 and the National Judicial Appointments Commission in 2015. Though it was possible for the legislature to nullify the effect of the Supreme Court order by again making a law to restore the previous position, it might have possibly triggered a battle between the judiciary and the legislature led by the government.

The current status of confusion over social media communication in India is not conducive for business. There is a lack of clarity as to what can be the repercussions in case something is amiss in the messages and who else, besides the sender and receiver, can be hauled up. The companies providing the social network platforms clearly are of the opinion that it is not their job, and it is beyond their technical capability, to filter each and every message and find out different connotations and implications of the language used, which may itself be coded or camouflaged. The innocent users are terrified so as not to get caught on the wrong foot. The hardened professional rumour-mongers are surreptitiously busy finding ways of surviving and thriving in the state of confusion. However, the tussle between the government and the social media companies is ongoing. The Government of India wishes to shift the onus on to these companies of keeping the content clean. *The Economic Times* reported:

> The government is considering a move to shift the responsibility for ensuring that social media is free from harmful content to platforms such as WhatsApp, Facebook and Telegram from users, besides the companies having management teams based in India, telecom secretary Aruna Sundararajan told ET. That's part of focussed efforts by the government to make them more accountable amid security concerns. "The committee which I'm part of is primarily looking into a few key aspects, including shift of accountability from a user to a social platform, as users are sometimes unaware and innocently retweet or forward content, so much higher standards of accountability for platforms are needed," she said in an interview.[17]

We need clarity regarding social media. And the sooner the better. Besides issues of security and accountability, there are surely concerns regarding intellectual property rights violation, as users are either not informed about them adequately or somehow the process of copying text, images, videos and so on is simplified and has been made possible with a click of the mouse.

While communicating, businesspersons often pick up things from the internet and now because of the ease of copying material—text, photographs, audio, video, graphics and so on—many of them due to inadvertence, not intention, there are violations of copyright. Search engines such as Google have made it extremely easy to find almost anything in a fraction of seconds. A number of features used by Google have made it possible to download a lot of material, irrespective of the copyright claim of the author. Social media platforms are abuzz with such activities where a lot of material is forwarded mindlessly by the recipients and extensively used to create a lot of literary and artistic work without duly acknowledging the copyright owner. This is not acceptable in the world we are living in with internet connectivity bringing people from any part of the world close to each other, without even bothering about the geographical

[17] Onus of keeping social media safe may shift from users to Facebook & WhatsApp: Telecom Secy; The Economic Times, 22 Sep 2018; https://economictimes.indiatimes.com/tech/internet/onus-of-keeping-social-media-safe-may-shift-from-users-to-facebook-whatsapp-telecom-secy/articleshow/65907922.cms

boundaries and the distance of tens of thousands of miles. International legal treaties aim at protecting the intellectual property across the globe, but different legal systems in different countries—with varied levels of enforcement of the black letter law—have been posing serious challenges in creating a homogeneous and uniform system. In such a scenario, the responsibility of creating a legally correct system lies with the market leader by conforming to the highest standards of execution and incorporating the best practices in its protocol. Equally strong business entities in a mutually dependent system, with symbiotic relationship, have the ability of compelling each other to listen to the dynamic requirements and keep on tweaking their business model occasionally. The rigidity to continue with established style of business does not help and may lead to legal action and erosion of goodwill and reputation. Willingness to settle a contentious issue and enter into a deal is a good sign, exuding positive vibes, for businesses. Google and Getty images did the same.

Google, Getty Images and Legal Periphery

In February 2018, Google entered into a deal with Getty Images and settled an ongoing litigation between them primarily regarding the use of images easily available on Google while surfing for any information. Google had accepted to remove the "View Image" button, a link which had easily allowed the users to click on an image and download it without leaving the Google page or without visiting the hosting website displaying the image.

Getty Images is a stock photo agency which makes money by selling the copyright in photographs it owns or by licencing the usage of such photographs. Over the years Getty Images has managed to have a huge collection of photographs and videos both by engaging photographers and also using the easily available photographs—related to history, nature, events and so on. It has on several occasions found itself on the wrong side of the law as it has been charged with infringement of copyright. Most of such cases have been settled by making a one-time lump-sum payment to the complainant.

It had been the turn of Getty Images to test the legal framework available in the United States and the European Union to protect its own intellectual property—copyright in images. Google had, in the recent past, been embroiled in a number of legal issues in several jurisdictions of the world particularly for privacy and personal rights, improper and illegal data collection, sharing of data without authority for consideration, abusing its dominant position in the market and the like. The last thing Google would have liked at that stage was to continue with uncertain litigation with Getty Images. It was reported:

> Today, Getty Images and Google announced the forming of a multiyear global licensing partnership, nearly two years after Getty filed a competition law complaint against Google with the European Commission. As part of the partnership, Google will be modifying its image search to improve attribution of contributors' work. The changes will also include making copyright disclaimers more prominent and removing view image links to the image URL.[18]

Getty Images had filed a competition law related case in the European Union accusing Google of using its image scraping techniques to display image search results. This is nothing new as for the last several years since the technology service providers have started creating platform for making content easily available, there have been in general accusations made by content providers—music, films, literature, images and the like—that the technology companies are more inclined not to pay attention to the copyright-related issues and are more than willing to allow any and every user to exploit the content available on their platform. Despite several complaints and court cases initiated by content creators, technology companies have been taking shelter under the legislative framework—the Digital Millennium Copyright Act—which has been a boon for the technology companies by allowing them legitimately to extend the services provided by the ever-evolving technology.

It has always been found very difficult—if not impossible—to police the content by the technology companies, and, thus, these companies have been strategically arguing that the onus of pointing out the instances of copyright violation lies on the content providers, and once they notify the technology companies about such an infringement, it is the duty of such a company to take corrective measures which include immediate takedown of the disputed material. However, identical or similar material can easily be uploaded again by different users, and it is truly burdensome for the

[18] Google will make copyright disclaimers more prominent in image search; 9 Feb 2018; The Verge; https://www.theverge.com/2018/2/9/16994508/google-copyright-disclaimers-getty-images-search

copyright owner to keep sending such notices perpetually to the technology service provider.

The business decision made by Google to settle the matter with Getty Images made tremendous sense as the bargaining power of Google in negotiation, though it was extremely high, got somewhat eroded due to the strict legal enforcement in the United States and the European Union. Court decisions had not been quite favourable for Google. Even in India it had to face a penalty of less than US$20 million—quantum itself does not signify the importance of the decision in India—with a legal possibility of appealing the decision in a higher judicial forum.

Google had, on the other hand, successfully settled the matter with Uber regarding the confidential information for driverless car technology. It had been a season of settlements, and amicable settlements between disputing parties are a sure sign of highly evolved jurisdictions as the parties do not wish to remain living in high levels of uncertainty coupled with the threat of exemplary damages.

The Indian legal environment for business somehow does not provide for exemplary damages—though the black letter law nowhere bars it—and most of the businesses continue testing the stretchable legal periphery without really bothering about the consequences of final decisions. Speedier decisions with realistic damages will surely do some good for businesses in the country.

Conclusion

The users should not get caught in the crossfire between big technology giants. Businesspersons mostly use the otherwise legally forbidden material unintentionally and usually not for pure commercial gains. Using such material for upgrading their websites or mobile apps is done without proper legal understanding and awareness. The role of the government and regulatory bodies is to create more awareness so that businesses, particularly small- and medium-sized companies, do not resort to simply copying material for their own use. It is quite certain that if they know that it is not legally permissible and penal action can be taken against them, most of them will refrain from doing it. Besides the issue of ethical conduct, law itself is an important guiding factor. The dynamic nature of law provides a guarantee in most of the evolved jurisdictions that an effective legal framework would be created so that the erring technology companies do not simply get away. Enforcement of the existing laws with interpretation made with extrapolation due to changed circumstances can really be helpful; however, it will be better if new laws are enacted to take care of the ever-changing face of technology and social media. With faster telecommunication methods and powerful gadgets, the digital world is bound to be the real happening place, and thus it is important for the law to keep pace with the challenges and changes happening so that this benign technology can be used for social welfare and public interest rather than it being misused by mischief mongers and extremists. Just like the kitchen knife, which can be used to even kill a person, benign technologies like social media have been misused and abused with almost no effort. Such is the great impact of social media on common people that whatever may be available in visual form is often taken as the gospel truth, which in fact may be doctored, absolutely fake, dated, from some other similar location, or modified with endless applications possible even with inexpensive gadgets. Companies and businesspersons do need to be extra careful so that they do not fall into the trap of anti-social elements. Also, they have to be cautious of the fact that the social media platforms have an undeniable role in creating negative image of any business, even if an initial thread starts with a fake message sent by a disgruntled and vindictive customer. Appropriate action at the right time for countering such messages has to be done otherwise negative sentiments can spread like wildfire.

Business communication in today's world and the world of tomorrow will primarily be by using social media platforms. Business leaders can possibly make social media their friend by understanding it better and walking in step with it.

CHAPTER 7

Speech Is Silver, Silence Is Golden

Often we have seen people meditating by keeping their eyes closed and remaining silent for a long period of time. Silence is supposed to be letting a person look inside, introspect, or when coupled with meditation, it means a state of hollowness where nothing is allowed to pervade. Silence helps a person to concentrate and focus on certain inner thoughts and thereby eliminate the clutter of useless thoughts and too much noise. True silence makes it possible for a person to hear the real music of life and enjoy the notes of positivity. Silence also plays an important role in avoiding the turbulence of unrestricted flow of words and thoughts, which often result in dissipation of energy without resulting in something fruitful. That is why it is said in Latin *"silentium est aurum,"* which means silence is golden.

Human beings, by their very nature, are gregarious. Most of them are sociable, outgoing, extrovert, expressive and love the company of others. Sometimes, some of the people, who otherwise are quite sociable, may not like to mix with others due to certain reasons, whereas some people usually do not like to mix with others and are quite introvert. Behaviour of individuals depends on a number of factors and most of them are guided by the mood of the person at that moment. We are here not discussing the psychological aspects of why certain people do not want to interact with others generally, but we're trying to understand how remaining silent mostly, or pushing one's temperament towards using fewer words than normally used, facilitates the business interests of business leaders. It is

A. K. Agarwal, *Legal Language and Business Communication*,
https://doi.org/10.1007/978-981-13-7534-7_7

true that when a person speaks too much, there's always a chance to reveal what is not required to be revealed at all. Expectations of the world are also higher from a garrulous person who typically speaks a lot and thus shares a lot of information. There is, however, a possibility that a particular person is smart enough not to share the vital details, and he just mixes most of his conversation with either the information which is easily available in the public domain or with words which are almost equivalent to noise and carry no meaning.

It is often said that people of great wisdom and knowledge do not speak too much, whereas people with little learning tend to speak very often just to show off whatever knowledge they have, or rather the lack of it camouflaged by pompous words, quotations and namedropping. However, the reverse is always not true. It cannot be simply concluded that all the people who tend to remain silent are persons of great knowledge and wisdom. There is a possibility that a person might not be able to speak at all and hence remains silent because his knowledge on the subject is absolutely zero, and even if he wishes to somehow show off his understanding and comprehension, there is simply nothing on which he can rely upon and initiate a conversation. Similarly, it is also not true that all the people who speak a lot are people with little learning. Therefore, this simple test of being silent on one extreme and being loquacious on the other end of the spectrum does not help us to conclude about the knowledge and wisdom a person may have.

Silence, therefore, is a double-edged sword. It has to be used prudently to be effective and observers must infer the meaning wisely. It is a matter of an individual's judgment to realise when to remain silent so as to make an impact. It's again a matter of exercise of discretion to speak freely and vent out all the thoughts if the situation so demands. It can, therefore, be easy to understand that there is no one basic fundamental principle to guide the action of business leaders, or for that matter anyone, as to when to remain silent, when to say a few words and when to speak freely. It all depends on context and that is why effective business leaders choose the right moment for this very purpose.

Silence should not be construed as weakness or cowardice. Typically, very strong persons do not unnecessarily speak and let others read their mind by analysing every word spoken by them. Rather, they tend to remain silent and let the world guess and anticipate as to what they might be thinking and what their next step can be. It is often said that words are like arrows, and once they are out of the quiver, they cannot be taken back.

Is Remaining Silent Ethical?

It is a difficult question to be answered as it depends on the context. Remaining silent can be a matter of choice in certain situations and for certain individuals when the situation so demands that silence is better than speaking; however, ethical norms locally have to be considered while choosing to remain silent. While talking about ethical norms it is important to understand that there are certain universal ethical norms which are accepted at all the places and by all the people and at all points in time. There are, at the same time, certain local ethical norms which may be stricter than the universal ethical standards. It depends on the geographical location, a particular profession, any specific business organisation, a particular community and so on. Very often it is observed that ethical standards of a particular profession—for instance, the medical profession—are surely higher than what are to be followed in the society in general.

It would be really unacceptable for a doctor to not reply to the query—howsoever childish, naïve or at times foolish it may be—of the patient and choose to remain silent. Very busy doctors are obviously not expected to reply to each and every query but they're expected to explain the most important aspects and thereafter leave the routine and unimportant issues to be taken care of either by a junior doctor or by providing a piece of paper with frequently asked questions answered. In today's world, things have become easier when busy persons can simply provide a web link which can take care of all such routine queries. However, in no case a professional can afford to remain silent and not answer a query. It is considered to be unprofessional not to respond, and whether it is ethical or unethical, it can be dealt according to the ethical standards followed for that particular profession.

For businesspersons it is difficult to choose to remain silent whether it is a conversation between a business and business or between a business and consumer. An employer may choose to remain silent vis-à-vis its employees for a certain period of time, as the employer is commanding a higher bargaining power, but after a certain period of time, or after the occurrence of certain events, the employer is bound to speak. In communication between business to business, businesspersons or business managers or business leaders ought to speak with clarity and communicate with the other party precisely and concisely as to what they wish to convey to the other party. Silence can in no way be an option. But, there are certain situations in which a business manager can choose to remain silent depending on the repetitive nature of the incidents. For instance, if a company A wishes to acquire company B, and sends an offer, then company B is ethically, and according to business practices, bound to respond. But if company B has denied the offer along with an unambiguous statement that the company is not for sale and is not at all interested in entertaining any offers for acquisition, thereafter company B is under no ethical obligation to respond and can safely remain silent to any new offers made by company A.

Remaining silent should not be construed to be acceptance under all circumstances. It is quite possible that the person did not speak and preferred to remain silent for a certain reason which may not be apparent. The person may not be in a mood to speak, may be extremely tired, may be just fed up with too many questions asked, or may simply not have the answer to those questions, or may be shocked and dumbstruck at the offer made. In some of these and so many other situations, it is ethically not necessary for the person to speak. Remaining silent in such situations is not ethically wrong; however, the dividing line between the right and wrong is very thin, and a slight change in the facts and circumstances of the case may completely change the expectation from a person. Thus, in situations of distress and disasters, individuals manning enquiry counters, telephone lines and helplines cannot prefer to remain silent even though they may be dead tired after continuously working for two or more shifts or bored to tears by repeating the same information umpteen number of times. The situation demands that they have to speak, and not only just speak, they must speak with clarity, sufficient energy and positivity and also transmitting a bundle of hope to the enquirer.

Celebrating Silence

Silence has also been celebrated in constitutions and it is well known that the British constitution is unwritten and relies on customs, practices and traditions which truly guide the conduct of the people, and wherever there is a doubt as what could have been the intention of the earlier generations, it is interpreted and guided by the people of the present generation, taking into consideration the changing times and keeping in mind the aspirations of the people. In his book, *The Silence of Constitutions*, Michael Foley had written that

> *Just as silence is seen as denoting a presumptive agreement, so basic unanimity is seen as allowing for constitutional silence. Accordingly the constitution becomes the projection of that sort of implicit reciprocity that can be deferred to without formal agreement or declaration. The end result is one of a constitution for a people with no need for a constitution and, therefore, with a constitution which embodies that lack of need.*[1]

Silence and abeyance signify advanced constitutional culture. But, silence often leads to ambiguity. However, in evolved jurisdictions and particularly when mature people interact with each other, silence is dealt with in an agreeable and amicable manner without too much emphasis on ambiguity. Rather, mature people try to avoid any ambiguity and do not resort to corrosive and abrasive conduct which may result in souring of relationships. It is extremely important for business managers to take care of the silence on the part of their business partners and their own silence also needs to be dealt with due respect and dignity. Thus, silence on the part of business leaders is usually assumed to be a sophisticated and resilient conduct which means that he keeps the cards close to his chest but also leaves the door always open for issues to be reconcilable.

Silence by many persons is deliberate for the reason of retaining flexibility and not taking a stand. It helps in avoiding potential conflicts by allowing a person to shift his position on certain issues, which may not be as clear as day and night, but may be fuzzy like the dawn and dusk. Issues which immediately may appear to be unresolvable can get resolved with a little effort if a party, or preferably if both the parties in a dispute or conflict, chooses to remain silent even if for a short period of time. Too much interexchange of words and thoughts may make the business parties too much familiar, and, as the adage goes, familiarity breeds contempt. It somehow happens that the more a person speaks, or opens up before others, the more his thoughts—both good and bad, and sometimes ugly as well—are known to the listeners and to the counterparts in business and the like. It is quite possible that they may stop giving due respect to the speaker as they get to know about all his bad qualities also.

Silence has been celebrated for a long time by teachers who force their students in the class to remain silent and think about the problem at hand. Teaching disciples to remain silent and then channelise all the energy internally and focus on a specific issue is very difficult. Even more difficult

[1] Foley, Michael, "The Silence of Constitutions," Routledge, New York, 1989, p. 90.

is to make the disciples remain silent and do nothing. It may seem to some persons as sheer waste of time to just remain silent and not do anything—physically or mentally—but it is the exercise which strengthens the inner core without being degraded by baser thoughts. When individuals arrive at this state of attaining the inner peace, it becomes very easy to accept views of others. Though it is not simple to reach this state of mind, conscious efforts do help in covering some distance and coming nearer to the state of bliss. This can be said to be the continuous journey to attainment of the highest levels of tolerance resulting in self-acquired harmony.

Parties to any conflict, dispute, argument and the like can comfortably reach consensus with silence being used as a vital tool in the process. Instead of arguments, the focus is more on agreements. It may appear to be clichéd, but there is merit in this statement that willingness to agree gives much better results to the opposing parties. And, this willingness can germinate from silence. It is, however, necessary that both the parties think alike and are ready to introspect, remain silent for most of the time and thus cooperate to reach a decision. Are we not asking for the moon? Yes, surely. When parties are in a dispute, how can one expect them to think alike? In most of the practical situations, it is one party which has to remain silent for most of the time, but not let go of the opportunity when it must speak. That approach definitely makes a difference. Thus, it is proper to celebrate silence.

Silence as Acceptance in Business Contracts

The fundamental principle of a contract is that it initiates with an *offer* and when the offer is *accepted* it becomes a contract, provided all other conditions are fulfilled with regard to the age of majority of the parties concerned, legal consideration involved, the object of the contract being legal, the parties to be of sound mind, the parties' intention to create a contractual relationship, and a meeting of the minds between the parties. For an offer made, acceptance has to be unconditional and absolute, and in case it is not so, the acceptance itself does not result in the formation of contract, but is deemed to be a counter-offer. Hence, tremendous importance is given in contracts to acceptance, which must be free consent of the party to whom the offer has been made, who is also known as the offeree, whereas the person who makes the offer is known as the offeror.

Without going into the legal jargon of offeror and offeree, it is important to understand that the acceptance has to be duly signified and cannot be merely a state of mind where a person has mentally decided to accept the offer but has not communicated the acceptance. Such a state of mental acceptance is deemed to be no acceptance in the eyes of the law. It is, therefore, vital to communicate acceptance so that the offer can be converted into a contract.

There is, however, one interesting situation where the offer itself mentions that if there is no reply within a certain period of time the offer would be deemed to be accepted. What shall be the legal position of such offers where silence is deemed to be acceptance? It is clearly the position in law that there has to be some response made as acceptance—it may be a formal and express acceptance, or it may simply be an implied acceptance by doing something which is required to be done according to the conditions mentioned in the offer. In either of the cases, the acceptance has to be signified and complete silence is not considered acceptance.

Thus, what shall be the legal position of the following offer?

An offer is made to a certain person that if the offeror doesn't hear from the offeree within a period of ten days that the offeree is willing to sell his old car for a particular sum of money, it would be deemed to be acceptance by the offeree and the offeror would have a legal right created under the contract law to get the possession of the car after payment of the sum of money mentioned in the offer.

Common sense and reasonableness tell us that a number of such offers can be made to any individual and it will become extremely difficult, or next to impossible, to respond to each and every such offer made. Obviously, the sum of money quoted in the offer would be lower than the market rate of the car and the offeror would be trying to misuse the legal technicality that the offeree has not responded and kept silent, and hence it could easily be inferred that the offeree has accepted the offer. If this has been the position of law, precious time and energy would be simply wasted in rejecting such frivolous offers. That, precisely, is not the purpose of law; it is not supposed to make life difficult for the people. And, that is why silence is not deemed to be acceptance under the contract law.

Silence, therefore, is not golden as far as contracts are concerned. There must be an external manifestation, some overt act, of acceptance. Otherwise, it can be considered as a forced promise on the offeree resulting into a contract when silence is deemed to be acceptance. In the cases when some action by the offeree is expected as a part of the terms of the offer, and when those actions are performed, these are said to be *unilateral* promises where the offeror has made the conditions in such a way that the offeree simply needs to accept by performance. But even in those cases, that performance cannot be reckoned by remaining silent, which means no overt action on the part of the offeree is done.

It is a costly affair to respond to offers made and businesses consider it to be important to compare the costs of sending acceptances and rejections. It all depends on the probability of acceptance of an offer made. Assuming the cost of communicating acceptance and rejection to be the same, and if the rate of acceptance is half or more, it makes sense to have a silent-acceptance method. However, in the long run it is important to be on the right side of the law and take abundant precaution so as not to get mired in litigation later on. After going through these issues under consideration, it emerges that it is prudent not to accept silence as acceptance and insist on some action, howsoever small it may be, to signify acceptance.

Non-Disclosure Agreements: Anthony Levandowski, Google, Uber and Otto

Anthony Levandowski had a meteoric rise and fall. And the reason was simple: he did not remain silent when he was supposed to be. Keeping one's lips sealed is essential when one is working on a confidential project and more so when the law has the binding effect due to contractual terms. He had worked for about nine years at Google and then formed his own company Otto, which was acquired by Uber. He was made the head of the self-driving car project at Uber and was later fired by Uber for issues related to breach of confidentiality.

The actions of technology giant Alphabet and Uber, the cab aggregator company, in March 2017 had been watched anxiously by the legal and business fraternity, particularly those dealing with resolution of business disputes. In a move, which was anticipated by many legal experts earlier, Uber had told a court in San Francisco that it would have preferred to have the matter resolved by way of arbitration rather than in a court of law. However, it is for the court to decide whether arbitration would be permissible as the method for resolution of this dispute or not.

A little background will help to understand the dispute. It is well known that some of the top technology companies were pumping a lot of time, effort and money in developing and fine-tuning a driverless car and technology related to it. Alphabet—the parent company of Google—had created a subdivision for this very purpose and named it Waymo. As any researcher and other employees working with these companies are working on cutting-edge technology solutions, it is quite natural for them to sign a *non-disclosure agreement* along with a *non-compete clause*, which makes it mandatory for them not to join a competitor after leaving the previous employer within a reasonable period of time, usually called the cooling off period.

Equally important, if not more, is the *confidentiality clause*, which, as the name suggests, makes it binding for the person not to disclose anything confidential to the project in particular and anything related to the overall business in general to any person who is not authorised to know it. Despite a very strict legal environment in the United States about the protection of trade secrets through confidentiality clauses in employment contracts, there have been several incidents, which have included the top-notch companies, where individuals have used obvious methods to gather confidential information in a retrievable form: left the job; joined a competitor; and the competitor thereafter raced ahead in business. Interestingly, there are legal methods by which the aggrieved company can sue the competitor, even though there has been no contract between them, and can also sue the employee who took away confidential information and trade secrets for the benefit of the competitor and to the disadvantage of the previous employer.

Levandowski used to work at Waymo and one day just before quitting the job and joining Uber, he downloaded more than 14,000 confidential documents. This appears to be an open and shut case with hardly anything needed to be proved that he took away with him sensitive information about the technology which was proprietary in nature. Given the tremendous potential business benefits at stake, Waymo—that is Google and Alphabet with deep pockets—fought a tough legal battle, both arbitration and litigation. The matter had been filed in San Francisco court against both Levandowski and Uber.

In March 2017, Uber picked up the employment contract of Levandowski with Waymo and highlighted the arbitration clause which was broad in nature and insisted on arbitration instead of court proceedings. Why did Uber do so?

In the recent past Uber had been emboldened by its success in arbitration proceedings against its drivers, who had filed a petition in San Francisco court claiming that they were Uber employees and not working on contract and that's why they should be provided all the benefits which were statutorily mandated to be given to the employees. In those cases as well, Uber had argued that while agreeing to the terms and conditions and downloading the app on their smartphones the drivers had agreed to the arbitration clause and hence the issue had to be decided in arbitration. The court had decided in Uber's favour.

The method of arbitration gives the flexibility and independence to choose an expert as the arbitrator(s)—the individual or individuals making the decision—and the confidential nature of the proceedings insulates the parties from negative publicity at least till the time the award is challenged in any court of law. In most of the highly technical matters, it makes sense that a subject matter expert, rather than a generalist judge, decides the issue; however, in the instant case it was a question of simple breach of contractual obligation by divulging confidential information, and the action against Uber by Waymo would have been in the nature of a tortious claim, which had to be decided by a court of law. Still the matter was referred to arbitration.

A year later in April 2018, Waymo, that is, Google, and Uber settled the matter with undisclosed terms. However, Waymo did not settle with Levandowski and is still pursuing the matter in private arbitration. There is also the dispute over $120 million incentive paid to him while he was working with Waymo. All this happened because he did not keep his lips sealed.

Confidentiality in Arbitration

The arbitration proceedings are conducted in private and hence confidentiality is ensured. Arbitration is a method of resolution of disputes which is done in a formal, though harmonious, and amicable manner between the parties in the presence of external arbitrator or arbitrators who are subject matter experts. There is almost complete flexibility in conducting the arbitration proceedings which have one of the most important aspects of being confidential in nature as contradistinguished from courts which are public places. Arbitrator and lawyers concerned with arbitration matters are supposed to keep the matter confidential and not talk about it in public.

It is however remarkable to note that the confidentiality clause is not an overarching clause and has to be interpreted according to the facts and circumstances of each case. But, even in the absence of such a clause, there is an implicit understanding that confidentiality has to be maintained. Therefore, what is covered by the confidentiality clause needs to be clarified at the outset to avoid any confusion. Also, arbitration proceedings are in different stages—submission of claim, submission of counter-claim if any, rebuttal, supporting documents, oral evidence, arguments, decision and so on. It is quite possible that the level of confidentiality is not the same at each and every stage. Some of the documents may be only for the arbitrators and only if the arbitrators permit, they can be shared with the other party. The method by which the documents or other evidence have been procured may have a bearing on the level of confidentiality expected from the parties. The level of confidentiality becomes almost zero when the matter reaches a court of law, as the courts are public places and until and unless the matter is being heard *in camera*[2] and the judges have ordered the entire proceedings or part thereof to remain confidential, the proceedings become open to public scrutiny and anyone can witness them. The media in normal circumstances is allowed to report the proceedings to the public at large.

The aspect of remaining silent about arbitration proceedings in general, not in a court of law, has far-reaching consequences. Silence often is inferred as opacity which is not the norm in public accountability. Transparency is the key word in business dispute resolution; however, the essential feature of arbitration is that not all the proceedings in an arbitration matter are opaque and confidential. Thus, it can be said that there is discretion to be exercised, either to speak up or to remain silent. Thus, there is selective confidentiality, but in most of the cases, confidentiality is almost complete. And that is precisely one of the main reasons as to why disputing parties prefer to get their matters resolved through arbitration.

Despite such freedom to be exercised regarding speaking and remaining silent to the parties, lawyers and other persons involved, the duty to remain silent is strictly imposed on the arbitrators. The members of the arbitral tribunal do discuss, and are expected to do so without any restriction and hesitation, among themselves about the matter to be decided. They are not supposed to—neither ethically nor legally—talk about the issues concerned to anyone else. But, what about seeking an expert's opinion? This is a dilemma which the arbitrators have to handle very delicately. Professionally, they are required to decide the matter on their own, but if there is a ticklish issue which requires a little bit of advice which the

[2] *in camera* is a Latin phrase which is usually used in legal proceedings and means in private; in the judge's chambers, where public and press do not have access. Such proceedings are held in highly sensitive matters, according to the discretion of the judge, which may not be fit to be heard in the open court. There should not be any confusion regarding the word camera in the phrase. *in camera* does not mean that proceedings have to be video recorded.

arbitrators themselves are not able to handle, they can get it resolved by an expert on that issue, provided the facts of the case are not disclosed to the expert. The question has to be framed in such a manner so that the expert is not able to identify the facts of the case—the parties involved, the events, the timeline, place and so on. It must be camouflaged properly.

Making everyone involved in the arbitration proceedings maintain silence—to a large extent—is typically done in an implied manner, without signing any contract for this purpose. Experienced individuals involved do understand it and are also expected to guide and groom the rookies. Cultivating discreetness is not easy, and it can best be rubbed off by seasoned persons on the youngsters and inexperienced persons.

When Silence Is Unwanted: Rustling Sound Added to Silent Leaf by Nissan

Business communication is not the only way individuals communicate with each other, it can even be the product which communicates. If it does not communicate, it may at least send a one-way communicating signal in form of a sound to warn the users and others in close proximity. In 2010–2011, the Japanese automobile company Nissan produced electric vehicle and branded it Leaf; it was such an engineering marvel that at low speeds it did not produce any sound and was just noiseless. It was silent. Can there be a problem with the silence of the car called Leaf? Yes, there was a problem that the regulators complained that the noiseless vehicle was hazardous on the street as the other vehicles and individuals in close proximity could not get any warning signals from the moving car and they would not be cautioned to move away or take appropriate action. The human mind gets alerted at the slightest of the stimuli, and sound is surely one of them, and in the absence of the stimuli the human mind would not guide the body to take any action. The reflexes of the body tend to become slow or not act at all when the surrounding environment is highly comfortable without any perceptible variations.

Though the automobile Leaf had been a fantastic work of great precision, yet its silence created problems regarding its commercial prospects. The company was forced by the legal and regulatory agencies to add artificial sound to get the impact of a moving vehicle at low speeds. Above a speed of roughly 30 km an hour, there is noticeable sound due to the rubbing of the tyres on the road as frictional forces act leading to creation of some noise. However, at low speeds the rubbing of the tyres does not create noise which can be noticed by a normal human ear. Therefore, the problem had been at lower speeds which the regulators wanted to address.

The company had to decide what sound to add. With tens of thousands of sounds available—and all of them simple digital form—there was no paucity of solutions. Plenty was the problem. The company worked on this problem for a reasonable period of time and researched on every aspects before deciding on a particular sound to be used. It worked with people without sight, people who have assisted them, individuals and companies providing sound effects to movies, psychologists working on effects of sound on human mind, and also worked with experts on different types of sounds to be used as audible warnings. It later on settled for a soft whine which proportionally changed its intensity as the car sped up. The company released a statement, which *inter alia* mentioned:

> *While silence is golden, it does present practical challenges...*[3]

Adding sound was not without opposition. It was argued by scientists, researchers and environmental experts that silence is one of the greatest virtues and cherished goals of living in the civilised world and that they have really worked hard to get an engineering marvel with this noiseless vehicle. Electric cars, unlike the fossil fuel consuming vehicles which produce high decibel noises due to the internal combustion process, are differentiated and uniquely characterised by their silent performance. This has been one of the most important targets set by the designers and researchers while working at the drawing board. Legal and regulatory authorities were defeating the very purpose of this research and nullifying the positive aspects of the noiseless vehicle.

These sounds have been added now to almost all the electric cars produced by different car companies all over the world, but Nissan was the first major car company to do so.

While talking about the fossil fuel consuming vehicles, Harley-Davidson considers its engine's sound of *"potato potato potato..."* to be unique and had even applied for a sound mark—a trademark granted by the trademark registry—but had failed to get it as each engine makes its own sound which may be almost similar but not identical to that made by the engine

[3] The Washington Post, "Nissan adds noises to Leaf electric vehicle as safety precaution," June 12, 2010, http://www.washingtonpost.com/wp-dyn/content/article/2010/06/11/AR2010061105343.html?noredirect=on

of the other motorcycle. Engine tuning experts vouch for the perfection achieved in tuning an engine by finely adjusting its inlet and exhaust to get the perfect sound produced by the engine. Several of the automobile companies take pride in the unique sound produced by the engines of their products, particularly the motorcycles. There are enthusiasts who will go to any extent to get a particular sound to be produced by the engines of their prized motorcycles. There are contests and competitions organised for motorcycle riders to excel in letting the engines of their motorcycles produce different sounds, and the most popular ones are intermittent gunshots, variations of the screeching sounds of the tyres on the road, whistling sound and so on and so forth.

For a very long time there has been a tremendous effort by automobile engineers in getting a proper balance between the level of sound produced by the engines and power generated by them. The simple rule is: the higher the exhaust of the engine, the higher the power produced. The amount of exhaust depends on, and is directly proportional to, the fuel burned inside the engine cavity. And the higher the exhaust, the higher the sound produced. Thus, in a civilised society there has been an effort to somehow get a reasonable balance between power and sound, and for this purpose a device commonly called as the *"silencer"* is used. Undoubtedly, there have been efforts to make the engine less noisy yet more powerful.

Can anyone imagine a racing car without sound?

The technology regarding silencers has been developing rapidly and in today's world it is not uncommon to find ordinary cars fitted with a silencer using the latest technology to be almost noiseless; however, these are the cars which do not get used in car races. The racing cars have very high power producing engines with very high exhausts. The sound produced is also phenomenal and it increases manifold due to the addition of the sound produced by the friction of the rubbing of car tyres at the racing track at very high speeds. It is all high speed and high decibel with a rush of adrenaline that make car racing truly adventurous. The moment we remove sound from that, there is hardly any fun.

The same applies to horse races and chariot races—as in the famous movie *Ben-Hur* of 1959. This movie was a remake of the 1925 silent film, which obviously did not have the impact of the sound and thus the energy and enthusiasm created with the addition of sound were missing. Galloping horses, without any sound, do not make any sense and are difficult to be imagined. The associated sound of the heavy impact of the horseshoe on the ground, along with the neighing and whinnying of the horses, in a true sense completes the picture and can hold the onlookers in awe. It was the impact of sound, not silence, which made the 1959 *Ben-Hur* the fastest and highest grossing film of that year. It was, after the masterpiece *Gone with the Wind*—featuring Clark Gable and Vivien Leigh—the second-highest grossing movie till that time of cinema history. The movie had won a record 11 Academy Awards, and surely the sound effects, not silence, had contributed in a major way in its success.

The movie *Ben-Hur* is also famous for its fantastic film score, which is the background music originally composed for a specific film. The film score of this movie was composed by Miklós Rózsa and has been considered to be one of the longest ever composed film score, with a very impressive overture at the beginning. The overture—not silence—at the start of the movie has been a great attraction and, till date, viewers vouch for the impact of the starting music helping them transcend mentally to an era of kings, queens, horses and palaces and the times when men fought like real men. Brute power, not acknowledged and appreciated in today's world, was the sole criterion of winning bouts of wrestling, horse racing and battles, and anything and everything related to sheer masculine prowess and machoism. However, the music also mixes the unique touch of love, compassion, empathy and simple kindness for the fellow human beings.

Thus, the music exceptionally blends the tough and soft aspects of man. No wonder, the opening music of the film simply lifts the viewers and softly places them in that time period so that when in the opening scenes of the movie there are descriptions of the Nativity of Jesus and life at that time period. Viewers don't get any sudden jerks as the mind has already tuned in with that age. That's the beauty of the opening music.

Whether movies, horses, motorcycles or cars, silence does not embellish them. Though silence may be golden in several contexts, yet many a time silence is not cherished. This is therefore a matter of judgment for business leaders as to when to prefer silence so as to give a fillip to sale and thus profit and when not to remain silent. The law can on most of the occasions provide necessary and useful guidance, still it remains a business decision and not purely a legal decision. Business communication is gainfully benefitted by the choices of making the right noises at the right time and at the right place, which also includes the choice of not making any noise and hence keeping silent.

Uber Apology: Trouble in London and Rest of Europe

In September 2017, the transport regulator in the city of London, Transport for London—TfL—did not renew Uber's licence to operate as the taxi aggregator. Such a decision by the regulator became a major problem for the company and it had to tackle it at the highest levels. It had to handle three parties at one time—the government and regulators, the drivers, and the most important being the consumers. Besides taking legal action, the company had to handle the communication with all the three in a tactful manner. It required efforts to be made by the company's Chief Executive, Dara Khosrowshahi, to placate all the three.

One important thing done by him at that time was to apologise on behalf of the company in an open letter for all the mistakes made by the company with regard to operation of taxi services everywhere, particularly in the city of London. It has been very well known that the traditional taxi operators in London were finding it difficult to compete with the services provided by Uber to passengers at a cut-throat price along with tremendous convenience which could never ever be offered by the traditional cab operators.

According to the company, there were more than 40,000 taxi drivers in London providing their services to Uber and there were more than 3.5 million customers who will be using the services of the company at least once every three months. London being such a prime market for the company would not be taken easily and lightly by the top management, and, hence, the non-renewal of the licence by TfL was surely panicky for the company. One wrong word on behalf of the company in the communication to the stakeholders could have been disastrous and, therefore, the company thought it is better to not give detailed explanation while apologising. It could be said to be a very pragmatic tactical move by the Chief Executive as he did not open all the cards and still tried his best to keep the hopes alive by using a multipronged strategy of starting a public relations exercise along with triggering off the legal remedies available to the company.

Moreover, the communication lines were kept open with the transport regulator and also the government in London. Another channel was to communicate with the drivers who were the most disgruntled and disappointed lot. This was not at all an easy exercise and required clarity of thought along with a sense of purpose to take the discussions forward with them. Though very tough stands were taken by the parties—drivers on one side and the company management on the other side—it was quite obvious from the very beginning that the final decision would not be possible only with the negotiations between these two parties as the transport regulator and the government had also intervened into the matter with the moral high ground of working in public interest.

Undoubtedly, for a democratically elected local government, public interest is paramount and it is really easy for the government and the regulator to hold on to that aspect steadfastly while making any argument, whether during private negotiations or while making a public statement. They might have several other aspects to be taken care of, as well as certain political leaders might have their own hidden agenda. Tactfully, they did not spell out all the things while discussing it either with the taxi aggregator or addressing the media. Easily, they can be quite selective in making their arguments, as well as defences known to the other parties or public in general.

Unfortunately, for the traditional taxi drivers, the luxury of remaining silent, or disclosing as little as possible, was not available because they were the aggrieved parties and while making any allegations they are expected, both by law and proprietary, that they should make all the averments clearly so as to give the other party a fair chance to negate any of those allegations. It is not only complete and cogent allegations which have to be made, admissible evidence also has to be adduced, which, of course, cannot be accomplished by remaining silent. Thus, the aggrieved party has to prepare a detailed account of all the irritants while making a presentation to the government or the regulator, and the same draft can be converted to a petition to be filed in a court of law by structuring it in the required format using the necessary legal jargon.

On a petition filed by two Uber drivers, the employment tribunal had decided against Uber and had granted the worker status to the drivers which was not acceptable to Uber as the grant of such a status to the drivers would have meant providing all the benefits such as medical, holiday and pension, which would have negatively impacted its business model and thus Uber had appealed against this decision in the Employment Appeal Tribunal. In November 2017, Uber lost the case there also and had been left with the option of appealing in the Court of Appeal and thereafter to the UK Supreme Court. As this would have meant a fairly longish legal journey, Uber had decided to file an application in the UK Supreme Court praying to directly hear the matter bypassing the Court of Appeal.

The rule of law has two important aspects—substantive law and procedural law. The substantive law determines the consequences of certain actions; however, the procedural law lays down the method which has to be followed to reach such a conclusion. In legal proceedings, hierarchy of courts and due process are of immense importance in strong legal jurisdictions—the United Kingdom surely can claim to have one of the well-established legal systems with the rule of law and due process deeply ingrained—which typically do not allow any court to deviate from the set legal procedure. In early December 2017, unsurprisingly, the UK Supreme Court did not agree with Uber's prayer as could have been easily anticipated by any legal observer. It is almost a purely commercial matter and courts eschew from taking up such cases out of turn. Such exceptions may be made for matters pertaining to violation of human rights or fundamental rights.

Immediately thereafter, on 20 December 2017, Uber suffered another blow from the European Court of Justice,[4] though the matter was not directly related to the British taxi drivers in London. In a case which was filed by the taxi drivers Association of Barcelona, the European Court of Justice at Luxembourg ruled that Uber was a transport company which meant that the company had to follow stricter regulation and licencing mechanism applicable to any taxi operator within the European Union. After Brexit, Uber drivers in London and the services provided by the company in the United Kingdom will not directly be within the jurisdiction of the European Court of Justice; however, as it is a fuzzy area while the entire proceedings of Brexit take place, the company has to deal with a lot of uncertainty which, surely, has been damaging to its business prospects.

At times it is not prudent to remain silent as Uber has learned the hard way in this case decided in the European Court of Justice. It was on 29 October 2014 that Association of taxi drivers in Barcelona—Elite Taxi—had brought an action against Uber in Commercial Court in Barcelona, primarily on the ground that Uber was indulging in unfair trade practices and infringing the existing legislation. Uber had always claimed that it was only a technology service provider for aggregating taxis and that it was not in the business of providing taxi services. To that extent Uber had not

[4] Asociación Profesional Élite Taxi v. Uber Systems Spain SL, ECJ, 20 December 2017, Case C 434/15, http://curia.europa.eu/juris/document/document.jsf?text=uber%2Bbarcelona&docid=198047&pageIndex=0&doclang=EN&mode=req&dir=&occ=first&part=1&cid=203989#ctx1

clarified its stand to convince the parties concerned and also not tried its best to have a healthy competitive relationship with the rivals. The company was aggressive from the very beginning and was also quite silent about the moves it had made—which is quite well-recognised in the business fraternity as a strategy to remain agile and make the best use of any available opportunity. But, when a business company wishes to avoid litigation and not get embroiled into unnecessary interpretation of the existing legislation, it is usually advisable to double check with the implementing authorities as to what practical meaning one can draw from the black letter law.

However, whenever a business decides to first act and thereafter face the legal consequences, typically strong legal environments do not treat such players with leniency. The courts and the implementing authorities are ruthless and the entire business plan may go haywire.

Uber has to deal with local laws in different jurisdictions and hence it may be logical to adapt its position according to the local requirements and also be open about its stand keeping in mind the big picture of its global business model. Concealing less and revealing more—that is, not remaining silent for longish periods of time which may be perceived as a tactical move to hide and cover relevant information—is usually becoming a global practice, and is often made a statutory requirement in several jurisdictions.

Thus, silence may not always be golden. And, citizens in a true democracy should not be expected to remain silent as was evident in Chennai in India some time back.

Freedom of Speech and Sheep to the Slaughter

In May 2015, according to media reports, the Indian Institute of Technology (IIT) Madras—a premier technology institute in India—had banned a students' group allegedly for criticising the Prime Minister of India. This was most unfortunate and needed to be condemned. The contents of the discussion—oral or written—were not material as we are not competent as a judicial body to make a decision on their propriety and legality. What was unacceptable was the fact that the student body had been banned and a gag order passed. Silence of this nature cannot be celebrated. It is undesirable and unacceptable.

Voltaire, the famous French writer and historian, had said,

> *I disapprove of what you say, but I will defend to the death your right to say it.*

The same is true about the rights of individuals in India—a mature democracy—to say what they want to say. The law on the subject is very well developed and evolved and there was rather no need for an educational institution to resort to a gag order. The law could surely have taken its own course in case something was amiss.

Students in any college, and IIT Madras is no exception, are usually of the age of majority, 18 and above. A very few in their first year of study may be less than 18 years old. Thus, almost the entire student body is eligible to vote. For real democratic forces to shape the society, it is essential that the members of the society discuss, deliberate and debate. Students have to actively participate in such debates and discussions to sharpen their minds and understand the issues being faced by the country, the world and the human beings in the right perspective.

Needless to say that any such debate would be meaningless without talking about certain key individuals—those individuals who are responsible for decision-making at the top and their actions shape the destiny of the nation. The Prime Minister of India is undoubtedly the *de facto* head of the country and willy-nilly would be referred. As is said that one may like him or dislike him, but it is not possible to ignore him. Thus, it is quite natural for college students in India to talk about the Prime Minister of the country. Rather, it would be abnormal if they don't.

Education, after all, is a training of the mind. Democracy is based on dissent. Putting the two together, it can easily be inferred that among others, dissenting in a civilised manner is an important goal of good and meaningful education. If young citizens of India simply bow their heads to everything mentioned by authority, there would hardly be any difference between them and cattle. In no way we are suggesting that there is a need to oppose and question everything. However, it is desirable that everything is tested on the anvil of reasonableness, prudence and propriety.

We are reminded of what George Washington, the first President of the United States, had said,

> *If the freedom of speech is taken away then dumb and silent we may be led, like sheep to the slaughter.*

It would be the biggest disservice to the nation to treat sharp and intelligent young students like sheep. What will happen to the spark in debates which may cause revolutions? We are talking about revolution of ideas, thoughts and possibilities. Who will tell the students to be "possibility thinkers"? Do we want to create mechanised graduates equivalent to robots who have been provided with some artificial intelligence as deemed fit by the creator? Or, do we want the nation to be led by thinking individuals? The choice is with us.

The fact of the matter is that even that choice is not with us. Victor Hugo had said it so succinctly,

No army can stop an idea whose time has come.

We must stop treating young students as sheep. They must be allowed to speak their mind, within the reasonable boundaries of decency and courtesy. The communication through the electronic media is very fast and can be quite damaging in the shortest possible time and hence the cyber law in India tries to regulate it. But, sometimes the law can be against the principles enshrined in the Constitution of India as fundamental rights. Such a law has to be nullified by the Supreme Court as was done in 2015 about Section 66A of the Information Technology Act, 2000.

Section 66A of Information Technology Act Was Gone in 2015 in India

In March 2015, there was jubilation all around about the striking down of Section 66A of the Information Technology Act, 2000, by the Supreme Court of India. As had been reported governments of the day—of different coalitions at the centre and different parties in provinces—had preferred to use the law on several occasions. It did not sit silently on the statute book.

This section was added by an amendment in 2008 and was meant to provide punishment for sending offensive messages through communication service, which included information shared via a computer resource or a communication device. It was meant for those messages which were known to be false but were sent for the purpose of causing annoyance, inconvenience, danger, obstruction, insult, injury, criminal intimidation, enmity, hatred or ill will. Thus, the section's ambit was very wide and could have included almost anything and everything.

It is obvious that governments and administration do not like dissent, opposition, criticism and harsh words. It is easier to muffle and gag discomforting voices in a dictatorship; however, democracy is a different game altogether. The entire idea of democracy is based on dissent: *vox populi*, the voice of the people. Realistically speaking, the moment the voice of an ordinary citizen is gagged, it is the beginning of the end of democracy. So, there was no surprise that both the coalition governments at the centre in India—the United Progressive Alliance (UPA) and the National Democratic Alliance (NDA) governments—had favoured this section, which was introduced during the time of the UPA. The section simply gave much more power to the government functionaries, particularly the police, to take action on the basis of communication under Section 66A.

This was nothing new as governments of the day would usually try to get more and more powers to have an iron grip on the subjects. It is still very much the mind-set of rulers versus ruled. The more the power, the easier it is to manage. Thus, it would have been unwise to think that there shall be no efforts made by the government to circumvent this judgment. As had been written at that time that there may be steps taken to beat it in spirit and make all possible interpretations of the black letter law to expand the powers. The ultimate effort may be to try to nullify the impact of this judgment by using the amendment route on the basis of the moral high ground of safeguarding the security of the nation and public interest. Another interesting mechanism may be somehow controlling the expansion of the internet and connectivity through mobile phone technology with certain clauses so that the desired result is achieved in a circuitous manner. Almost all of these were tried in one way or the other by the administration, which faced challenge every time in the court.

That highlights the importance of the free and fair judiciary in a democratic country committed to the rule of law. Any such action taken by the government can again be challenged in the court to see the real effect of the doctrine of separation of powers—legislature, executive and judiciary—and the concept of judicial review. The final test shall be the interpretation of "reasonable restrictions," a power provided under the constitution. In India there is no absolute free speech and reasonable restrictions can be imposed. The grounds on which it can be done are many, but primarily they deal with public interest and national security.

Regarding gagging, it's not only the government, the judiciary also has the power of contempt of court, which though used sparingly, has been debated every now and then. Most of the time, since India became Republic, the courts have exercised this power maturely and with great restraint. However, there has been misuse, at times, by certain individuals to teach a lesson to someone who has been speaking too much.

Now is the time when a much liberal interpretation should be adopted for the contempt of court. The people of India do need freedom to talk about the ills prevailing in the judicial system. There have been many instances of financial and personal misconduct which have come out in open but are hardly discussed because of the fear of the law of contempt of court. These simply cannot be brushed under the carpet. Rampant corruption and inbuilt inefficiencies will surely be the first two topics discussed on social media. And, thus, there cannot be a muffled and silent democracy.

Judicial Volcano: *Silentium Est Aurum*

In January 2018, we witnessed the unprecedented—four judges of the Supreme Court of India had held a press conference and had washed dirty linen in public. The judicial volcano, which must have been building up for quite some time, had erupted. They had accused that the Chief Justice of India had been unfairly allotting cases to judges and that everything was not fine with the way things had been going on in the Supreme Court.[5]

It is not very often that such serious accusations are made against the highest judicial authority—the Chief Justice of India—in the country and must be the very first time when they have been made by brother judges and that too in public.

Issues against the working of the judges are typically raised by lawyers, political masters, media persons, the so-called civil society, at time disgruntled litigants, and habitually by everyone to label the working of the judicial system as slow and tardy. But, the insiders, taking the job onto themselves, are rather strange. There must have been compelling circumstances to warrant such an action. Or, it could have been sheer helplessness coupled with frustration which might have led them to take the unparalleled step.

Let us have the constitutional position clear.

The judges of the Supreme Court and the High Courts—excluding the Chief Justice—called puisne (pronounced puny) judges are in no way inferior or subordinate to the Chief Justice as far as judicial competence and

[5] Supreme Court crisis: All not okay, democracy at stake, say four senior-most judges, The Hindu BusinessLine, January 12, 2018, https://www.thehindubusinessline.com/news/supreme-court-crisis-all-not-okay-democracy-at-stake-say-four-seniormost-judges/article10028921.ece

power are considered. They are not bound by a non-judicial observation made by the Chief Justice, who including the Chief Justice of India (CJI), is simply *primus inter peres*—first among equals. Administrative powers of the Chief Justice give him the edge over other judges, which must be exercised with caution and due discretion, and not arbitrarily. Exercise of discretion has to be tested on "reason and relevance." In judicial matters, the Chief Justice, while sitting in a bench with other brother and sister judges, in no way has veto power. Often there have been judgments pronounced with the Chief Justice being in minority position, and that is also the case in the US Supreme Court and courts in other evolved jurisdictions.

Keeping the flock together is difficult, and when it is about the intelligent and constitutionally powerful judges, the task even for the Chief Justice is not easy. Dissent is the bedrock of democracy. Independent and fair judiciary cannot even be imagined without the right to disagree.

In a sense, the judicial volcanic eruption is a positive development which vindicates the stand that each judge has a mind of his own, and has been provided with sufficient protection by the Constitution of India which ensures that he is not always trying to figure out the mood of the head of the institution, and, thus, can think and work truly independently. Unfortunately, but true, there are several institutions where one is made to understand by the head from day one that one's survival depends on following and practising "your wish is my command" without fail. Robustness of the constitution is thereby proved.

Head of any institution has to take people along, and many a time there are dissenters, trouble-makers, people speaking the truth in the bluntest manner, people lacking diplomacy and tact, people hell-bent on making the life of the head difficult at every given opportunity and so on and so forth. How can one keep everyone aligned to the vision and mission? With menial workers, it can be by using carrot and stick policy, but, with intelligent class, discussion appears to be the only method. Higher the level of intellect, higher should be the level of engagement in debates, deliberations, arguments and counter-arguments. Intellectual superiority, rather than one's position, should be the factor determining what view should prevail.

In such situations, absence of discussion is a sure sign of decay. Without going into the merits of the instant matter, one can easily say that judges are ought to speak through their judgments and to quote Francis Bacon, "a much talking judge is an ill-tuned cymbal." Issues could have been resolved by talking as the legendary Chief Justice Marshall of the US Supreme Court—he was the Chief Justice for more than three decades—

used to do. He said, "to listen well is as powerful a means of communication and influence as to talk well."

No wonder, if speech is silver, silence is gold—*silentium est aurum*—definitely in the case of judges. Of late, the higher judiciary in India has been managing—directly or indirectly—the game of cricket in the country as there have been serious issues about the management of the game, which is a big money spinner. Besides being a sport, it is huge business. Should the cricketers on the field speak or remain silent? This question has arisen on several occasions when the players have not conducted themselves well at the filed.

Cricketers or Gladiators: Where Are the Gentlemen?

In March 2017, India had won the cricket test series against Australia. This test series would long be remembered not for India's win but for extinguishing the spirit of the game of cricket. Some of the cricketers had conducted themselves more like gladiators and the cricket ground had looked more like the Roman Colosseum. Adrenaline had rushed rapidly to peak levels with decency, silence, sobriety and tolerance being given unceremonious burial.[6]

Cricket still is considered a gentleman's game and it is the duty of cricketers—on-field and off-field—to maintain the dignity and glory of the game. At no point in time, any one of them should be allowed to behave in a manner which is unbecoming of a true cricketer. And it is the solemn duty of the management, howsoever difficult and unpalatable it may appear, to chastise erring—not only in their professional performance but also in their conduct in general—players in a commensurate manner.

Interestingly, the cricket management in India at that time had been chosen by the Supreme Court of India and hence, willy-nilly, was under some sort of control of the court. The top cricketers not only play for the nation—irrespective of the country they play for—they serve as role models for generations. Where are the role models? Some of the cricketers' body language, gestures, lip movements, acrobatics, victory dances and crass monkey jumps *ipso facto* disqualify them from being any type of role model, regardless of their performance in the game.

[6]Virat Kohli rages at rival Steve Smith's "cheating" as India vs Australia turns ugly, The Independent, March 7, 2017, https://www.independent.co.uk/sport/cricket/virat-kohli-steve-smith-india-vs-australia-a7615701.html

Some of the inter-player communication on the ground which is not supposed to be heard by others—but thanks to the highly evolving technology which almost takes a TV viewer right to the spot of action or brings that slice of playing arena right inside the living room—has become audible. This is not good news for players who hardly have any control over their words. They need to be trained to think ten times before blurting out the unspeakable. After all, it's a cricket ground and not the Speakers' Corner in Hyde Park in London, which gives anyone an absolute right of free speech.

If speech is silver, silence is gold.

Many a time, it is important to understand the value of *"sob"*—acronym for sophisticated overt behaviour—which differentiates a well-cultured democratic person willing to practise tolerance from that of a savage, crass, thoughtless moron. Democracy thrives on the basic principle of agreeing to disagree and willingness to engage in a decent cordial dialogue.

The worst impression the adolescents—for them cricketers are demigods—can get is to believe that "this" is the way to behave and because my "hero" is doing it, so it must be the gold standard of behaviour. And, also, they get the impression that "this" is the way one can win, and winners should do it. Most unfortunate! After all, actions speak louder than words. It is the bounden duty of the heroes of the cricketing world, irrespective of nationalities and irrespective of the fact as to for which team they play, to conduct themselves in a pristine manner. Their aggression and foul words can be damaging to impressionable minds.

Cricket's visual treat is available almost 24×7 on one TV channel or another. Alfred Hitchcock did not shoot *Psycho* in colour as he was of the opinion that the visual impact on viewers of too much blood would be too gory. Thus, the damage which aggression in cricket can cause is immense. It is the need of the hour to regulate cricketers' behaviour and penalise erring players suitably. There must be enough deterrent effect in the penal action. No one is above the spirit of the game, which truly is to play like a gentleman.

Like tea, a man's best (or worst) colours come out in hot water. Emotional stability is essential. Let your game speak. Even if it is becoming fashionable to be aggressive, there is a thin dividing line between being aggressive and being abusive. Raising the voice, using expletives, hurling abuses and so on and so forth do not go well with the game of cricket. It might have been the norm in the Roman Colosseum where gladiators fought violently with other gladiators and wild animals, but we are talking about cricket.

Let cricket remain a gentleman's game. Television ratings and business get boosted with such unexpected turn of events on the field but this is not the way to communicate to the world the game of cricket. Silence still is a virtue in the game of cricket, and in the long run is good for business as well.

Conclusion

Silence is a wonderful thing for hermits in stages but for businesspersons it may not have the purpose when direct communication is required to clear the air and not have any confusion at all. Clarity of purpose and certainty are two most important cherished values for businesses and in the absence of these there can be a lot many disputes arising because of miscommunication or no communication at all. Silence, therefore, can only be exercised as an option when it helps to promote business but at the same time keeps the businessperson on the right side of the law and also on the ethical side according to the circumstances. Moving a little bit away from being totally silent can be "being brief" and businesspersons do exercise this option while dealing with other parties in the highly contextual culture, a culture of business in which it is not required to explicitly either speak or write the entire narrative, and only the relevant words and phrases are suffice keeping in mind the background of the previous conversation and the trail of letters or emails. It is quite common to continue to reply to that same email by both parties and after passage of time there may be dozens of emails going back and forth but having all the information in one single email thread.

Brevity of communication should never be confused with making communication ambiguous or incomplete. If silence can create a lot of problems, too brief a communication may also lead the parties into trouble by not answering the relevant portions necessary to be taken care of and thus leaving the communication to be not of much use. For critical legal scrutiny, each and every word and punctuation mark of the communication are important and hence while replying on the go, particularly using electronic means of communication, one should be wary of the fact that the message really conveys what the sender wants to convey. In case of after sending the message he realises that there has been a mistake, corrective measures should be taken immediately without any delay, which include the foremost measure of sending another communication clearly in bold letters that the previous message should be ignored and the intended message will soon be delivered. Remaining silent at that time can create numerous problems including contractual obligations with extremely heavy damages to be paid. To avoid legal action, one has to act with alacrity in the given circumstances.

Silence is golden, and brevity is the soul of wit, but not always. A businessperson has to exercise the discretion of choosing what to do to be on the right side of the law as well as effective in business. There cannot be a clear-cut standard operating procedure.

Correction to: Legal Language and Business Communication

CORRECTION TO:

A. K. Agarwal, *Legal Language and Business Communication*,
https://doi.org/10.1007/978-981-13-7534-7

The original version of this book was published with missing front matter elements. The preface, dedication, and an about the author section have been added.

The updated original online version of the book can be found at
https://doi.org/10.1007/978-981-13-7534-7

A. K. Agarwal, *Legal Language and Business Communication*,
https://doi.org/10.1007/978-981-13-7534-7_8

The manufacturer's authorised representative in the EU is Springer Nature Customer Service Centre GmbH, Europaplatz 3, 69115 Heidelberg, Germany. If you have any concerns regarding our products, please contact ProductSafety@springernature.com

Printed and bound by CPI Group (UK) Ltd, Croydon, CR0 4YY

25/09/2026

02222897-0002